BABY & KIDS
CROCHET
Style

30 Patterns for Stunning Heirloom Keepsakes,
Adorable Nursery Décor and Boutique-Quality Accessories

JENNIFER DOUGHERTY
Author of *Crochet Style* and Founder of Crochet by Jennifer

Photography by April Patterson (AppleTree Photography)

PAGE
PAGE STREET
PUBLISHING CO.

PAGE STREET
PUBLISHING CO.

First published in 2018 by

Page Street Publishing Co.

27 Congress Street, Suite 105

Salem, MA 01970

www.pagestreetpublishing.com

Distributed by Macmillan, sales in Canada by The Canadian Manda Group.

22   21   20   19   18   1   2   3   4   5

ISBN-13: 978-1-62414-605-3

ISBN-10: 1-62414-605-8

Library of Congress Control Number: 2018933900

Cover and book design by Rosie Gutmann for Page Street Publishing Co.

Photography by April Patterson

Printed and bound in China

DEDICATED TO MY BEAUTIFUL DAUGHTERS, KATRINA AND TARYN. OFTEN THE INSPIRATION FOR NEW DESIGNS, BOTH OF MY GIRLS HAVE BEEN WONDERFUL MODELS FOR ME OVER THE PAST SEVERAL YEARS.

Contents

INTRODUCTION

Over the years, my pattern-writing style has evolved into a distinct combination of detailed instructions and textured designs. I remember when I was young and I would try to work from a pattern book and the wording was so vague that I would often give up in defeat because I wasn't sure where to place the stitch. I knew how to make all the stitches. I just didn't know where to place them if the pattern wasn't specific enough. I strive to be very clear when I specify where and how to work a stitch, and my followers have learned to expect that. It does make my patterns wordier and much longer than the typical pattern out there, but I hope it helps avoid any possible confusion. Most of all, I love designing and I love texture, so I almost always design for an intermediate skill level. Although this is not a teaching or beginner-level crochet book, many of the designs included are achievable for a determined crocheter at an advanced-beginner skill level.

In my first book, *Crochet Style*, the focus was mainly on trendy designs for adults with some sizes for children also included. In this book, I have focused on babies and children, but I have also included numerous patterns that go all the way up to adult sizes. Here you'll find traditional baby gifts along with photography style props that any crocheter can make and sell in their home-based business. Balancing out those patterns are many new textured hat designs for all ages, as well as a few of my favorites. I have always made a point to include as many sizes as possible in my patterns—and this book is no exception. I hope you enjoy this collection as much as I've enjoyed putting it together!

My original crochet patterns are also available on Etsy, Ravelry and Craftsy. You can find more information about my patterns and books at crochetbyjennifer.com. Now go grab your hook and yarn, and get ready to crochet something fabulous!

Jennifer

1

HEIRLOOM KEEPSAKES & BABY SHOWER GIFTS

Handmade baby items are a special gift for any expecting parent, and they often become treasured keepsakes to be handed down to the next generation. Choose from small projects such as the Revelation Baby Bonnet (page 24), or tackle something bigger such as the Chunky Chevron Car Seat Canopy Cover (page 31). Make a beautifully coordinated set with the Snow Flurry Baby Bonnet (page 17) and Snow Flurry Baby Blanket (page 21). Whichever you choose, it's sure to be a welcome gift for any parent.

DEDICATION BABY BONNET

With a subtle weave texture, the Dedication Baby Bonnet is a classic design that is suitable for both boys and girls. It's perfect for special occasions such as blessings or christenings, and it's also a great choice for casual outings.

SKILL LEVEL: Intermediate

MATERIALS

TOOLS	Stitch marker, measuring tape, yarn needle
YARN	2 oz (57 g) or less of #4 worsted weight yarn
GAUGE	Diameter of circle after Rnd 5 should measure approximately 4" (10 cm) with 6 mm hook
HOOK SIZE	"J" (6 mm) for bonnet and "H" (5 mm) for edging/ties

BONNET SIZE CHART

NEWBORN	12-13" (31-33 cm) circumference, finished bonnet approximately 5" x 5" (13 x 13 cm)
0-3 MONTHS	13-14" (33-36 cm) circumference, finished bonnet approximately 5.5" x 5.5" to 6" x 6" (14 x 14 cm to 15 x 15 cm)
3-6 MONTHS	14-16" (36-41 cm) circumference, finished bonnet approximately 6.5" x 6.5" (17 x 17 cm)
6-12 MONTHS	16-18" (41-46 cm) circumference, finished bonnet approximately 7" x 7" (18 x 18 cm)
TODDLER	18-20" (46-51 cm) circumference, finished bonnet approximately 7.5" x 7.5" (19 x 19 cm)

ABBREVIATIONS USED

ST(S)	stitch(es)
CH	chain stitch
RND(S)	round(s)
SC	single crochet
HDC	half double crochet
MB ST	mini bean stitch
SP	space
SL ST	slip stitch
SK	skip
EA	each
PREV	previous
YO	Yarn Over
RS	Right Side

SPECIAL STITCH DEFINITION

MINI BEAN STITCH (MB ST): Insert hook in next st, YO, draw up a loop (2 loops on hook), YO, insert hook in same st, YO, draw up a loop (4 loops on hook), YO, pull through all 4 loops on hook, ch 1 (counts as "top" of the mini bean stitch).

TIP: HOW TO GET THE PERFECT BONNET SIZE AND SHAPE

When completed, lay the bonnet flat to measure both the height and width. If the bonnet flares out or doesn't have the overall rounded shape of a circle (the height should not be taller than the width after adding the final edging), then you can either take out the edging row and continue with the width to make it a larger size, or redo the last few rows with a smaller hook. The finished bonnet should be approximately the same height and width.

NEWBORN DEDICATION BABY BONNET

Use "J" (6 mm) hook, or match gauge checkpoint after Rnd 5.

NOTE: *The beginning of this bonnet is worked in continuous rounds. Do not ch 2 or join except Rnd 1. Move the stitch marker after each round.*

RND 1: Magic ring, ch 2, work 8 hdc in ring, join with sl st in first hdc. (8)

OR ch 2, work 8 hdc in 2nd ch from hook, join with sl st in first hdc. (8)

RND 2: (sc, hdc) in first st, work 2 hdc in ea remaining st to end of rnd, do not join. (16)

RND 3: *hdc in next st, 2 hdc in next st*, repeat between *...* to end of rnd. (24)

RND 4: *hdc in next 2 sts, 2 hdc in next st*, repeat between *...* to end of rnd. (32)

RND 5: *hdc in next 3 sts, 2 hdc in next st*, repeat between *...* to end of rnd. (40)

GAUGE CHECKPOINT: *Diameter of the circle should measure approximately 4" (10 cm) here.*

NOTE: *The pattern is now worked back and forth in rows instead of rounds.*

ROW 1: sc in next st, sl st in next st, ch 2, mb st in next st, *sk next st, mb st in next st*, repeat between *...* to last 4 sts (do not count the sl st where the ch 2 begins), leave last 4 sts unworked. (18 mb sts)

NOTE: *Because the last mb st of Row 1 is completed with a ch 1, Row 2 actually starts with a total of ch 2 (ch 1 + ch 1, turn).*

ROW 2: ch 1, turn, mb st in base of ch 2, *sk next ch-1 sp, mb st in next st*, repeat between *...* to end of row, last mb st will be on the "side" of the last mb st (first mb st from prev row). (18 mb sts)

REPEAT ROW 2 until the bonnet measures approximately 4.5 to 5" (11 to 13 cm) from the center of the magic ring to the edge of the bonnet, end with a RS (outside of bonnet facing) row.

NOTE: *Switch to an "H" (5 mm) hook (or 1 to 2 sizes smaller than the gauge) for the edging. The bonnet should be approximately the same height and width. See Tip on page 11.*

EDGING WITH CROCHETED TIES: *ch 40 (or to desired length), sl st in 2nd ch from hook and in ea ch back down to bonnet*, sc evenly across bottom of bonnet to other corner, repeat between *...* for second tie, sc across last row (around face), fasten off with invisible join (or sl st) in last st before first tie. Weave in ends.

0-3 MONTHS DEDICATION BABY BONNET

Use "J" (6 mm) hook, or match gauge checkpoint after Rnd 5.

NOTE: *The beginning of this bonnet is worked in continuous rounds. Do not ch 2 or join except Rnd 1. Move the stitch marker after each round.*

RND 1: Magic ring, ch 2, work 8 hdc in ring, join with sl st in first hdc. (8)

OR ch 2, work 8 hdc in 2nd ch from hook, join with sl st in first hdc. (8)

RND 2: (sc, hdc) in first st, work 2 hdc in ea remaining st to end of rnd, do not join. (16)

RND 3: *hdc in next st, 2 hdc in next st*, repeat between *...* to end of rnd. (24)

RND 4: *hdc in next 2 sts, 2 hdc in next st*, repeat between *...* to end of rnd. (32)

RND 5: *hdc in next 3 sts, 2 hdc in next st*, repeat between *...* to end of rnd. (40)

GAUGE CHECKPOINT: *Diameter of the circle should measure approximately 4" (10 cm) here.*

RND 6: *hdc in next 4 sts, 2 hdc in next st*, repeat between *...* to end of rnd. (48)

NOTE: *The pattern is now worked back and forth in rows instead of rounds.*

ROW 1: sc in next st, sl st in next st, ch 2, mb st in next st, *sk next st, mb st in next st*, repeat between *...* to last 4 sts (do not count the sl st where the ch 2 begins), leave last 4 sts unworked. (22 mb sts)

NOTE: *Because the last mb st of Row 1 is completed with a ch 1, Row 2 actually starts with a total of ch 2 (ch 1 + ch 1, turn).*

ROW 2: ch 1, turn, mb st in base of ch 2, *sk next ch-1 sp, mb st in next st*, repeat between *...* to end of row, last mb st will be on the "side" of the last mb st (first mb st from prev row). (22 mb sts)

REPEAT ROW 2 until the bonnet measures approximately 5.5 to 6" (14 to 15 cm) from the center of the magic ring to the edge of the bonnet, end with a RS (outside of bonnet facing) row.

NOTE: *Switch to an "H" (5 mm) hook (or 1 to 2 sizes smaller than the gauge) for the edging. The bonnet should be approximately the same height and width. See Tip on page 11.*

EDGING WITH CROCHETED TIES: *ch 45 (or to desired length), sl st in 2nd ch from hook and in ea ch back down to bonnet*, sc evenly across bottom of bonnet to other corner, repeat between *...* for second tie, sc across last row (around face), fasten off with invisible join (or sl st) in last st before first tie. Weave in ends.

3-6 MONTHS DEDICATION BABY BONNET

Use "J" (6 mm) hook, or match gauge checkpoint after Rnd 5.

NOTE: *The beginning of this bonnet is worked in continuous rounds. Do not ch 2 or join except Rnd 1. Move the stitch marker after each round.*

RND 1: Magic ring, ch 2, work 8 hdc in ring, join with sl st in first hdc. (8)

OR ch 2, work 8 hdc in 2nd ch from hook, join with sl st in first hdc. (8)

RND 2: (sc, hdc) in first st, work 2 hdc in ea remaining st to end of rnd, do not join. (16)

RND 3: *hdc in next st, 2 hdc in next st*, repeat between *...* to end of rnd. (24)

RND 4: *hdc in next 2 sts, 2 hdc in next st*, repeat between *...* to end of rnd. (32)

RND 5: *hdc in next 3 sts, 2 hdc in next st*, repeat between *...* to end of rnd. (40)

GAUGE CHECKPOINT: *Diameter of the circle should measure approximately 4" (10 cm) here.*

RND 6: *hdc in next 4 sts, 2 hdc in next st*, repeat between *...* to end of rnd. (48)

RND 7: *hdc in next 5 sts, 2 hdc in next st*, repeat between *...* to end of rnd. (56)

NOTE: *The pattern is now worked back and forth in rows instead of rounds.*

ROW 1: sc in next st, sl st in next st, ch 2, mb st in next st, *sk next st, mb st in next st*, repeat between *...* to last 4 sts (do not count the sl st where the ch 2 begins), leave last 4 sts unworked. (26 mb sts)

NOTE: *Because the last mb st of Row 1 is completed with a ch 1, Row 2 actually starts with a total of ch 2 (ch 1 + ch 1, turn).*

ROW 2: ch 1, turn, mb st in base of ch 2, *sk next ch-1 sp, mb st in next st*, repeat between *...* to end of row, last mb st will be on the "side" of the last mb st (first mb st from prev row). (26 mb sts)

REPEAT ROW 2 until the bonnet measures approximately 6 to 6.5" (15 to 17 cm) from the center of the magic ring to the edge of the bonnet, end with a RS (outside of bonnet facing) row.

NOTE: *Switch to an "H" (5 mm) hook (or 1 to 2 sizes smaller than the gauge) for the edging. The bonnet should be approximately the same height and width. See Tip on page 11.*

EDGING WITH CROCHETED TIES: *ch 50 (or to desired length), sl st in 2nd ch from hook and in ea ch back down to bonnet*, sc evenly across bottom of bonnet to other corner, repeat between *...* for second tie, sc across last row (around face), fasten off with invisible join (or sl st) in last st before first tie. Weave in ends.

6-12 MONTHS DEDICATION BABY BONNET

Use "J" (6 mm) hook, or match gauge checkpoint after Rnd 5.

NOTE: *This bonnet is worked in continuous rounds. Do not ch 2 or join. Move marker after each round.*

RND 1: Magic ring, ch 2, work 8 hdc in ring, join with sl st in first hdc. (8)

OR ch 2, work 8 hdc in 2nd ch from hook, join with sl st in first hdc. (8)

RND 2: (sc, hdc) in first st, work 2 hdc in ea remaining st to end of rnd, do not join. (16)

RND 3: *hdc in next st, 2 hdc in next st*, repeat between *...* to end of rnd. (24)

RND 4: *hdc in next 2 sts, 2 hdc in next st*, repeat between *...* to end of rnd. (32)

RND 5: *hdc in next 3 sts, 2 hdc in next st*, repeat between *...* to end of rnd. (40)

> **GAUGE CHECKPOINT:** *Diameter of the circle should measure approximately 4" (10 cm) here.*

RND 6: *hdc in next 4 sts, 2 hdc in next st*, repeat between *...* to end of rnd. (48)

RND 7: *hdc in next 5 sts, 2 hdc in next st*, repeat between *...* to end of rnd. (56)

RND 8: *hdc in next 13 sts, 2 hdc in next st*, repeat between *...* to end of rnd. (60)

> **NOTE:** *The pattern is now worked back and forth in rows instead of rounds.*

ROW 1: sc in next st, sl st in next st, ch 2, mb st in next st, *sk next st, mb st in next st*, repeat between *...* to last 4 sts (do not count the sl st where the ch 2 begins), leave last 4 sts unworked. (28 mb sts)

> **NOTE:** *Because the last mb st of Row 1 is completed with a ch 1, Row 2 actually starts with a total of ch 2 (ch 1 + ch 1, turn).*

ROW 2: ch 1, turn, mb st in base of ch 2, *sk next ch-1 sp, mb st in next st*, repeat between *...* to end of row, last mb st will be on the "side" of the last mb st (first mb st from prev row). (28 mb sts)

REPEAT ROW 2 until the bonnet measures approximately 6.5 to 7" (17 to 18 cm) from the center of the magic ring to the edge of the bonnet, end with a RS (outside of bonnet facing) row.

> **NOTE:** *Switch to an "H" (5 mm) hook (or 1 to 2 sizes smaller than the gauge) for the edging. The bonnet should be approximately the same height and width. See Tip on page 11.*

EDGING WITH CROCHETED TIES: *ch 55 (or to desired length), sl st in 2nd ch from hook and in ea ch back down to bonnet*, sc evenly across bottom of bonnet to other corner, repeat between *...* for second tie, sc across last row (around face), fasten off with invisible join (or sl st) in last st before first tie. Weave in ends.

TODDLER DEDICATION BABY BONNET

Use "J" (6 mm) hook, or match gauge checkpoint after Rnd 5.

NOTE: *The beginning of this bonnet is worked in continuous rounds. Do not ch 2 or join except Rnd 1. Move stitch marker after each round.*

RND 1: Magic ring, ch 2, work 8 hdc in ring, join with sl st in first hdc. (8)

OR ch 2, work 8 hdc in 2nd ch from hook, join with sl st in first hdc. (8)

RND 2: (sc, hdc) in first st, work 2 hdc in ea remaining st to end of rnd, do not join. (16)

RND 3: *hdc in next st, 2 hdc in next st*, repeat between *...* to end of rnd. (24)

RND 4: *hdc in next 2 sts, 2 hdc in next st*, repeat between *...* to end of rnd. (32)

RND 5: *hdc in next 3 sts, 2 hdc in next st*, repeat between *...* to end of rnd. (40)

GAUGE CHECKPOINT: *Diameter of the circle should measure approximately 4" (10 cm) here.*

RND 6: *hdc in next 4 sts, 2 hdc in next st*, repeat between *...* to end of rnd. (48)

RND 7: *hdc in next 5 sts, 2 hdc in next st*, repeat between *...* to end of rnd. (56)

RND 8: *hdc in next 6 sts, 2 hdc in next st*, repeat between *...* to end of rnd. (64)

NOTE: *The pattern is now worked back and forth in rows instead of rounds.*

ROW 1: sc in next st, sl st in next st, ch 2, mb st in next st, *sk next st, mb st in next st*, repeat between *...* to last 4 sts (do not count the sl st where the ch 2 begins), leave last 4 sts unworked. (30 mb sts)

NOTE: *Because the last mb st of Row 1 is completed with a ch 1, Row 2 actually starts with a total of ch 2 (ch 1 + ch 1, turn).*

ROW 2: ch 1, turn, mb st in base of ch 2, *sk next ch-1 sp, mb st in next st*, repeat between *...* to end of row, last mb st will be on the "side" of the last mb st (first mb st from prev row). (30 mb sts)

REPEAT ROW 2 until the bonnet measures approximately 7 to 7.5" (18 to 19 cm) from the center of the magic ring to the edge of the bonnet, end with a RS (outside of bonnet facing) row.

NOTE: *Switch to an "H" (5 mm) hook (or 1 to 2 sizes smaller than the gauge) for the edging. The bonnet should be approximately the same height and width. See Tip on page 11.*

EDGING WITH CROCHETED TIES: *ch 60 (or to desired length), sl st in 2nd ch from hook and in ea ch back down to bonnet*, sc evenly across bottom of bonnet to other corner, repeat between *...* for second tie, sc across last row (around face), fasten off with invisible join (or sl st) in last st before first tie. Weave in ends.

SNOW FLURRY BABY BONNET

This elegant baby bonnet uses an intricate combination of puff stitches and chains to create wonderful texture and beautiful style. Add the coordinating Snow Flurry Baby Blanket (page 21) for an extra special gift.

SKILL LEVEL: Intermediate

MATERIALS

TOOLS	Stitch marker, measuring tape, yarn needle
YARN	3.5 oz (99 g) or less of #4 worsted weight yarn. This pattern was designed and tested with 50/50 cotton/acrylic blend yarns. You may have different results with other fibers.
GAUGE	Diameter of circle after Rnd 4 should measure approximately 3.5" (9 cm) (or 3.25" [8.3 cm] for newborn)
HOOK SIZE	"J" (6 mm) crochet hook, or to match gauge checkpoint given after Rnd 4 for all sizes except newborn. Newborn: "I" (5.5 mm) or to match alternate gauge checkpoint given on page 18.

BONNET SIZE CHART

PREEMIE/DOLL	10-12" (25-30 cm) circumference, finished bonnet approximately 4.5" x 4.5" (11 x 11 cm)
NEWBORN	12-13" (30-33 cm) circumference, finished bonnet approximately 5" x 5" (13 x 13 cm)
0-3 MONTHS	13-14" (33-36 cm) circumference, finished bonnet approximately 6" x 6" (15 x 15 cm)
3-6 MONTHS	14-16" (36-41 cm) circumference, finished bonnet approximately 6.5" x 6.5" (17 x 17 cm)
6-12 MONTHS	16-18" (41-46 cm) circumference, finished bonnet approximately 7" x 7" (18 x 18 cm)
TODDLER	18-20" (46-51 cm) circumference, finished bonnet approximately 7.5" x 7.5" (19 x 19 cm)

ABBREVIATIONS USED

ST(S)	stitch(es)
CH OR CH-SP(S)	chain stitch or chain space(s)
SC	single crochet
HDC	half double crochet
DC	double crochet
PUFF ST	puff stitch
PUFF ST SHELL	puff stitch shell
V-ST	v-stitch
SL ST	slip stitch
RND(S)	round(s)
SK	skip
EA	each
BEG	beginning
PREV	previous
YO	Yarn Over
WS	Wrong Side

SPECIAL STITCHES DEFINITIONS

PUFF STITCH (PUFF ST): [YO, insert hook in indicated stitch, YO, draw up loop] 3 times in same stitch, YO, draw through all 7 loops on hook.

PUFF STITCH SHELL (PUFF ST SHELL): [(puff st, ch 3) twice, puff st] in indicated stitch or space.

V-STITCH (V-ST): (dc, ch 1, dc) in indicated stitch or space.

SNOW FLURRY BABY BONNET (ALL SIZES)

Use "J" (6 mm) hook, or match gauge checkpoint after Rnd 4.

NEWBORN SIZE ONLY: Use "I" (5.5 mm) hook, or to match adjusted gauge checkpoint of 3.25" after Rnd 4.

> **NOTE:** *The beginning of this bonnet is worked in continuous rounds. Do not ch 2 or join except for Rnd 1. After completing each round, add a stitch marker around the loop left on the hook. Move the stitch marker with each round.*

RND 1: Magic ring, ch 2, work 8 hdc in ring, join with sl st in first hdc. (8)

OR ch 2, work 8 hdc in 2nd ch from hook, join with sl st in first hdc. (8)

RND 2: (sc, hdc) in first st, work 2 hdc in ea remaining st to end of rnd, do not join. (16)

RND 3: *hdc in next st, 2 hdc in next st*, repeat between *...* to end of rnd. (24)

RND 4: *hdc in next 2 sts, 2 hdc in next st*, repeat between *...* to end of rnd. (32)

END HERE for preemie/doll, continue with Row 1 (below).

> **GAUGE CHECKPOINT:** *Diameter of the circle should measure approximately 3.5" (9 cm) here for all sizes except Newborn (3.25" [8.3 cm] for Newborn).*

RND 5: *hdc in next 3 sts, 2 hdc in next st*, repeat between *...* to end of rnd. (40)

END HERE for newborn and 0-3 months, continue with Row 1 (below).

RND 6: *hdc in next 4 sts, 2 hdc in next st*, repeat between *...* to end of rnd. (48)

END HERE for 3-6 months, continue with Row 1 (page 17).

RND 7: *hdc in next 5 sts, 2 hdc in next st*, repeat between *...* to end of rnd. (56)

END HERE for 6-12 months, continue with Row 1 (page 17).

RND 8: *hdc in next 6 sts, 2 hdc in next st*, repeat between *...* to end of rnd. (64)

END HERE for toddler, continue with Row 1 (page 17).

> **NOTE:** *The pattern is now worked back and forth in rows instead of rounds. Work Row 1 according to size and continue with Row 2.*

ROW 1 FOR SIZES: preemie/doll, newborn, 0-3 months

sc in next st, sl st in next st, (ch 3, puff st) in same st as ch 3, ch 1, *sk next 3 sts, v-st in next st, sk next 3 sts, puff st shell in next st, ch 1*, repeat to the last 7 sts (don't count the sl st where the ch 3 begins), sk next 3 sts, work 2 dc in next st, leave remaining 3 sts unworked.

ROW 1 FOR SIZES: 3–6 months, 6–12 months, toddler

SC in next st, sl st in next st, (ch 3, puff st) in same st as ch 3, ch 1, sk next 2 sts, v-st in next st, sk next 3 sts, puff st shell in next st, ch 1, *sk next 3 sts, v-st in next st, sk next 3 sts, puff st shell in next st, ch 1*, repeat to the last 8 sts (don't count the sl st where the ch 3 begins), sk next 2 sts, work 2 dc in next st, leave remaining 5 sts unworked.

ROW 2: (all sizes) ch 3, **turn,** puff st in next dc, ch 1, *v-st in center puff st of next puff st shell, puff st shell in next v-st ch-1 sp, ch 1*, repeat between *...* to end of row, ending with 2 dc in top of beg ch 3.

REPEAT ROW 2 until the bonnet reaches the following measurement, end with a WS row (inside of bonnet facing out):

PREEMIE/DOLL	Approximately 4.5" (11 cm) from center of magic ring to edge of bonnet
NEWBORN	Approximately 5" (13 cm) from center of magic ring to edge of bonnet
0–3 MONTHS	Approximately 5.5–6" (14–15 cm) from center of magic ring to edge of bonnet
3–6 MONTHS	Approximately 6.5" (17 cm) from center of magic ring to edge of bonnet
6–12 MONTHS	Approximately 7" (18 cm) from center of magic ring to edge of bonnet
TODDLER	Approximately 7.5" (19 cm) from center of magic ring to edge of bonnet

NOTE: *Lay the bonnet flat after working the last row. If the bonnet flares out or doesn't have the rounded shape of a circle (the bonnet should not be taller than the width after adding the final edgings), then either take out the edging row and continue with the width to make it a larger size, or redo with a smaller hook. The finished bonnet should be approximately the same height and width.*

EDGING

ch 1, turn, sc in same st as ch 1 and next dc, *3 sc in ea of next two ch-3 sps, 2 sc in ch-1 sp of next v-st*, repeat between *...* to end of row, sc in top of beg puff st and in top of turning ch. Do not fasten off. Continue with Bottom Edging.

BOTTOM EDGING (WITH CROCHETED TIES): *ch 40–50 for smaller sizes or 50–60 for the larger sizes (or to desired length), sl st in 2nd ch from hook and in ea ch back down to bonnet*, sl st in bonnet to join, sc evenly across bottom of bonnet to opposite corner, repeat between *...* for second tie, fasten off with invisible join (or sl st) in bonnet. Weave in ends.

SNOW FLURRY BABY BLANKET

An heirloom piece for sure, the Snow Flurry Baby Blanket perfectly complements the Snow Flurry Baby Bonnet (page 17). With the same intricate combination of puff stitches and chains, it includes a delicate ruffle edge to give it an extra feminine touch. Make the matching set for a fantastic baby gift that is sure to be appreciated.

SKILL LEVEL: Intermediate

MATERIALS

TOOLS	Measuring tape, yarn needle
YARN	14 oz (397 g) or less of #4 worsted weight yarn for 24" x 24" (61 x 61 cm) size (Hobby Lobby Baby Bee Hushabye in "Naked" is pictured). This pattern was designed and tested with cotton or cotton blend yarns. You may have different results with other fibers.
GAUGE	15 stitches and 7 rows in dc = 4" x 4" (10 x 10 cm) with 6 mm hook
HOOK SIZE	"J" (6 mm) crochet hook, or to match gauge

ABBREVIATIONS USED

ST(S)	stitch(es)
CH	chain stitch
SC	single crochet
DC	double crochet
SL ST	slip stitch
SK	skip
SP	space
EA	each
BEG	beginning
YO	Yarn Over

SIZE CHART (COMMON BLANKET SIZES BABY–TEEN)

LOVEY	10" x 10" (25 x 25 cm)
SECURITY	14" x 17" (36 x 43 cm)
LAYERING BLANKET	12" x 12" (30 x 30 cm) to 15" x 15" (38 x 38 cm)
PROP BLANKET	18" x 18" (46 x 46 cm) up to 20" x 20" (51 x 51 cm)
STROLLER	30" x 40" (76 x 102 cm)
BASSINET	16" x 36" (41 x 91 cm)
CRADLE	20" x 36" (51 x 91 cm)
PACK 'N PLAY	26" x 36" (66 x 91 cm)
CRIB	30" x 36" (76 x 91 cm) up to 45" x 60" (114 x 152 cm)
RECEIVING	24" x 24" (61 x 61 cm) up to 36" x 36" (91 x 91 cm)
INFANT	24" x 30" (61 x 76 cm) up to 36" x 48" (91 x 122 cm)
TODDLER	36" x 48" (91 x 122 cm)
CHILD	42" x 48" (107 x 122 cm)
TEEN	48" x 60" (122 x 152 cm)

SPECIAL STITCHES DEFINITIONS

PUFF STITCH (PUFF ST): [YO, insert hook in indicated stitch, YO, draw up loop] 3 times in same stitch, YO, draw through all 7 loops on hook.

PUFF STITCH SHELL (PUFF ST SHELL): [(puff st, ch 3) twice, puff st] in indicated stitch or space.

V-STITCH (V-ST): (dc, ch 1, dc) in indicated stitch or space.

SNOW FLURRY BABY BLANKET

Use "J" (6 mm) hook and #4 worsted weight yarn.

NOTE: *This blanket can be made in any size. To adjust the width, ch any multiple of 8 plus 5 for foundation chain, ch 6 more (counts as beginning ch 6). Substitute this number for the beginning chain number listed in the Foundation Row. To adjust the length, add more rows. (The beginning chain listed below will result in approximately 23–24" [58–61 cm] for the width.)*

FOUNDATION ROW: ch 91, puff st in 7th ch from hook, ch 1, *sk 3 ch sts, v-st in next ch, sk 3 ch sts, puff st shell in next ch, ch 1*, repeat between *...* to last 4 ch sts, sk 3 ch sts, work 2 dc in last ch.

ROW 1: (ch 6, turn, puff st) in first dc, ch 1, *v-st in center puff st of next puff st shell, puff st shell in next v-st ch-1 sp, ch 1*, repeat between *...* to end of row, ending with 2 dc in 3rd ch of beg ch-6.

REPEAT Row 1 until the blanket is the desired length.

TIP: *If the edging is "pulling," use more stitches. If the edging is "ruffling," use fewer stitches.*

EDGING RND 1: ch 1, turn, *sc in ea of next 2 sts, 2 sc in ea of next 2 ch-3 sps, 2 sc in next ch-1 sp*, repeat to end, sc in ea of last 2 sts, work 4 sc in last ch-sp to go around corner, sc evenly along the side of the blanket (work 4 sc in ea corner) and repeat for the other 2 sides, sl st in first st to join.

EDGING RND 2: ch 1, do not turn, sc in ea st (work 3 sc in ea corner st) around entire blanket, sl st in first st to join.

FINAL EDGING: ch 4 (counts as sc plus ch 3), do not turn, sc in same st as ch 4, *sk next st, (sc, ch 3, sc) in next st* repeat around entire blanket (work [sc, ch 3, sc, ch 3, sc] in corner sts), fasten off with invisible join (or sl st) in first st to join. Weave in ends.

REVELATION BABY BONNET

The Revelation Baby Bonnet has a unique texture that looks great on both sides. Although it looks complicated, the pattern repeat is easy to memorize, and the result is impressive.

SKILL LEVEL: ◼️◻️ Intermediate

MATERIALS

TOOLS	Stitch marker, measuring tape, yarn needle
YARN	4 oz (113 g) or less of #4 worsted weight yarn
GAUGE	Diameter of circle after Rnd 5 should measure approximately 4" (10 cm) with "J" (6 mm) hook
HOOK SIZE	"J" (6 mm) or to match gauge checkpoint after Rnd 5 for each size

BONNET SIZE CHART

NEWBORN	12–13" (30–33 cm) circumference, finished bonnet approximately 5" x 5" (13 x 13 cm)
0–3 MONTHS	13–14" (33–36 cm) circumference, finished bonnet approximately 6" x 6" (15 x 15 cm)
3–6 MONTHS	14–16" (36–41 cm) circumference, finished bonnet approximately 6.5" x 6.5" (17 x 17 cm)
6–12 MONTHS	16–18" (41–46 cm) circumference, finished bonnet approximately 7" x 7" (18 x 18 cm)
TODDLER	18–20" (46–51 cm) circumference, finished bonnet approximately 7.5" x 7.5" (19 x 19 cm)

ABBREVIATIONS USED

ST(S)	stitch(es)
CH	chain stitch
SC	single crochet
HDC	half double crochet
DC	double crochet
TR	treble crochet
SL ST	slip stitch
RND(S)	round(s)
SK	skip
EA	each
PREV	previous
YO	Yarn Over

SPECIAL STITCHES DEFINITIONS

TREBLE CROCHET (TR): YO twice, insert hook in st and pull up a loop (4 loops on hook), YO, draw through 2 loops (3 loops on hook), YO, draw through 2 loops (2 loops on hook), YO, draw through last 2 loops.

CROSS STITCH (CROSS-ST): Skip next ch-2 space, dc in next ch-2 space, working behind first dc, dc in skipped ch-2 space.

PUFF STITCH (PUFF ST): [YO, insert hook in indicated st, YO, draw up a loop] 3 times in same st or space, YO, draw through all 7 loops on hook.

TIP (HOW TO GET THE PERFECT BONNET SIZE AND SHAPE)

When completed, lay the bonnet flat to measure both height and width. If the bonnet flares out or doesn't have the overall rounded shape of a circle (the height should not be taller than the width after adding the final edging), then you can either take out the edging row and continue with the width to make it a larger size, or redo the last row or two with a smaller hook. The finished bonnet should be approximately the same height and width.

NEWBORN REVELATION BABY BONNET

Use "J" (6 mm) hook, or match gauge checkpoint after Rnd 5.

NOTE: *The beginning of this bonnet is worked in continuous rounds. Do not ch 2 or join except Rnd 1. Move the stitch marker after each round. When working in a skipped stitch, work behind (under) the first dc made.*

RND 1: Magic ring, ch 2, work 8 hdc in ring, join with sl st in first hdc. (8)

OR ch 2, work 8 hdc in 2nd ch from hook, join with sl st in first hdc. (8)

RND 2: (sc, hdc) in first st, work 2 hdc in ea remaining st to end of rnd, do not join. (16)

RND 3: *hdc in next st, 2 hdc in next st*, repeat between *...* to end of rnd. (24)

RND 4: *hdc in next 2 sts, 2 hdc in next st*, repeat between *...* to end of rnd. (32)

RND 5: *hdc in next 3 sts, 2 hdc in next st*, repeat between *...* to end of rnd. (40)

GAUGE CHECKPOINT: *Diameter of the circle should measure approximately 4" (10 cm) here.*

NOTE: *The pattern is now worked back and forth in rows instead of rounds.*

ROW 1: sc in next st, sl st in next st, ch 3 (counts as first dc), sk next st, dc in next st, dc in skipped st, *dc in next st, sk next st, dc in next st, dc in skipped st*, repeat between *...* to last 4 sts (don't count the sl st where the ch 3 begins), dc in next st, leave last 3 sts unworked. (12 dc + crossed dc combos and 1 dc)

ROW 2: ch 1, turn, sc in first dc, *ch 2, puff st (see Special Stitches Definitions, page 24) in center (between stitches) of next cross-st, ch 2**, sc in next dc*, repeat between *...*, end last repeat at **, sc in second ch of beg ch-3 of prev row. (12 sc + puff st combos and 1 sc)

ROW 3: ch 3, turn, *cross-st (see Special Stitches Definitions)**, tr in next sc*, repeat between *...* to end of row, end last repeat at **, dc (counts as last tr) in first sc of prev row. (1 ch 3 and 12 cross-st + tr combos)

ROW 4: ch 1, turn, sc in first tr, *ch 2, puff st in center (between stitches) of next cross-st, ch 2**, sc in next tr*, repeat between *...*, end last repeat at **, sc in second ch of beginning ch-3 of prev row. (12 sc + puff st combos and 1 sc)

REPEAT ROWS 3 AND 4 until the bonnet measures approximately 4.5 to 5" (11 to 13 cm) from the center of the magic ring to the edge of the bonnet (end with Row 3).

EDGING WITH CROCHETED TIES: If bonnet is "flaring," use a smaller hook for this section. See Tip on page 11. *ch 40 (or to desired length), sl st in 2nd ch from hook and in ea ch back down to bonnet*, sc evenly across bottom of bonnet to other corner, repeat between *...* for second tie, sc across last row (around face), fasten off with invisible join (or sl st) in last st before first tie. Weave in ends.

0-3 MONTHS REVELATION BABY BONNET

Use "J" (6 mm) hook, or match gauge checkpoint after Rnd 5.

NOTE: *The beginning of this bonnet is worked in continuous rounds. Do not ch 2 or join except Rnd 1. Move stitch marker after each round. When working in a skipped st, work behind (under) the first dc made.*

RND 1: Magic ring, ch 2, work 8 hdc in ring, join with sl st in first hdc. (8)

OR ch 2, work 8 hdc in 2nd ch from hook, join with sl st in first hdc. (8)

RND 2: (sc, hdc) in first st, work 2 hdc in ea remaining st to end of rnd, do not join. (16)

RND 3: *hdc in next st, 2 hdc in next st*, repeat between *...* to end of rnd. (24)

RND 4: *hdc in next 2 sts, 2 hdc in next st*, repeat between *...* to end of rnd. (32)

RND 5: *hdc in next 3 sts, 2 hdc in next st*, repeat between *...* to end of rnd. (40)

GAUGE CHECKPOINT: *Diameter of the circle should measure approximately 4" (10 cm) here.*

RND 6: *hdc in next 9 sts, 2 hdc in next st*, repeat between *...* to end of rnd. (44)

NOTE: *The pattern is now worked back and forth in rows instead of rounds.*

ROW 1: sc in next st, sl st in next st, ch 3 (counts as first dc), sk next st, dc in next st, dc in skipped st, *dc in next st, sk next st, dc in next st, dc in skipped st*, repeat between *...* to last 5 sts (don't count the sl st where the ch 3 begins), dc in next st, leave last 4 sts unworked. (13 dc + crossed dc combos and 1 dc)

ROW 2: ch 1, turn, sc in first dc, *ch 2, puff st (see Special Stitches Definitions, page 24) in center (between stitches) of next cross-st, ch 2**, sc in next dc*, repeat between *...*, end last repeat at **, sc in second ch of beg ch-3 of prev row. (13 sc + puff st combos and 1 sc)

ROW 3: ch 3, turn, *cross-st (see Special Stitches Definitions, page 24)**, tr in next sc*, repeat between *...* to end of row, end last repeat at **, work dc (counts as last tr) in first sc of prev row. (1 ch 3 and 13 cross-st + tr combos)

ROW 4: ch 1, turn, sc in first tr, *ch 2, puff st in center (between stitches) of next cross-st, ch 2**, sc in next tr*, repeat between *...*, end last repeat at **, sc in second ch of beginning ch-3 of prev row. (13 sc + puff st combos and 1 sc)

REPEAT ROWS 3 AND 4 until the bonnet measures approximately 5.5 to 6" (14 to 15 cm) from the center of the magic ring to the edge of the bonnet (end with Row 3).

EDGING WITH CROCHETED TIES: If the bonnet is "flaring," use a smaller hook for this section. See Tip on page 11. *ch 45 (or to desired length), sl st in 2nd ch from hook and in ea ch back down to bonnet*, sc evenly across bottom of bonnet to other corner, repeat between *...* for second tie, sc across last row (around face), fasten off with invisible join (or sl st) in last st before first tie. Weave in ends.

3-6 MONTHS REVELATION BABY BONNET

Use "J" (6 mm) hook, or match gauge checkpoint after Rnd 5.

NOTE: *The beginning of this bonnet is worked in continuous rounds. Do not ch 2 or join except Rnd 1. Move stitch marker after each round. When working in a skipped stitch, work behind (under) the first dc made.*

RND 1: Magic ring, ch 2, work 8 hdc in ring, join with sl st in first hdc. (8)

OR ch 2, work 8 hdc in 2nd ch from hook, join with sl st in first hdc. (8)

RND 2: (sc, hdc) in first st, work 2 hdc in ea remaining st to end of rnd, do not join. (16)

RND 3: *hdc in next st, 2 hdc in next st*, repeat between *...* to end of rnd. (24)

RND 4: *hdc in next 2 sts, 2 hdc in next st*, repeat between *...* to end of rnd. (32)

RND 5: *hdc in next 3 sts, 2 hdc in next st*, repeat between *...* to end of rnd. (40)

GAUGE CHECKPOINT: *Diameter of the circle should measure approximately 4" (10 cm) here.*

RND 6: *hdc in next 4 sts, 2 hdc in next st*, repeat between *...* to end of rnd. (48)

NOTE: *The pattern is now worked back and forth in rows instead of rounds.*

ROW 1: sc in next st, sl st in next st, ch 3 (counts as first dc), dc in next st, working behind first dc made, dc in same st as ch 3, *dc in next st, sk next st, dc in next st, dc in skipped st*, repeat between *...* to last 4 sts (don't count the sl st where the ch 3 begins), dc in same st as first dc of the last crossed pair, leave last 4 sts unworked (15 dc + crossed dc combos and 1 dc).

ROW 2: ch 1, turn, sc in first dc, *ch 2, puff st (see Special Stitches Definitions, page 24) in center (between stitches) of next cross-st, ch 2**, sc in next dc*, repeat between *...*, end last repeat at **, sc in second ch of beg ch-3 of prev row. (15 sc + puff st combos and 1 sc)

ROW 3: ch 3, turn, *cross-st (see Special Stitches Definitions, page 24)**, tr in next sc*, repeat between *...* to end of row, end last repeat at **, work dc (counts as last tr) in first sc of prev row. (1 ch 3 and 15 cross-st + tr combos)

ROW 4: ch 1, turn, sc in first tr, *ch 2, puff st in center (between stitches) of next cross-st, ch 2**, sc in next tr*, repeat between *...*, end last repeat at **, sc in second ch of beginning ch-3 of prev row. (15 sc + puff st combos and 1 sc)

REPEAT ROWS 3 AND 4 until the bonnet measures approximately 6 to 6.5" (15 to 17 cm) from the center of the magic ring to the edge of the bonnet (end with Row 3).

EDGING WITH CROCHETED TIES: If the bonnet is "flaring," use a smaller hook for this section. See Tip on page 11. *ch 50 (or to desired length), sl st in 2nd ch from hook and in ea ch back down to bonnet*, sc evenly across bottom of bonnet to other corner, repeat between *...* for second tie, sc across last row (around face), fasten off with invisible join (or sl st) in last st before first tie. Weave in ends.

6-12 MONTHS REVELATION BABY BONNET

Use "J" (6 mm) hook, or match gauge checkpoint after Rnd 5.

NOTE: *The beginning of this bonnet is worked in continuous rounds. Do not ch 2 or join except Rnd 1. Move stitch marker after each round. When working in a skipped stitch, work behind (under) the first dc made.*

RND 1: Magic ring, ch 2, work 8 hdc in ring, join with sl st in first hdc. (8)

OR ch 2, work 8 hdc in 2nd ch from hook, join with sl st in first hdc. (8)

RND 2: (sc, hdc) in first st, work 2 hdc in ea remaining st to end of rnd, do not join. (16)

RND 3: *hdc in next st, 2 hdc in next st*, repeat between *...* to end of rnd. (24)

RND 4: *hdc in next 2 sts, 2 hdc in next st*, repeat between *...* to end of rnd. (32)

RND 5: *hdc in next 3 sts, 2 hdc in next st*, repeat between *...* to end of rnd. (40)

GAUGE CHECKPOINT: *Diameter of circle should measure approximately 4" (10 cm) here.*

RND 6: *hdc in next 4 sts, 2 hdc in next st*, repeat between *...* to end of rnd. (48)

RND 7: *hdc in next 11 sts, 2 hdc in next st*, repeat between *...* to end of rnd. (52)

NOTE: *The pattern is now worked back and forth in rows instead of rounds.*

ROW 1: sc in next st, sl st in next st, ch 3 (counts as first dc), dc in next st, working behind first dc made, dc in same st as ch 3, *dc in next st, sk next st, dc in next st, dc in skipped st*, repeat between *...* to last 5 sts (don't count the sl st where the ch 3 begins), dc in same st as first dc of the last crossed pair, leave last 5 sts unworked. (16 dc + crossed dc combos and 1 dc)

ROW 2: ch 1, turn, sc in first dc, *ch 2, puff st (see Special Stitches Definitions, page 24) in center (between stitches) of next cross-st, ch 2**, sc in next dc*, repeat between *...*, end last repeat at **, sc in second ch of beg ch-3 of prev row. (16 sc + puff st combos and 1 sc)

ROW 3: ch 3, turn, *cross-st (see Special Stitches Definitions, page 24)**, tr in next sc*, repeat between *...* to end of row, end last repeat at **, work dc (counts as last tr) in first sc of prev row. (1 ch 3 and 16 cross-st + tr combos)

ROW 4: ch 1, turn, sc in first tr, *ch 2, puff st in center (between stitches) of next cross-st, ch 2**, sc in next tr*, repeat between *...*, end last repeat at **, sc in second ch of beginning ch-3 of prev row. (16 sc + puff st combos and 1 sc)

REPEAT ROWS 3 AND 4 until the bonnet measures approximately 6.5 to 7" (17 to 18 cm) from the center of the magic ring to the edge of the bonnet (end with Row 3).

EDGING WITH CROCHETED TIES: If bonnet is "flaring," use a smaller hook for this section. See Tip on page 11. *ch 55 (or to desired length), sl st in 2nd ch from hook and in ea ch back down to bonnet*, sc evenly across bottom of bonnet to other corner, repeat between *...* for second tie, sc across last row (around face), fasten off with invisible join (or sl st) in last st before first tie. Weave in ends.

TODDLER REVELATION BABY BONNET

Use "J" (6 mm) hook, or match gauge checkpoint after Rnd 5.

NOTE: *The beginning of this bonnet is worked in continuous rounds. Do not ch 2 or join except Rnd 1. Move stitch marker after each round. When working in a skipped stitch, work behind (under) the first dc made.*

RND 1: Magic ring, ch 2, work 8 hdc in ring, join with sl st in first hdc. (8)

OR ch 2, work 8 hdc in 2nd ch from hook, join with sl st in first hdc. (8)

RND 2: (sc, hdc) in first st, work 2 hdc in ea remaining st to end of rnd, do not join. (16)

RND 3: *hdc in next st, 2 hdc in next st*, repeat between *...* to end of rnd. (24)

RND 4: *hdc in next 2 sts, 2 hdc in next st*, repeat between *...* to end of rnd. (32)

RND 5: *hdc in next 3 sts, 2 hdc in next st*, repeat between *...* to end of rnd. (40)

GAUGE CHECKPOINT: *Diameter of the circle should measure approximately 4" (10 cm) here.*

RND 6: *hdc in next 4 sts, 2 hdc in next st*, repeat between *...* to end of rnd. (48)

RND 7: *hdc in next 5 sts, 2 hdc in next st*, repeat between *...* to end of rnd. (56)

NOTE: *The pattern is now worked back and forth in rows instead of rounds.*

ROW 1: sc in next st, sl st in next st, ch 3 (counts as first dc), dc in next st, working behind first dc made, dc in same st as ch 3, *dc in next st, sk next st, dc in next st, dc in skipped st*, repeat between *...* to last 6 sts (don't count the sl st where the ch 3 begins), dc in same st as first dc of the last crossed pair, leave last 6 sts unworked. (17 dc + crossed dc combos and 1 dc)

ROW 2: ch 1, turn, sc in first dc, *ch 2, puff st (see Special Stitches Definitions, page 24) in center (between stitches) of next cross-st, ch 2**, sc in next dc*, repeat between *...*, end last repeat at **, sc in second ch of beg ch-3 of prev row. (17 sc + puff st combos and 1 sc)

ROW 3: ch 3, turn, *cross-st (see Special Stitches Definitions, page 24)**, tr in next sc*, repeat between *...* to end of row, end last repeat at **, work dc (counts as last tr) in first sc of prev row. (1 ch 3 and 17 cross-st + tr combos)

ROW 4: ch 1, turn, sc in first tr, *ch 2, puff st in center (between stitches) of next cross-st, ch 2**, sc in next tr*, repeat between *...*, end last repeat at **, sc in second ch of beg ch-3 of prev row. (17 sc + puff st combos and 1 sc)

REPEAT ROWS 3 AND 4 until the bonnet measures approximately 7 to 7.5" (18 to 19 cm) from the center of the magic ring to the edge of the bonnet (end with Row 3).

EDGING WITH CROCHETED TIES: If the bonnet is "flaring," use a smaller hook for this section. See Tip on page 11. *ch 60 (or to desired length), sl st in 2nd ch from hook and in ea ch back down to bonnet*, sc evenly across bottom of bonnet to other corner, repeat between *...* for second tie, sc across last row (around face), fasten off with invisible join (or sl st) in last st before first tie. Weave in ends.

CHUNKY CHEVRON CAR SEAT CANOPY COVER

Thick and squishy, the Chunky Chevron Car Seat Canopy Cover serves an important purpose in any cold climate. Perfect for keeping the draft off baby, the trendy chevron stripes appeal to almost everyone. This one always elicits compliments from anyone who sees it being used.

SKILL LEVEL: Easy

MATERIALS

TOOLS	Stitch markers, measuring tape, 2 buttons (approximately 1⅛" [28 mm]), needle and thread, large yarn needle (for weaving in ends)
YARN	2 skeins (10.5 oz [300 g] each) of Bernat Blanket yarn, or any similar #6 super bulky weight yarn
GAUGE	Gauge checkpoint given in pattern after Row 3
HOOK SIZE	"P" (10 mm) Boye hook. Other brands may vary in size; be sure to match mm size.

SIZE CHART

ONE SIZE FITS MOST	Finished dimensions approximately 26–28" (66–71 cm) wide and 36–38" (91–97 cm) long

ABBREVIATIONS USED

ST(S)	stitch(es)
CH	chain stitch
SP(S)	space(s)
SC	single crochet
HDC	half double crochet
DC	double crochet
TREBLE	treble crochet
SL ST	slip stitch
SK	skip
EA	each
BEG	beginning
PREV	previous
YO	Yarn Over

CHUNKY CHEVRON CAR SEAT CANOPY BLANKET

Use #6 super bulky weight yarn and "P" (10 mm) hook, or match gauge checkpoint after Row 3.

NOTE: *Keep the tension loose. Do not crochet tightly in this pattern.*

ROW 1: With Color A, ch 68, 2 sc in second ch from hook, sc in ea of next 4 chs, sk next 2 chs, sc in ea of next 4 chs, *3 sc in next ch, sc in ea of next 4 chs, sk next 2 chs, sc in ea of next 4 chs*, repeat between *...* to end of row, 2 sc in last ch. (6 chevron "points")

ROW 2: ch 1, turn, 2 sc in first sc, sc in ea of next 4 sc, sk next 2 sc, sc in ea of next 4 sc, *3 sc in next sc, sc in ea of next 4 sc, sk next 2 sc, sc in ea of next 4 sc*, repeat between *...* to end of row, 2 sc in last sc (see Note to the right).

NOTE: *There are two options for this blanket. Each color can be carried up the side of the blanket (if an edging will be added this will be easier), or fasten each color off and work the ends in. Do not pull the yarn too tight if it is being carried or it will make the side of the blanket curl up. Keep the tension loose and pull each stitch up higher on the hook, if necessary.*

ROW 3: Pull up a loop of Color B, pull Color A tight over it, ch 1, turn, 2 sc in first sc, sc in ea of next 4 sc, sk next 2 sc, sc in ea of next 4 sc, *3 sc in next sc, sc in ea of next 4 sc, sk next 2 sc, sc in ea of next 4 sc*, repeat between *...* to end of row, 2 sc in last sc.

GAUGE CHECKPOINT: *The width of the blanket should be approximately 28 to 30" (71 to 76 cm) wide. If the gauge does not match, either adjust the tension or change the hook size.*

REPEAT ROWS 2 AND 3, alternating colors A and B after 2 rows of each color, until the blanket reaches approximately 36 to 38" (91 to 97 cm) in height (measure from the points of the chevrons).

(OPTIONAL) EDGING

Sc evenly around the entire edge of the blanket (work 3 sc in ea corner). Fasten off. Weave in ends.

BUTTON STRAPS (MAKE TWO)

Use #6 super bulky weight yarn and "P" (10 mm) hook

NOTE: *If you crochet loosely, use a smaller hook so the straps are more solid.*

ROW 1: ch 5, sc in second ch from hook and ea st to end of row. (4)

ROW 2: ch 1, turn, sc in ea st to end of row. (4)

REPEAT ROW 2 until there are a total of 15 rows, or the button strap measures approximately 10″ (25 cm) long (see Tip below).

> **TIP:** *If the blanket is too wide, the bottom front corners will drag on the floor. If the blanket is a little too wide, make the straps shorter (to hold the blanket up higher on the car seat handle). If it's not wide enough, use the suggested length above so the blanket isn't too short on the sides (leaving gaps).*

ROW 3: ch 3 (counts as a dc), turn, dc in ea st to end of row (the middle space between the stitches of this row will serve as the button hole). (4)

ROW 4: ch 1, turn, sc in ea st to end of row. Before fastening off, test button hole with desired button. Make adjustments to Row 3 if necessary. (Use shorter or taller sts [hdc or tr] to change height.) Fasten off. Weave in ends with large yarn needle.

ASSEMBLY

Sew a button on the end of the button strap that is opposite the button hole (about a half inch [1.3 cm] from each edge). Repeat for the second button strap.

> **NOTE:** *For best results, I recommend draping the car seat canopy over the exact car seat on which it will be used. If a car seat isn't available, use the photo below for placement.*

Using stitch markers, mark the locations for the button straps approximately one-third of the way down from the top and one-third of the way in from each side (see photo). Using a yarn needle and long tail end, stitch the straps securely on the blanket.

BORDERLINE CAR SEAT CANOPY COVER

Designed with cold weather in mind, this car seat cover is amazingly soft and warm. It's made with super bulky yarn to work up fast and keep the chill away from baby in windy climates.

SKILL LEVEL: ⬤▬▬ Easy

MATERIALS

TOOLS	Stitch markers, measuring tape, 2 buttons (approximately 1⅛" [28 mm]), needle and thread, large yarn needle (for weaving in ends)
YARN	**COLOR A:** 2 skeins (10.5 oz [300 g] each) Bernat Blanket yarn (or any #6 super bulky weight yarn) **COLOR B:** 1 skein (10.5 oz [300 g]) Bernat Blanket yarn (or any #6 super bulky weight yarn)
GAUGE	Gauge checkpoint given in pattern after Row 3
HOOK SIZE	"M/N" (9 mm) or "P" (10 mm) hook. Brands may vary in size, be sure to match mm size.

SIZE CHART

ONE SIZE FITS MOST	Finished dimensions approximately 30" (76 cm) wide and 36 to 38" (91 to 97 cm) long

ABBREVIATIONS USED

ST(S)	stitch(es)
CH	chain stitch
SC	single crochet
HDC	half double crochet
DC	double crochet
TR	treble crochet
DC3TOG	double crochet 3 stitches together
SC3TOG	single crochet 3 stitches together
SL ST	slip stitch
RND(S)	round(s)
SK	skip
SP	space
EA	each
RS	Right Side
WS	Wrong Side
YO	Yarn Over

SPECIAL STITCHES DEFINITIONS

DOUBLE CROCHET 3 STITCHES TOGETHER (DC3TOG):
YO and insert hook in stitch indicated, YO and draw up a loop, YO and draw through 2 loops, *YO and insert hook in next st, YO and draw up another loop, YO and draw through 2 loops*, repeat between *...* in next st, YO and draw through all 4 loops on hook.

SINGLE CROCHET 3 STITCHES TOGETHER (SC3TOG):
Pull up a loop in each of next 3 stitches, YO and draw through all 4 loops on hook.

JOINING WITH SC: Begin with a slipknot on hook, insert hook in stitch indicated, YO and pull up a loop, YO and draw through both loops.

BORDERLINE CAR SEAT CANOPY

Use #6 super bulky weight yarn and a 9–10 mm crochet hook, or match gauge checkpoint after Row 3.

WITH COLOR A, ch 58. (To adjust size, ch any multiple of 6 + 4)

ROW 1: (RS) dc in 4th ch from hook (3 skipped ch sts count as a dc), dc in next ch, dc3tog over next 3 ch sts, dc in next ch, *3 dc in next ch, dc in next ch, dc3tog, dc in next ch*, repeat between *...* to last ch, dc in ea of last 2 ch sts.

ROW 2: (WS) ch 3 (counts as first dc), turn, dc in same st as ch 3, dc in next dc, dc3tog, dc in next dc, *3 dc in next dc, dc in next dc, dc3tog, dc in next dc*, repeat between *...* to last dc, work 2 dc in last dc. Finish off.

ROW 3: With RS facing, join Color B with sc in first dc (see Joining with SC under Special Stitches Definitions [page 35]), sc in same st as joining, sc in next dc, sc3tog, sc in next dc, *3 sc in next dc, sc in next dc, sc3tog, sc in next dc*, repeat between *...* to last dc, work 2 sc in last dc.

GAUGE CHECKPOINT: *The width of the blanket should be approximately 30" (76 cm) wide here. If the gauge does not match, either adjust the tension or change the hook size.*

ROW 4: (WS) ch 1, turn, 2 sc in first sc, sc in next sc, sc3tog, sc in next sc, *3 sc in next sc, sc in next sc, sc3tog, sc in next sc*, repeat between *...* to last sc, work 2 sc in last sc. Finish off.

ROW 5: With RS facing, join Color A with sl st in first sc, ch 3, dc in same st as ch 3, dc in next sc, dc3tog, dc in next sc, *3 dc in next sc, dc in next sc, dc3tog, dc in next sc*, repeat between *...* to last sc, work 2 dc in last sc.

REPEAT ROWS 2–5 until the blanket measures approximately 36 to 38" (91 to 97 cm) in height.

EDGING: (see Tip below) sc evenly around the entire edge of the blanket (work 3 sc in corners). Fasten off with invisible join in first sc, or repeat round if desired (work 2 sc in ea of the 3 corner sc for a second round). Weave in ends.

TIP: *Measure the width of blanket after completing the first edging round. If it's too wide, the bottom front corners will touch the floor. If it's not wide enough, there will be gaps on the sides. It is easy to adjust the width by an inch or two (3 to 5 cm) by adding extra edging rounds.*

BUTTON STRAPS (MAKE TWO)

Use #6 super bulky weight yarn and "P" (10 mm) hook.

NOTE: *If you crochet loosely, use a smaller hook so the straps are more solid.*

ROW 1: ch 5, sc in second ch from hook and ea st to end of row. (4)

ROW 2: ch 1, turn, sc in ea st to end of row. (4)

REPEAT ROW 2 until there are a total of 15 rows, or the button strap measures approximately 10" (25 cm) long (see Tip on page 34).

ROW 3: ch 3 (counts as a dc), turn, dc in ea st to end of row (the middle space between the stitches of this row will serve as the button hole). (4)

ROW 4: ch 1, turn, sc in ea st to end of row. Before fastening off, test button hole with desired button. Make adjustments to Row 3 if necessary. (Use shorter or taller sts [hdc or tr] to change height.) Fasten off. Weave in ends with large yarn needle.

ASSEMBLY

Sew a button on the end of button strap that is opposite the button hole (about a half inch [1.3 cm] from each edge). Repeat for the second button strap.

NOTE: *For best results, I recommend draping the car seat canopy over the exact car seat for which it is meant. If a car seat isn't available, use the photo below for placement.*

Using stitch markers, mark the locations for the button straps approximately one-third of the way down from the top and one-third of the way in from each side (or approximately 6" [15 cm] apart, see photo). Using a yarn needle and long tail end, stitch the straps securely on the blanket.

WINDCHILL HOODED BUTTON-UP BABY COCOON

With its fabulous texture and stylish design, this hooded cocoon is sure to be a treasured heirloom gift. Cozy and warm, babies will love it too!

SKILL LEVEL: ▰▱ Intermediate

MATERIALS

TOOLS	Measuring tape, yarn needle, 10-18 buttons, needle and thread
YARN	400-600 yards (366-549 m) of #5 bulky weight yarn (depending on size), Bernat Home Dec is pictured (gauge may vary with other chunky yarns due to the difference in fiber type)
GAUGE	Gauge checkpoint given in pattern after Row 3
HOOK SIZE	9 mm hook (or one hook size larger than recommended for yarn)

SIZE CHART

PREEMIE COCOON	16-18" (41-46 cm) circumference, 14" (36 cm) length
NEWBORN COCOON	18-20" (46-51 cm) circumference, 18" (46 cm) length
0-3 MONTHS COCOON	20-22" (51-56 cm) circumference, 20" (51 cm) length
3-6 MONTHS COCOON	22-24" (56-61 cm) circumference, 22" (56 cm) length

ABBREVIATIONS USED

ST(S)	stitch(es)
CH	chain stitch
SC	single crochet
DC	double crochet
FPDC	front post double crochet
SL ST	slip stitch
SK	skip
SP	space
EA	each
BEG	beginning
PREV	previous
YO	Yarn Over
RS	Right Side
WS	Wrong Side
BLO	Back Loop Only

SPECIAL STITCHES DEFINITIONS

FRONT POST DOUBLE CROCHET (FPDC): Working from the front side of the work, YO and insert the hook from right to left under the post of the double crochet indicated from the previous row, YO and pull up a loop, [YO and draw through 2 loops] twice.

CLUSTER: 3 fpdc worked around a sc (term used for stitch count purposes only in this pattern).

WINDCHILL HOODED BUTTON-UP BABY COCOON (ALL SIZES)

Use 9 mm hook and #5 bulky yarn, or see Note below for adjustments.

NOTE: *This pattern can be adapted for other yarn weights. Use a multiple of 4 plus 2 for the Foundation Row and match the width and length in the size chart (measure width after completing a few rows; length is determined by how many rows are added in total). Use a hook at least one size larger than the recommended hook for the yarn because the stitch is very heavy.*

FOUNDATION ROW: ch (34, 38, 42, 46), sc in back loop of 2nd ch from hook and ea ch to end of row. (33, 37, 41, 45)

ROW 1: ch 2 (counts as a dc), turn, sk first sc (base of ch 2), dc in next st, *sc in next st, sk next st, work 3 fpdc around next sc, sk next st*, repeat between *...* to last 3 sts, sc in next st, dc in ea of last 2 sts. (7, 8, 9, 10 clusters plus 2 dc and a sc at ea end of row)

ROW 2 (RS): ch 2 (counts as a dc), turn, sk first 2 dc, *work 3 fpdc around next sc, sc in center st of next 3 fpdc*, repeat between *...* to end of row, ending with 3 fpdc around last sc, sk next dc, dc in top of turning ch. (8, 9, 10, 11 clusters and a dc at ea end of row)

ROW 3 (WS): ch 2 (counts as a dc), turn, sk first st (base of ch 2), dc in next st (first of 3 fpdc from prev row), *sc in next st (center of 3 fpdc), sk next st, work 3 fpdc around next sc, sk next st*, repeat to last 3 sts, sc in next st, dc in ea of last 2 sts. (7, 8, 9, 10 clusters plus 2 dc and a sc at ea end of row)

GAUGE CHECKPOINT: *Width of the cocoon should match the following measurement on the right (length will be determined by how many rows are added); see Note to the right.*

PREEMIE:	9-10" (23-25 cm) wide
NEWBORN	10-11" (25-28 cm) wide
0-3 MONTHS	11-12" (28-30 cm) wide
3-6 MONTHS	12-13" (30-33 cm) wide

NOTE: *The width can be slightly bigger (for a less snug fit) but do not make it smaller.*

REPEAT ROWS 2 AND 3 until the cocoon reaches approximately the following length:

PREEMIE:	34" (86 cm)
NEWBORN	42" (107 cm)
0-3 MONTHS	46" (117 cm)
3-6 MONTHS	50" (127 cm)

> **NOTE:** *The cocoon will be a very long skinny rectangle at this point. Now one short end will be seamed together to form the hood.*

HOOD: ch 1, turn, fold last completed end to opposite end of row (keeping RS on inside), sl st across both sides to middle of row (which is now the point of the hood), fasten off. Turn RS out.

> **NOTE:** *Start on the opposite end of the long rectangle to add the ribbing. The slip stitch ribbing is attached as it is worked, so there's no sewing together at the end! Work slip stitches loosely.*

RIBBING

With RS facing, attach yarn on bottom corner, ch 1, sc in ea st across bottom short end of long rectangle, rotate so you are now working along one long side (with RS of work facing you), ch 6, turn, sl st in 2nd ch from hook and in ea of next 4 ch sts back down to cocoon, sl st in cocoon to join, *ch 1, turn, sk the first sl st, sl st in BLO of next 5 sts, ch 1, turn, sl st in BLO of next 5 sts back to cocoon, sl st in cocoon to join*, repeat between *...* ALL the way around cocoon to the first sc (work stitches farther apart on hood so ribbing curves in a little), ending with invisible join in end of first sl st row completed.

ASSEMBLY

Fold the bottom end of the rectangle up to about 1" (3 cm) below where the hood ends (making sure RS is the "outside" of the cocoon). Determine how many buttons will be needed by laying them out on each side of the ribbing (they will be sewn through the front ribbing only). Sew the buttons on each side as desired (buttons are decorative only and not functional). There are two different options (after adding the buttons) for stitching the sides of the cocoon together. Using a yarn needle and the same yarn, the cocoon can either be stitched together on the outer edges of the ribbing (see the cream cocoon in the photos [page 41]), or stitched together where the ribbing meets the cocoon (see the gray cocoon in the photos [pages 40 and 42]). To use, simply slide the baby in the cocoon.

TEXTURE WEAVE BABY BOOTIES

Using a traditional basket-weave texture, these booties are both warm and adorable. This is the perfect go-to pattern when you need a last-minute baby shower gift.

SKILL LEVEL: ⬛⬛⬜ Intermediate

MATERIALS

TOOLS	Stitch markers, measuring tape, yarn needle
YARN	3 oz (85 g) or less of #4 worsted weight yarn
GAUGE	Gauge checkpoint given in pattern after Row 3
HOOK SIZE	"G" (4 mm) or "H" (5 mm) hook or to match gauge (make sole and compare to size chart)

SIZE CHART AND GAUGE

Ages are approximate. *Please* measure baby's feet! Gauge checkpoint is also given in pattern for each size.

0–3 MONTHS	3.5" (9-cm) sole
3–6 MONTHS	4" (10-cm) sole
6–12 MONTHS	4.5" (11-cm) sole

ABBREVIATIONS USED

ST(S)	stitch(es)
CH	chain stitch
SC	single crochet
HDC	half double crochet
DC	double crochet
FPSC	front post single crochet
FPDC	front post double crochet
BPDC	back post double crochet
HDC2TOG	half double crochet 2 stitches together
SL ST	slip stitch
RND(S)	round(s)
EA	each
BEG	beginning
PREV	previous
BLO	Back Loop Only
RS	Right Side
WS	Wrong Side
YO	Yarn Over

SPECIAL STITCHES DEFINITIONS

FRONT POST SINGLE CROCHET (FPSC): Insert the hook from the front side of the work (right to left) under the post of the indicated stitch, YO and pull up a loop, YO and draw through 2 loops.

FRONT POST DOUBLE CROCHET (FPDC): Working from the front side of the work, YO and insert the hook from right to left under the post of the double crochet indicated from the previous round, YO and pull up a loop, [YO and draw through 2 loops] twice.

BACK POST DOUBLE CROCHET (BPDC): Working from the back side of the work, YO and insert the hook from right to left over the post of the double crochet indicated from the previous round, YO and pull up a loop, [YO and draw through 2 loops] twice.

HALF DOUBLE CROCHET 2 STITCHES TOGETHER (HDC2TOG): [YO, insert hook in next stitch, YO and pull up a loop] twice, YO and draw through all 5 loops on hook.

0-3 MONTHS TEXTURE WEAVE BOOTIES

Use "G" (4 mm) or "H" (5 mm) hook, or match gauge checkpoint after Rnd 2.

(SOLE) RND 1: ch 11, place stitch marker around loop on hook, 2 hdc in 3rd ch from hook, hdc in ea of next 7 ch, 6 hdc in last ch. Turn work so you are now working on the opposite side of the foundation ch, hdc in ea of next 7 sts, 2 hdc in last st, join with sl st in stitch with marker. (24)

(SOLE) RND 2: ch 1 (does not count as a st), place stitch marker around loop on hook, work 2 sc in base of ch 1, sc in ea of next 7 sts, hdc in next st, dc in next st, 2 dc in next 5 sts, dc in next st, hdc in next st, sc in ea of next 7 sts, 2 sc in last st, join with sl st in stitch with marker. (32)

GAUGE CHECKPOINT: *Measure the length of the sole; it should be approximately 3.5" (9 cm) here. If not, adjust the hook size and redo.*

RND 3: ch 2 (does not count as a st), place stitch marker around loop on hook, working in BLO for entire rnd, hdc in same st as ch 2 and next 13 sts, hdc2tog twice, hdc in next 14 sts, join with sl st in stitch with marker. (30)

NOTE: *The side with the unused front loops is the bottom of the sole. Turn and work in the opposite direction after each round to keep the back seam straight. Add a stitch marker to the loop around the hook after the beginning ch 2. At the end of the round, join in the stitch with the stitch marker (top of ch 2). To work with WS facing means to have the inside of the bootie facing you. To work with RS facing means to have the outside of the bootie facing you.*

RND 4: (WS) ch 2 (does not count as a st), turn (now working in both loops again and in opposite direction), hdc in same st as ch 2 and next 10 sts, (hdc2tog) 4 times, hdc in next 11 sts, join with sl st in top of ch 2. (26)

RND 5: (RS) ch 2 (does not count as a st), turn, hdc in same st as ch 2 and next 8 sts, (hdc2tog) 4 times, hdc in next 9 sts, join with sl st in top of ch 2. (22)

RND 6: (WS) ch 2 (does not count as a st), turn, hdc in same st as ch 2 and next 6 sts, (hdc2tog) 4 times, hdc in next 7 sts, join with sl st in top of ch 2. (18)

RND 7: (RS) ch 2 (counts as a dc), turn, dc in next 7 sts, 2 dc in ea of next 2 sts, dc in next 8 sts, join with sl st in top of ch 2. (20)

NOTE: *All rounds will be worked from the RS from this point (do not turn). The "fpsc and ch 2" at the beginning of the following rounds creates a stitch that looks like a fpdc. Be sure to crochet the fpsc tightly around the post so it doesn't bulge at the base of the ch 2. It is correct if it looks very similar to a fpdc. Starting the round in this fashion (instead of a standard ch 2) will result in a seam that is almost completely invisible.*

RND 8: (do not ch or turn) fpsc around beg ch 2 from prev rnd, ch 2 (counts as first fpdc), fpdc around next st, bpdc around next 2 sts, *fpdc around next 2 sts, bpdc around next 2 sts*, repeat between *...* to end of rnd, join with sl st in top of ch 2. (20)

RND 9: fpsc around beg ch 2 from prev rnd, ch 2 (counts as first fpdc), fpdc around next fpdc, bpdc around ea of next 2 bpdc, *fpdc around ea of next 2 fpdc, bpdc around ea of next 2 bpdc*, repeat between *...* to end of rnd, join with sl st in top of ch 2. (20)

RND 10: sl st in next st, fpsc around first bpdc of prev rnd, ch 2 (counts as first fpdc), fpdc around next bpdc, bpdc around ea of next 2 fpdc, *fpdc around ea of next 2 bpdc, bpdc around ea of next 2 fpdc*, repeat between *...* to end of rnd, join with sl st in top of ch 2. (20)

RND 11: Repeat Rnd 9. Fasten off with invisible join in top of ch 2. Weave in ends.

REPEAT the instructions for the second bootie.

OPTIONAL: Thread a piece of yarn (or ch a short tie) through base of Rnd 7.

3-6 MONTHS TEXTURE WEAVE BOOTIES

Use "G" (4 mm) or "H" (5 mm) hook, or match gauge checkpoint after Rnd 3.

(SOLE) RND 1: ch 11, place stitch marker around loop on hook, 2 hdc in 3rd ch from hook, hdc in ea of next 7 ch, 6 hdc in last ch. Turn work so you are now working on the opposite side of the foundation ch, hdc in ea of next 7 sts, 2 hdc in last st, join with sl st in stitch with marker. (24)

(SOLE) RND 2: ch 1 (does not count as a st), place stitch marker around loop on hook, work 2 sc in base of ch 1, sc in ea of next 7 sts, hdc in next st, dc in next st, 2 dc in next 5 sts, dc in next st, hdc in next st, sc in ea of next 7 sts, 2 sc in last st, join with sl st in stitch with marker. (32)

(SOLE) RND 3: ch 1 (does not count as a st), place stitch marker around loop on hook, work 2 sc in base of ch 1, sc in ea of next 10 sts, [2 sc in next st, sc in next st] 5 times, sc in ea of next 10 sts, 2 sc in last st, join with sl st in stitch with marker. (39)

> **GAUGE CHECKPOINT:** *Measure the length of the sole; it should be approximately 4" (10 cm) here. If not, adjust the hook size and redo.*

RND 4: ch 2 (does not count as a st), place stitch marker around loop on hook, working in BLO for entire rnd, hdc in same st as ch 2 and next 18 sts, hdc2tog, hdc in next 18 sts, join with sl st in stitch with marker. (38)

> **NOTE:** *The side with the unused front loops is the bottom of the sole. Turn and work in the opposite direction after each round to keep the back seam straight. Add a stitch marker to the loop around the hook after the beginning ch 2. At the end of the round, join in the stitch with the stitch marker (top of ch 2). To work with WS facing means to have the inside of the bootie facing you. To work with RS facing means to have the outside of the bootie facing you.*

RND 5: (WS) ch 2 (does not count as a st), turn (now working in both loops again and in opposite direction), hdc in same st as ch 2 and next 14 sts, (hdc2tog) 4 times, hdc in next 15 sts, join with sl st in top of ch 2. (34)

RND 6: (RS) ch 2 (does not count as a st), turn, hdc in same st as ch 2 and next 12 sts, (hdc2tog) 4 times, hdc in next 13 sts, join with sl st in top of ch 2. (30)

RND 7: (WS) ch 2 (does not count as a st), turn, hdc in same st as ch 2 and next 10 sts, (hdc2tog) 4 times, hdc in next 11 sts, join with sl st in top of ch 2. (26)

RND 8: (RS) ch 2 (does not count as a st), turn, hdc in same st as ch 2 and next 8 sts, (hdc2tog) 4 times, hdc in next 9 sts, join with sl st in top of ch 2. (22)

> **NOTE:** *All rounds will be worked from the RS from this point (do not turn). The "fpsc and ch 2" at the beginning of the following rounds creates a stitch that looks like a fpdc. Be sure to crochet the fpsc tightly around the post so it doesn't bulge at the base of the ch 2. It is correct if it looks very similar to a fpdc. Starting the round in this fashion (instead of a standard ch 2) will result in a seam that is almost completely invisible.*

RND 9: (RS) ch 2 (counts as a dc), dc in next 9 sts, 2 dc in next st, dc in next st, 2 dc in next st, dc in next 9 sts, join with sl st in top of ch 2. (24)

RND 10: (do not ch or turn) fpsc around beg ch 2 from prev rnd, ch 2 (counts as first fpdc), fpdc around next st, bpdc around next 2 sts, *fpdc around next 2 sts, bpdc around next 2 sts*, repeat between *...* to end of rnd, join with sl st in top of ch 2. (24)

RND 11: fpsc around beg ch 2 from prev rnd, ch 2 (counts as first fpdc), fpdc around next fpdc, bpdc around ea of next 2 bpdc, *fpdc around ea of next 2 fpdc, bpdc around ea of next 2 bpdc*, repeat between *...* to end of rnd, join with sl st in top of ch 2. (24)

RND 12: sl st in next st, fpsc around first bpdc of prev rnd, ch 2 (counts as first fpdc), fpdc around next bpdc, bpdc around ea of next 2 fpdc, *fpdc around ea of next 2 bpdc, bpdc around ea of next 2 fpdc*, repeat between *...* to end of rnd, join with sl st in top of ch 2. (24)

RND 13: Repeat Rnd 11. Fasten off with invisible join in top of ch 2. Weave in ends.

REPEAT the instructions for the second bootie.

OPTIONAL: Thread a piece of yarn (or ch a short tie) through base of Rnd 9.

6-12 MONTHS TEXTURE WEAVE BOOTIES

Use "G" (4 mm) or "H" (5 mm) hook, or match gauge checkpoint after Rnd 3.

(SOLE) RND 1: ch 11, place stitch marker around loop on hook, 2 hdc in 3rd ch from hook, hdc in ea of next 7 ch, 6 hdc in last ch. Turn work so you are now working on the opposite side of the foundation ch, hdc in ea of next 7 sts, 2 hdc in last st, join with sl st in stitch with marker. (24)

(SOLE) RND 2: ch 1 (does not count as a st), place stitch marker around loop on hook, work 2 sc in base of ch 1, sc in ea of next 7 sts, hdc in next st, dc in next st, 2 dc in next 5 sts, dc in next st, hdc in next st, sc in ea of next 7 sts, 2 sc in last st, join with sl st in stitch with marker. (32)

(SOLE) RND 3: ch 2 (does not count as a st), place stitch marker around loop on hook, work 2 hdc in base of ch 1, sc in ea of next 10 sts, [2 hdc in next st, hdc in next st] 5 times, sc in ea of next 10 sts, 2 hdc in last st, join with sl st in stitch with marker. (39)

GAUGE CHECKPOINT: *Measure the length of the sole; it should be approximately 4.5" (11 cm) here. If not, adjust the hook size and redo.*

RND 4: ch 2 (does not count as a st), place stitch marker around loop on hook, working in BLO for entire rnd, hdc in same st as ch 2 and next 18 sts, hdc2tog, hdc in next 18 sts, join with sl st in st with marker. (38)

NOTE: *The side with the unused front loops is the bottom of the sole. Turn and work in the opposite direction after each round to keep the back seam straight. Add a stitch marker to the loop around the hook after the beginning ch 2. At the end of the round, join in the stitch with the stitch marker (top of ch 2). To work with WS facing means to have the inside of the bootie facing you. To work with RS facing means to have the outside of the bootie facing you.*

RND 5: (WS) ch 2 (does not count as a st), turn (now working in both loops again and in opposite direction), hdc in same st as ch 2 and next 14 sts, (hdc2tog) 4 times, hdc in next 15 sts, join with sl st in top of ch 2. (34)

RND 6: (RS) ch 2 (does not count as a st), turn, hdc in same st as ch 2 and next 12 sts, (hdc2tog) 4 times, hdc in next 13 sts, join with sl st in top of ch 2. (30)

RND 7: (WS) ch 2 (does not count as a st), turn, hdc in same st as ch 2 and next 10 sts, (hdc2tog) 4 times, hdc in next 11 sts, join with sl st in top of ch 2. (26)

RND 8: (RS) ch 2 (does not count as a st), turn, hdc in same st as ch 2 and next 8 sts, (hdc2tog) 4 times, hdc in next 9 sts, join with sl st in top of ch 2. (22)

> **NOTE:** *All rounds will be worked from the RS from this point (do not turn). The "fpsc and ch 2" at the beginning of the following rounds creates a stitch that looks like a fpdc. Be sure to crochet the fpsc tightly around the post so it doesn't bulge at the base of the ch 2. It is correct if it looks very similar to a fpdc. Starting the round in this fashion (instead of a standard ch 2) will result in a seam that is almost completely invisible.*

RND 9: (RS) ch 2 (counts as a dc), dc in next 9 sts, 2 dc in next st, dc in next st, 2 dc in next st, dc in next 9 sts, join with sl st in top of ch 2. (24)

RND 10: (do not ch or turn) fpsc around beg ch 2 from prev rnd, ch 2 (counts as first fpdc), fpdc around next st, bpdc around next 2 sts, *fpdc around next 2 sts, bpdc around next 2 sts*, repeat between *...* to end of rnd, join with sl st in top of ch 2. (24)

RND 11: fpsc around beg ch 2 from prev rnd, ch 2 (counts as first fpdc), fpdc around next fpdc, bpdc around ea of next 2 bpdc, *fpdc around ea of next 2 fpdc, bpdc around ea of next 2 bpdc*, repeat between *...* to end of rnd, join with sl st in top of ch 2. (24)

RND 12: sl st in next st, fpsc around first bpdc of prev rnd, ch 2 (counts as first fpdc), fpdc around next bpdc, bpdc around ea of next 2 fpdc, *fpdc around ea of next 2 bpdc, bpdc around ea of next 2 fpdc*, repeat between *...* to end of rnd, join with sl st in top of ch 2. (24)

RND 13: Repeat Rnd 11. Fasten off with invisible join in top of ch 2. Weave in ends.

REPEAT the instructions for the second bootie.

OPTIONAL: Thread a piece of yarn (or ch a short tie) through base of Rnd 9.

SNOW BUNNY BABY BOOTIES

Keep baby's feet toasty warm with these fun booties topped off with an interesting "loopy" stitch. Pair them with the matching Snow Bunny Hat (page 197) for a complementing set.

SKILL LEVEL: ⬛⬜ Intermediate

MATERIALS

TOOLS	Stitch markers, measuring tape, yarn needle
YARN	3 oz (85 g) or less of #4 worsted weight yarn
HOOK SIZE	"G" (4 mm) or "H" (5 mm) hook or to match gauge (make sole and compare to size chart)

SIZE CHART AND GAUGE

Ages are approximate. *Please* measure baby's feet! Gauge checkpoint is also given in pattern for each size.

0–3 MONTHS	3.5" (9 cm) sole
3–6 MONTHS	4" (10 cm) sole
6–12 MONTHS	4.5" (11 cm) sole

ABBREVIATIONS USED

ST(S)	stitch(es)
CH	chain stitch
SC	single crochet
HDC	half double crochet
DC	double crochet
HDC2TOG	half double crochet 2 stitches together
SL ST	slip stitch
RND(S)	round(s)
EA	each
BEG	beginning
PREV	previous
BLO	Back Loop Only
FLO	Front Loop Only
RS	Right Side
WS	Wrong Side
YO	Yarn Over

SPECIAL STITCHES DEFINITIONS

HALF DOUBLE CROCHET 2 STITCHES TOGETHER (HDC2TOG): YO, insert hook in next stitch, YO and pull up a loop, twice, YO and draw through all 5 loops on hook.

0-3 MONTHS SNOW BUNNY BABY BOOTIES

Use "G" (4 mm) or "H" (5 mm) hook, or match gauge checkpoint after Rnd 2.

(SOLE) RND 1: ch 11, place stitch marker around loop on hook, 2 hdc in 3rd ch from hook, hdc in ea of next 7 ch, 6 hdc in last ch. Turn work so you are now working on the opposite side of the foundation ch, hdc in ea of next 7 sts, 2 hdc in last st, join with sl st in stitch with marker. (24)

(SOLE) RND 2: ch 1 (does not count as a st), place stitch marker around loop on hook, work 2 sc in base of ch 1, sc in ea of next 7 sts, hdc in next st, dc in next st, 2 dc in next 5 sts, dc in next st, hdc in next st, sc in ea of next 7 sts, 2 sc in last st, join with sl st in stitch with marker. (32)

> **GAUGE CHECKPOINT:** *Measure the length of the sole; it should be approximately 3.5" (9 cm) here. If not, adjust the hook size and redo.*

RND 3: ch 2 (does not count as a st), place stitch marker around loop on hook, working in BLO for entire rnd, hdc in same st as ch 2 and next 13 sts, hdc2tog twice, hdc in next 14 sts, join with sl st in stitch with marker. (30)

> **NOTE:** *The side with the unused front loops is the bottom of the sole. Turn and work in the opposite direction after each round to keep the back seam straight. Add a stitch marker to the loop around the hook after the beginning ch 2. At the end of the round, join in the stitch with the stitch marker (top of ch 2). To work with WS facing means to have the inside of the bootie facing you. To work with RS facing means to have the outside of the bootie facing you.*

RND 4: (WS) ch 2 (does not count as a st), turn (now working in both loops again and in opposite direction), hdc in same st as ch 2 and next 10 sts, (hdc2tog) 4 times, hdc in next 11 sts, join with sl st in top of ch 2. (26)

RND 5: (RS) ch 2 (does not count as a st), turn, hdc in same st as ch 2 and next 8 sts, (hdc2tog) 4 times, hdc in next 9 sts, join with sl st in top of ch 2. (22)

RND 6: (WS) ch 2 (does not count as a st), turn, hdc in same st as ch 2 and next 6 sts, (hdc2tog) 4 times, hdc in next 7 sts, join with sl st in top of ch 2. (18)

RND 7: (RS) ch 2 (does not count as a st), turn, dc in same st as ch 2 and next 7 sts, 2 dc in ea of next 2 sts, dc in next 8 sts, join with sl st in top of ch 2. (20)

> **NOTE:** *All rounds will be worked from the RS from this point (do not turn). Each of the following rounds is made up of two parts and will be worked in two rounds by first using the FLO for the "loops" (Rnd 1), then going around again and using the unused back loop (Rnd 2) for the dc stitches that provide the height of the bootie.*

RND 1: ch 5, sl st in FLO of same st as ch 5, *ch 5, sl st in FLO of next st*, repeat between *...* to end of rnd, join with sl in BLO of first st. (20 loops)

RND 2: ch 2 (does not count as a st), dc in BLO of same st as ch 2 and BLO of ea st to end of rnd, join with sl st in top of ch 2. (20)

REPEAT RNDS 1 AND 2 once. Fasten off with invisible join in top of ch 2.

WEAVE in ends. (Repeat for second bootie.)

OPTIONAL: Thread a piece of yarn (or ch a short tie) through base of Rnd 7.

3-6 MONTHS SNOW BUNNY BABY BOOTIES

Use "G" (4 mm) or "H" (5 mm) hook, or match gauge checkpoint after Rnd 3.

(SOLE) RND 1: ch 11, place stitch marker around loop on hook, 2 hdc in 3rd ch from hook, hdc in ea of next 7 ch, 6 hdc in last ch. Turn work so you are now working on the opposite side of the foundation ch, hdc in ea of next 7 sts, 2 hdc in last st, join with sl st in stitch with marker. (24)

(SOLE) RND 2: ch 1 (does not count as a st), place stitch marker around loop on hook, work 2 sc in base of ch 1, sc in ea of next 7 sts, hdc in next st, dc in next st, 2 dc in next 5 sts, dc in next st, hdc in next st, sc in ea of next 7 sts, 2 sc in last st, join with sl st in stitch with marker. (32)

(SOLE) RND 3: ch 1 (does not count as a st), place stitch marker around loop on hook, work 2 sc in base of ch 1, sc in ea of next 10 sts, [2 sc in next st, sc in next st] 5 times, sc in ea of next 10 sts, 2 sc in last st, join with sl st in stitch with marker. (39)

> **GAUGE CHECKPOINT:** *Measure the length of the sole; it should be approximately 4" (10 cm) here. If not, adjust the hook size and redo.*

RND 4: ch 2 (does not count as a st), place stitch marker around loop on hook, working in BLO for entire rnd, hdc in same st as ch 2 and next 18 sts, hdc2tog, hdc in next 18 sts, join with sl st in stitch with marker. (38)

> **NOTE:** *The side with the unused front loops is the bottom of the sole. Turn and work in the opposite direction after each round to keep the back seam straight. Add a stitch marker to the loop around the hook after the beginning ch 2. At the end of the round, join in the stitch with the stitch marker (top of ch 2). To work with WS facing means to have the inside of the bootie facing you. To work with RS facing means to have the outside of the bootie facing you.*

RND 5: (WS) ch 2 (does not count as a st), turn (now working in both loops again and in opposite direction), hdc in same st as ch 2 and next 14 sts, (hdc2tog) 4 times, hdc in next 15 sts, join with sl st in top of ch 2. (34)

RND 6: (RS) ch 2 (does not count as a st), turn, hdc in same st as ch 2 and next 12 sts, (hdc2tog) 4 times, hdc in next 13 sts, join with sl st in top of ch 2. (30)

RND 7: (WS) ch 2 (does not count as a st), turn, hdc in same st as ch 2 and next 10 sts, (hdc2tog) 4 times, hdc in next 11 sts, join with sl st in top of ch 2. (26)

RND 8: (RS) ch 2 (does not count as a st), turn, hdc in same st as ch 2 and next 8 sts, (hdc2tog) 4 times, hdc in next 9 sts, join with sl st in top of ch 2. (22)

> **NOTE:** *All rounds will be worked from the RS from this point (do not turn).*

RND 9: (RS) ch 2 (does not count as a st), dc in same st as ch 2 and next 9 sts, 2 dc in next st, dc in next st, 2 dc in next st, dc in next 9 sts, join with sl st in top of ch 2. (24)

NOTE: *Each of the following rounds is made up of two parts and will be worked in two rounds by first using the front loop for the "loops" (Rnd 1), then going around again and using the unused back loop (Rnd 2) for the dc stitches that provide the height of the bootie.*

RND 1: ch 5, sl st in FLO of same st as ch 5, *ch 5, sl st in FLO of next st*, repeat between *...* to end of rnd, join with sl in BLO of first st. (24 loops)

RND 2: ch 2 (does not count as a st), dc in BLO of same st as ch 2 and BLO of ea st to end of rnd, join with sl st in top of ch 2. (24)

REPEAT RNDS 1 AND 2 once. Fasten off with invisible join in top of ch 2.

WEAVE in ends. (Repeat for second bootie.)

OPTIONAL: Thread a piece of yarn (or ch a short tie) through base of Rnd 9.

6–12 MONTHS SNOW BUNNY BABY BOOTIES

Use "G" (4 mm) or "H" (5 mm) hook, or match gauge checkpoint after Rnd 3.

(SOLE) RND 1: ch 11, place stitch marker around loop on hook, 2 hdc in 3rd ch from hook, hdc in ea of next 7 ch, 6 hdc in last ch. Turn work so you are now working on the opposite side of the foundation ch, hdc in ea of next 7 sts, 2 hdc in last st, join with sl st in stitch with marker. (24)

(SOLE) RND 2: ch 1 (does not count as a st), place stitch marker around loop on hook, work 2 sc in base of ch 1, sc in ea of next 7 sts, hdc in next st, dc in next st, 2 dc in next 5 sts, dc in next st, hdc in next st, sc in ea of next 7 sts, 2 sc in last st, join with sl st in stitch with marker. (32)

(SOLE) RND 3: ch 2 (does not count as a st), place stitch marker around loop on hook, work 2 hdc in base of ch 1, sc in ea of next 10 sts, [2 hdc in next st, hdc in next st] 5 times, sc in ea of next 10 sts, 2 hdc in last st, join with sl st in stitch with marker. (39)

GAUGE CHECKPOINT: *Measure the length of the sole; it should be approximately 4.5" (11 cm) here. If not, adjust the hook size and redo.*

RND 4: ch 2 (does not count as a st), place stitch marker around loop on hook, working in BLO for entire rnd, hdc in same st as ch 2 and next 18 sts, hdc2tog, hdc in next 18 sts, join with sl st in st with marker. (38)

RND 5: (WS) ch 2 (does not count as a st), turn (now working in both loops again and in opposite direction), hdc in same st as ch 2 and next 14 sts, (hdc2tog) 4 times, hdc in next 15 sts, join with sl st in top of ch 2. (34)

RND 6: (RS) ch 2 (does not count as a st), turn, hdc in same st as ch 2 and next 12 sts, (hdc2tog) 4 times, hdc in next 13 sts, join with sl st in top of ch 2. (30)

RND 7: (WS) ch 2 (does not count as a st), turn, hdc in same st as ch 2 and next 10 sts, (hdc2tog) 4 times, hdc in next 11 sts, join with sl st in top of ch 2. (26)

RND 8: (RS) ch 2 (does not count as a st), turn, hdc in same st as ch 2 and next 8 sts, (hdc2tog) 4 times, hdc in next 9 sts, join with sl st in top of ch 2. (22)

RND 9: (RS) ch 2 (does not count as a st), dc in same st as ch 2 and next 9 sts, 2 dc in next st, dc in next st, 2 dc in next st, dc in next 9 sts, join with sl st in top of ch 2. (24)

RND 1: ch 5, sl st in FLO of same st as ch 5, *ch 5, sl st in FLO of next st*, repeat between *...* to end of rnd, join with sl st in BLO of first st. (24 loops)

RND 2: ch 2 (does not count as a st), dc in BLO of same st as ch 2 and BLO of ea st to end of rnd, join with sl st in top of ch 2. (24)

REPEAT RNDS 1 AND 2 once (or twice for a taller bootie). Fasten off with invisible join in top of ch 2.

WEAVE in ends. (Repeat for second bootie.)

OPTIONAL: Thread a piece of yarn (or ch a short tie) through base of Rnd 9.

2

PHOTOGRAPHY PROPS & NURSERY DÉCOR

Decorating a nursery and planning a newborn photo session are often the most anticipated events for new parents. In this chapter, you'll find several adorable projects—many that can make unique handmade gifts for expecting parents and serve a dual purpose as a prop or nursery decoration. Cover all your bases with the Faux Bearskin Nursery Rug (page 62): Use it for a newborn photography session, then use it to decorate the nursery! The Lion & Lioness Baby Bonnet (page 67) can also be multipurposed as a photo prop, Halloween costume accessory or just an everyday warm bonnet.

BEAR LOVEY PHOTO PROP

Whether you are making the Bear Lovey for a photography prop or a special gift for baby, you will love the option to swap out the lovey blanket for a different color or texture. Match the nursery décor or even a favorite outfit in a photo session.

SKILL LEVEL: ◼◼◻ Intermediate

MATERIALS

TOOLS	Stitch marker, measuring tape, 12–18 mm safety animal eyes, 15–21 mm safety bear/dog nose (eye/nose sizes can vary; anything within ranges listed will work), small amount of polyester fiberfill stuffing, yarn needle, button, needle and thread, bow hair-clip (optional)
YARN	2 oz (57 g) of #5 bulky "fur" type black yarn for head/ears (Lion Brand Luxe Fur is pictured), small amount of #4 worsted weight tan yarn for muzzle (Lion Brand Suede is pictured), and 4 oz (113 g) or less of #4 worsted weight yarn for blanket (Bernat Baby Blanket Tiny is pictured)
GAUGE	Gauge checkpoint listed in pattern after Rnd 4 of Bear Head
HOOK SIZE	"J" (6 mm) crochet hook, or to match yarn gauge

SIZE CHART

BEAR HEAD	Approximate dimensions are 10–12" (25–30 cm) circumference and 5" (13 cm) tall
LOVEY	Can be made in any size; 15" x 15" (38 x 38 cm) is a good standard size

DISCLAIMER

Buttons can be a safety hazard for babies and young children. NEVER leave a child unsupervised with this photo prop. If you are selling this item, please also warn your customers.

ABBREVIATIONS USED

ST(S)	stitch(es)
CH	chain stitch
SC	single crochet
DC	double crochet
SC2TOG	single crochet 2 stitches together
SL ST	slip stitch
RND(S)	round(s)
SK	skip
SP	space
EA	each
BEG	beginning
YO	Yarn Over

SPECIAL STITCHES DEFINITIONS

SINGLE CROCHET 2 STITCHES TOGETHER (SC2TOG):
Insert hook in stitch indicated, YO and draw up a loop, insert hook in next st, YO and draw up another loop. YO again and draw through all 3 loops on hook.

BEAR LOVEY PHOTO PROP

Work the entire pattern in the order listed.

EARS (MAKE 2)

Use #5 bulky weight black "fur" yarn and a "J" (6 mm) hook.

RND 1: ch 2, work 6 sc in 2nd ch from hook, do not join. (6)

RND 2: work 2 sc in ea st to end of rnd. (12)

FASTEN OFF with sl st (leave long tail to fasten onto head).

BEAR HEAD

Use #5 bulky weight black "fur" yarn and a "J" (6 mm) hook.

> **NOTE:** *This section is worked in continuous rounds. Do not join. Add marker and move with each round.*

RND 1: ch 2, work 6 sc in 2nd ch from hook, do not join. (6)

RND 2: work 2 sc in ea st to end of rnd. (12)

RND 3: *sc in next st, 2 sc in next st*, repeat between *...* to end of rnd. (18)

RND 4: *sc in ea of next 2 sts, 2 sc in next st*, repeat between *...* to end of rnd. (24)

> **GAUGE CHECKPOINT:** *Diameter of the circle should measure approximately 4" (10 cm) here.*

RND 5: sc in ea st to end of rnd. (24)

REPEAT RND 5 until the bear head measures approximately 3.5 to 4" (9 to 10 cm) from top to bottom (center of first round to edge). Do not fasten off yet.

EAR ASSEMBLY

Attach the ears to the head using the tail end of yarn. Set the bear head aside to make the muzzle.

MUZZLE

Use a contrasting (tan) yarn of your choice and a hook size appropriate to the yarn (making sure that the stitches are tight to securely hold the safety eyes and nose).

> **NOTE:** *This section is worked in continuous rounds. Do not join. Add marker and move with each round.*

RND 1: ch 2, work 8 sc in 2nd ch from hook, do not join. (8)

OR MAGIC ring, ch 1, work 8 sc in ring, do not join. (8)

RND 2: work 2 sc in ea st to end of rnd. (16)

RND 3: *sc in next st, 2 sc in next st*, repeat between *...* to end of rnd. (24)

FASTEN OFF (leave a long tail to fasten onto the head) with sl st (or invisible join).

FACE ASSEMBLY & STUFFING

Using a yarn needle and the tail end of your yarn, attach the muzzle to the head. Place the safety eyes through muzzle and attach the backs securely (see Disclaimer on page 59). Place the safety nose through the muzzle and attach the back securely. Stuff the bear head with a small amount of polyester fiberfill stuffing.

BEAR HEAD (CONTINUED)

Continuing with the bear head (to close up neck opening): *sc in next st, sc2tog over next 2 sts*, repeat between *…* to end of rnd, then work sc2tog until opening is almost closed. Stitch remaining space shut with tail end of yarn and yarn needle.

BUTTON (PHOTO PROP) OPTION

Sew an appropriate size button to the bottom of the head.

> **NOTE:** *If desired, the blanket can also be sewn onto the head for a permanent lovey option. However, the lovey should never be left unsupervised with babies.*

GRANNY SQUARE LOVEY BLANKET

Use #4 worsted weight yarn and "J" (6 mm) hook.

RND 1: ch 6, join with sl st to form a ring, ch 6 (counts as dc plus ch 3), [work 3 dc in ring, ch 3] 3 times, work 2 dc in ring, join with sl st in 3rd ch of beg ch-6.

> **TIP:** *At this point, test the size of the center opening with the button you wish to use. You can adjust the size by redoing the beginning chain with more (or fewer) chain stitches.*

RND 2: sl st in ch-3 sp directly below, ch 6 (counts as dc plus ch 3), work (3 dc, ch 1) in same sp, [sk next 3 dc, work (3 dc, ch 3, 3 dc, ch 1) in next corner ch-3 sp] 3 times, work 2 dc in beg ch-3 sp, join with sl st in 3rd ch of beg ch-6.

RND 3: sl st in ch-3 sp directly below, ch 6 (counts as dc plus ch 3), work (3 dc, ch 1) in same sp, [sk next 3 dc, 3 dc in next ch-1 sp, ch 1, sk next 3 dc, (3 dc, ch 3, 3 dc, ch 1) in next corner ch-3 sp] 3 times, repeat between [...] for 4th side, ending with 2 dc in beg ch-3 sp, join with sl st in 3rd ch of beg ch-6.

RND 4: sl st in ch-3 sp directly below, ch 6 (counts as dc plus ch 3), work (3 dc, ch 1) in same sp, *work (3 dc, ch 1) in each ch-1 sp to corner, work (3 dc, ch 3, 3 dc, ch 1) in corner ch-3 sp*, repeat between *…* to beg ch-sp, work 2 dc in beg ch-3 sp, join with sl st in 3rd ch of beg ch-6.

REPEAT RND 4 until the lovey blanket is the desired size (a 15″ [38-cm] square is a nice prop size). On the last round, fasten off with invisible join (or sl st) in 3rd ch of beg ch-6. To attach the blanket to the head, push the button through the center opening of the blanket.

FAUX BEARSKIN NURSERY RUG

The Faux Bearskin Nursery Rug pattern is a luxurious "no animals harmed" option for adorable nursery décor or the perfect photography prop. The entire body is actually crocheted, but it has the appearance of real fur to even experienced crocheters! This rug has so many options, and it is a favorite of both moms and photographers alike.

SKILL LEVEL: ◖■■▮ ▭ Intermediate

MATERIALS

TOOLS	Stitch markers, measuring tape, 18–24 mm safety animal eyes, 30–40 mm safety bear/dog nose (eye/nose sizes can vary; anything within ranges listed will work), small amount of polyester fiberfill stuffing, yarn needle (for weaving in ends)
COLOR SUGGESTIONS	**BLACK BEAR =** black fur, cream or tan muzzle, brown eyes **BROWN BEAR =** brown fur, brown or tan muzzle, brown or caramel eyes **POLAR BEAR =** white or cream fur, white or cream muzzle, brown eyes **PANDA BEAR =** white or cream fur, black ears/legs, black eye patches, brown eyes
YARN	**MUZZLE:** Small amount of desired color in either #4 worsted weight or #5 chunky weight yarn **BEAR "FUR":** 12–15 skeins of Red Heart Boutique Fur (or any #7 jumbo weight "fur" yarn) **PANDA "FUR":** 9 skeins of cream/white & 6 skeins of black Red Heart Boutique Fur (or any #7 jumbo weight "fur" yarn) **EYE PATCHES FOR PANDA:** Small amount of black #4 worsted weight yarn
GAUGE	**MUZZLE:** Gauge checkpoint of approximately 4" (10 cm) after Rnd 5 with 6 mm hook **FUR:** 4 stitches and 3 rows in sc = 4" x 4" (10 x 10 cm) with 10 mm hook
HOOK SIZES	"J" (6 mm) crochet hook for muzzle, "P" (10 mm) crochet hook for head, ears and body. Different brands vary. Match the mm size, not the letter.

RUG SIZE

ONE SIZE	Approximate dimensions of the finished rug are 25" (64 cm) wide and 40" (102 cm) long (including head and legs). The head is about 10–11" (25–28 cm) wide. The muzzle is approximately 5.5" (14 cm) wide (flat). The legs are approximately 10" (25 cm) long. Body (from neck to tip of tail) is approximately 23" (58 cm) long. All measurements (except muzzle) are taken after the edging has been added and can vary according to individual tension.

ABBREVIATIONS USED

ST(S)	stitch(es)
CH	chain stitch
SC	single crochet
HDC	half double crochet
DC	double crochet
TR	treble crochet
SC2TOG	single crochet 2 stitches together
SL ST	slip stitch
RND(S)	round(s)
SK	skip
SP(S)	space(s)
EA	each
YO	Yarn Over

SPECIAL STITCHES DEFINITIONS

SINGLE CROCHET 2 STITCHES TOGETHER (SC2TOG): Insert hook in stitch indicated, YO and draw up a loop, insert hook in next st, YO and draw up another loop. YO again and draw through all 3 loops on hook.

TREBLE CROCHET (TR): YO hook twice, insert hook in indicated st and pull up a loop (4 loops on hook), YO and draw through 2 loops (3 loops on hook), YO hook and draw through 2 loops (2 loops on hook), YO hook and draw through last 2 loops.

FAUX BEARSKIN NURSERY RUG

Work the entire pattern in the order listed. See page 66 for Panda Bear instructions.

MUZZLE

Use either #4 worsted weight or #5 chunky yarn and "J" (6 mm) hook.

RND 1: Magic ring, ch 1, work 8 sc in ring, join with sl st in first sc. (8)

OR ch 2, work 8 sc in 2nd ch from hook, join with sl st in first sc. (8)

RND 2: 2 sc in ea st to end of rnd, do not join (add st marker, move with ea rnd). (16)

RND 3: *sc in next st, 2 sc in next st*, repeat between *...* to end of rnd. (24)

RND 4: *sc in ea of next 2 sts, 2 sc in next st*, repeat between *...* to end of rnd. (32)

RND 5: *sc in ea of next 3 sts, 2 sc in next st*, repeat between *...* to end of rnd. (40)

GAUGE CHECKPOINT: *Diameter of the circle should measure approximately 4" (10 cm) here. (If substituting with a yarn with a larger gauge, stop when the circle reaches 4" [10 cm] even if it is fewer sts.)*

RND 6: sc in ea st to end of rnd. (40, or to match gauge)

REPEAT RND 6 until the muzzle measures approximately 3 to 3.5" (8 to 9 cm) from center of circle to edge.

LAST RND OF MUZZLE: *ch 1, sk next st, sc in next st*, repeat between *...* to end of rnd (this round leaves openings to attach the larger fur yarn with a larger hook). (20 ch-1 sps) Fasten off muzzle yarn. Weave in ends.

ALL FUR PARTS (HEAD, EARS, BODY)

Use #7 jumbo weight fur yarn and "P" (10 mm) hook.

FURRY PART OF HEAD

TIP: *The fur yarn is very forgiving if a stitch is missed or stitches are placed wrong. "Feel" for each stitch and count each round. It is more important to have the right number of stitches than to worry about the exact placement of each stitch. Pull each stitch up to a height of approximately 1" (3 cm) on the hook using the 10 mm hook and #7 jumbo yarn.*

RND 1: Attach fur yarn to any ch-1 sp, ch 1, sc in same ch-1 sp, *work 2 sc in next ch-1 sp, 1 sc in next ch-1 sp*, repeat between *...* to last st, 2 sc in last ch-1 sp, join with sl st in first sc. Add stitch marker. Move stitch marker after each rnd. (30)

RND 2: sc in ea st to end of rnd, join with sl st. (30)

REPEAT RND 2 until the furry section measures about 3–4" (8–10 cm) from where it was attached to muzzle to the last rnd completed.

RND 3: *sc2tog over next 2 sts*, repeat between *...* until there's an opening about 4" (10 cm) wide. Fasten off. Weave in all ends. Follow next steps in exact order.

EARS (MAKE TWO)

With fur yarn, ch 2, work 8 hdc in 2nd ch from hook. Fasten off leaving a 12" (30 cm) long tail to sew on to the head.

ASSEMBLY OF HEAD

Place the eyes and nose first, making sure they are centered just right. Place the eyes at the edge of the muzzle where it meets the fur. Then sew each ear onto the head with the tail end of the yarn and a yarn needle. Stuff head loosely with fiberfill stuffing.

BODY

ch 3, attach to one side of the opening on the back of the head, work approximately 4–5 sc stitches across the opening (closing up the opening as you go), ch an additional 3 past the opening. (This is Row 1 of the body that connects the neck to the head, and the ch 3 on each side forms the shoulders.)

> **TIP:** *The body increases by adding an extra stitch on each end of the row until it is determined that the body is wide enough (keeping in mind that an additional round will be worked around the entire body, which adds a significant amount to the width as well).*

ROW 2: ch 1, turn, 2 sc in 2nd ch from hook, sc in ea ch (and ea sc) to last ch, 2 sc in last ch.

ROW 3: ch 1, turn, 2 sc in the first st, sc in ea st to last st, 2 sc in last st.

REPEAT ROW 3 until the body is approximately 10 to 11" (25 to 28 cm) wide (my rugs were 16–18 sts wide). It's better to err on the side of "too small" here so you don't run out of yarn. You can add extra edging rounds later if you have enough yarn and want to make it bigger. Mark the first and last stitch of the last increase row with stitch markers (this is where each front leg will begin).

ROW 4: ch 1, turn, sc in ea st to end of row.

REPEAT ROW 4 until the body is approximately 18–19" (46 to 48 cm) long. (The final length and width will be larger because of the edging that will be added later.) Fasten off (or, if you have a full skein connected at this point, you can leave it attached to start one of the back legs).

FRONT LEGS

Attach the fur yarn at the end of one shoulder in a marked stitch (either one), ch 1 and work 4 sc (toward head). Ch 1 and turn, sc in ea st to end of row. Repeat until the leg is about 8" (20 cm) long. Fasten off. Repeat for the other front leg.

BACK LEGS

Attach fur yarn at bottom corner of body (either one), ch 1 and sc in next 4 sts toward bottom middle of body (where the tail will be). Ch 1 and turn, sc in ea st to end of row. Repeat until leg is about 8" (20 cm) long. Fasten off. Repeat for other back leg.

EDGING

Attach fur yarn anywhere on body, ch 1 and sc around entire body, including legs. When you reach the middle of the body between the back legs, work the following 5 sts so they are perfectly centered between back legs (tail): (hdc, dc, tr, dc, hdc)

> **TIP:** *If you have extra fur yarn left over and you want to make the rug longer and wider, you can add an extra edging round. In that case, you might want to work the "tail" stitches in the very last edging round so they don't lose their shape. Fasten off. Weave in all ends.*

PANDA BEAR INSTRUCTIONS

Follow pattern as written with the following changes:

BLACK EYE PATCH (MAKE TWO)

Using black #4 worsted weight yarn and a "J" (6 mm) hook, ch 9, hdc in 3rd ch from hook and ea of next 5 ch sts, work 6 dc in last ch st (curving around to go back the other direction after the 3rd dc), working on opposite side of row, hdc in next 6 ch sts, join with sl st in top of first st. Fasten off, leaving an 18" (46 cm) long tail end for sewing eye patch on muzzle.

Before following the instructions for the Assembly of Head, sew eye patches on each side of muzzle (where the muzzle meets the furry part of the head), with the wider end on the bottom, then continue with placing the safety eyes (at the smaller top end of each oval eye patch).

Follow the instructions for ears, using black fur yarn.

Start the body with cream/white fur yarn until you reach the shoulders, then switch to black fur yarn for about 3–4 rows (this will form the black stripe across the shoulders), then switch back to cream/white fur yarn for the rest of the body.

Make all four legs with black fur yarn. (Line each front leg up with the black shoulder stripe.) When working the edging, be sure to use the same colored yarn as the body part on which you are adding the edging.

> **DISCLAIMER:** *Please note that this rug is NOT a toy and should NEVER be left alone with young unsupervised children. If this rug is sold, please attach a safety warning.*

> **NOTE:** *If using as a rug on a nursery floor, please consider placing a nonslip pad underneath. For a safer option, consider hanging it on a wall or draping over a chair when not in use.*

LION & LIONESS BABY BONNET

So much fun for newborns and older children alike, the Lion Baby Bonnet is always a favorite. Make it without a mane and add a bow or flower for a lioness. Changing the yarn style or color for the mane can give you so many different looks that you might think it's a different pattern. Add a Baby Diaper Cover (page 74) with a lion tail (page 80) to complete the look.

SKILL LEVEL: Easy

MATERIALS

TOOLS	Stitch marker, measuring tape, latch hook (optional), yarn needle, bow/flower for "girl" hat (optional)
YARN	**BONNET:** 6 oz (170 g) or less of #4 worsted weight yarn (cream, tan, light brown, etc.). **MANE:** 2–4 oz (57–113 g) of Lion Brand Homespun in "spice" or "wildfire" or any "5" bulky or "6" super bulky weight chenille or fur type yarn in shades of orange/red/brown
GAUGE	15 stitches and 9 rows in hdc = 4" x 4" (10 x 10 cm) or see gauge checkpoint
HOOK SIZE	"J" (6 mm) hook or to match gauge, smaller hook for edging

BONNET SIZE CHART

PREEMIE/DOLL	10–12" (25–30 cm) circumference, finished bonnet approximately 4.5" x 4.5" (11 x 11 cm)
NEWBORN	12–13" (30–33 cm) circumference, finished bonnet approximately 5" x 5" (14 x 14 cm)
0–3 MONTHS	13–14" (33–36 cm) circumference, finished bonnet approximately 6" x 6" (15 x 15 cm)
3–6 MONTHS	14–16" (36–41 cm) circumference, finished bonnet approximately 6.5" x 6.5" (17 x 17 cm)
6–12 MONTHS	16–18" (41–46 cm) circumference, finished bonnet approximately 7" x 7" (18 x 18 cm)
TODDLER/CHILD	18–20" (46–51 cm) circumference, finished bonnet approximately 7.5" x 7.5" (19 x 19 cm)
TEEN/ADULT	20–22" (51–56 cm) circumference, finished bonnet approximately 8" x 8" (20 x 20 cm)

ABBREVIATIONS USED

ST(S)	stitch(es)
CH	chain stitch
SC	single crochet
HDC	half double crochet
SL ST	slip stitch
RND(S)	round(s)
SK	skip
EA	each

PREEMIE/DOLL LION BABY BONNET

NOTE: *Rnds 1-4 are worked in a continuous spiral. Add a stitch marker around the loop on the hook after completing Rnd 1 and move after each round. The beginning ch 2 does not count in stitch count.*

RND 1: Magic ring, ch 2, work 8 hdc in ring, join with sl st in top of ch 2. (8)

OR ch 2, 8 hdc in 2nd ch from hook, join with sl st in first hdc. (8)

RND 2: 2 hdc in ea st to end of rnd, do not join. (16)

RND 3: *hdc in next st, 2 hdc in next st*, repeat between *...* to end of rnd. (24)

RND 4: *hdc in ea of next 2 sts, 2 hdc next st*, repeat between *...* to end of rnd. (32)

GAUGE CHECKPOINT: *Total diameter of the circle should measure approximately 3.5" (9 cm) here.*

NOTE: *Pattern is now worked back and forth in rows instead of rounds from this point.*

ROW 5: (do not turn yet) hdc in ea of next 28 sts, leave last 4 sts unworked. (28)

ROW 6: ch 2, turn, hdc in same st as ch 2 and next 27 sts. (28)

REPEAT ROW 6 until measurement reaches 4.5" (11 cm) from center of magic ring to edge, end with a "right side" row (outside of bonnet facing you).

CONTINUE with Ties and Edging at end of pattern.

NEWBORN LION BABY BONNET

NOTE: *Rnds 1-5 are worked in a continuous spiral. Add a stitch marker around the loop on the hook after completing Rnd 1 and move after each round. The beginning ch 2 does not count in stitch count.*

RND 1: Magic ring, ch 2, work 8 hdc in ring, join with sl st in top of ch 2. (8)

OR ch 2, 8 hdc in 2nd ch from hook, join with sl st in first hdc. (8)

RND 2: 2 hdc in ea st to end of rnd, do not join. (16)

RND 3: *hdc in next st, 2 hdc in next st*, repeat between *...* to end of rnd. (24)

RND 4: *hdc in ea of next 2 sts, 2 hdc next st*, repeat between *...* to end of rnd. (32)

RND 5: *hdc in ea of next 3 sts, 2 hdc next st*, repeat between *...* to end of rnd. (40)

GAUGE CHECKPOINT: *Diameter of circle should measure 4.25 to 4.5" (about 11 cm) here.*

NOTE: *Pattern is now worked back and forth in rows instead of rounds from this point.*

ROW 6: (do not turn yet) hdc in ea of next 36 sts, leave last 4 sts unworked. (36)

ROW 7: ch 2, turn, hdc in same st as ch 2 and next 35 sts. (36)

REPEAT ROW 7 until measurement reaches 5" (13 cm) from center of magic ring to edge; end with a "right side" row (outside of bonnet facing you).

CONTINUE with Ties and Edging at end of pattern (page 73).

0–3 MONTHS LION BABY BONNET

NOTE: *Rnds 1–6 are worked in a continuous spiral. Add a stitch marker around the loop on the hook after completing Rnd 1 and move after each round. The beginning ch 2 does not count in stitch count.*

RND 1: Magic ring, ch 2, work 8 hdc in ring, join with sl st in top of ch 2. (8)

OR ch 2, 8 hdc in 2nd ch from hook, join with sl st in first hdc. (8)

RND 2: 2 hdc in ea st to end of rnd, do not join. (16)

RND 3: *hdc in next st, 2 hdc in next st*, repeat between *...* to end of rnd. (24)

RND 4: *hdc in ea of next 2 sts, 2 hdc next st*, repeat between *...* to end of rnd. (32)

RND 5: *hdc in ea of next 3 sts, 2 hdc next st*, repeat between *...* to end of rnd. (40)

GAUGE CHECKPOINT: *Total diameter of circle should measure approximately 4.25 to 4.5" (about 11 cm) here.*

RND 6: *hdc in ea of next 9 sts, 2 hdc next st*, repeat between *...* to end of rnd. (44)

NOTE: *Pattern is now worked back and forth in rows instead of rounds from this point.*

ROW 7: (do not turn yet) hdc in ea of next 38 sts, leave last 6 sts unworked. (38)

ROW 8: ch 2, turn, hdc in same st as ch 2 and next 37 sts. (38)

REPEAT ROW 8 until measurement reaches 5 to 5.5" (13–14 cm) from center of magic ring to edge; end with a "right side" row (outside of bonnet facing you).

CONTINUE with Ties and Edging at end of pattern (page 73).

3–6 MONTHS LION BABY BONNET

NOTE: *Rnds 1–6 are worked in a continuous spiral. Add a stitch marker around the loop on the hook after completing Rnd 1 and move after each round. The beginning ch 2 does not count in stitch count.*

RND 1: Magic ring, ch 2, work 8 hdc in ring, join with sl st in top of ch 2. (8)

OR ch 2, 8 hdc in 2nd ch from hook, join with sl st in first hdc. (8)

RND 2: 2 hdc in ea st to end of rnd, do not join. (16)

RND 3: *hdc in next st, 2 hdc in next st*, repeat between *...* to end of rnd. (24)

RND 4: *hdc in ea of next 2 sts, 2 hdc next st*, repeat between *...* to end of rnd. (32)

RND 5: *hdc in ea of next 3 sts, 2 hdc next st*, repeat between *...* to end of rnd. (40)

GAUGE CHECKPOINT: *Total diameter of circle should measure approximately 4.25 to 4.5" (about 11 cm) here.*

RND 6: *hdc in ea of next 9 sts, 2 hdc next st*, repeat between *...* to end of rnd. (44)

ROW 7: (do not turn yet) hdc in ea of next 40 sts, leave last 4 sts unworked. (40)

ROW 8: ch 2, turn, hdc in same st as ch 2 and next 39 sts. (40)

REPEAT ROW 8 until measurement reaches 5.5 to 6" (14 to 15 cm) from center of magic ring to edge, end with a "right side" row (outside of bonnet facing you).

CONTINUE with Ties and Edging at end of pattern.

6–12 MONTHS LION BABY BONNET

RND 1: Magic ring, ch 2, work 8 hdc in ring, join with sl st in top of ch 2. (8)

OR ch 2, 8 hdc in 2nd ch from hook, join with sl st in first hdc. (8)

RND 2: 2 hdc in ea st to end of rnd, do not join. (16)

RND 3: *hdc in next st, 2 hdc in next st*, repeat between *...* to end of rnd. (24)

RND 4: *hdc in ea of next 2 sts, 2 hdc next st*, repeat between *...* to end of rnd. (32)

RND 5: *hdc in ea of next 3 sts, 2 hdc next st*, repeat between *...* to end of rnd. (40)

GAUGE CHECKPOINT: *Total diameter of circle should measure approximately 4.25 to 4.5" (about 11 cm) here.*

RND 6: *hdc in ea of next 4 sts, 2 hdc next st*, repeat between *...* to end of rnd. (48)

ROW 7: (do not turn yet) hdc in ea of next 42 sts, leave last 6 sts unworked. (42)

ROW 8: ch 2, turn, hdc in same st as ch 2 and next 41 sts. (42)

REPEAT ROW 8 until measurement reaches 6 to 7" (15 to 18 cm) from center of magic ring to edge; end with a "right side" row (outside of bonnet facing you).

CONTINUE with Ties and Edging at end of pattern (page 73).

TODDLER/CHILD LION BABY BONNET

RND 1: Magic ring, ch 2, work 8 hdc in ring, join with sl st in top of ch 2. (8)

OR ch 2, 8 hdc in 2nd ch from hook, join with sl st in first hdc. (8)

RND 2: 2 hdc in ea st to end of rnd, do not join. (16)

RND 3: *hdc in next st, 2 hdc in next st*, repeat between *...* to end of rnd. (24)

RND 4: *hdc in ea of next 2 sts, 2 hdc next st*, repeat between *...* to end of rnd. (32)

RND 5: *hdc in ea of next 3 sts, 2 hdc next st*, repeat between *...* to end of rnd. (40)

> **GAUGE CHECKPOINT:** *Total diameter of circle should measure approximately 4.25 to 4.5" (about 11 cm) here.*

RND 6: *hdc in ea of next 4 sts, 2 hdc next st*, repeat between *...* to end of rnd. (48)

RND 7: *hdc in ea of next 5 sts, 2 hdc next st*, repeat between *...* to end of rnd. (56)

> **NOTE:** *Pattern is now worked back and forth in rows instead of rounds from this point.*

ROW 8: (do not turn yet) hdc in ea of next 50 sts, leave last 6 sts unworked. (50)

ROW 9: ch 2, turn, hdc in same st as ch 2 and next 49 sts. (50)

REPEAT ROW 9 until measurement reaches 7 to 7.5" (18 to 19 cm) from center of magic ring to edge; end with a "right side" row (outside of bonnet facing you).

CONTINUE with Ties and Edging at end of pattern (page 73).

TEEN/ADULT LION BABY BONNET

> **NOTE:** *Rnds 1–8 are worked in a continuous spiral. Add a stitch marker around the loop on the hook after completing Rnd 1 and move after each round. The beginning ch 2 does not count in stitch count*

RND 1: Magic ring, ch 2, work 8 hdc in ring, join with sl st in top of ch 2. (8)

OR ch 2, 8 hdc in 2nd ch from hook, join with sl st in first hdc. (8)

RND 2: 2 hdc in ea st to end of rnd, do not join. (16)

RND 3: *hdc in next st, 2 hdc in next st*, repeat between *...* to end of rnd. (24)

RND 4: *hdc in ea of next 2 sts, 2 hdc next st*, repeat between *...* to end of rnd. (32)

RND 5: *hdc in ea of next 3 sts, 2 hdc next st*, repeat between *...* to end of rnd. (40)

> **GAUGE CHECKPOINT:** *Total diameter of circle should measure approximately 4.25 to 4.5" (about 11 cm) here.*

RND 6: *hdc in ea of next 4 sts, 2 hdc next st*, repeat between *...* to end of rnd. (48)

RND 7: *hdc in ea of next 5 sts, 2 hdc next st*, repeat between *...* to end of rnd. (56)

RND 8: *hdc in ea of next 6 sts, 2 hdc next st*, repeat between *...* to end of rnd. (64)

ROW 9: (do not turn yet) hdc in ea of next 58 sts, leave last 6 sts unworked. (58)

ROW 10: ch 2, turn, hdc in same st as ch 2 and next 57 sts. (58)

REPEAT ROW 10 until measurement reaches 7.5 to 8" (19 to 20 cm) from center of magic ring to edge; end with a "right side" row (outside of bonnet facing you).

TIES AND EDGING (ALL SIZES)

CROCHETED TIES: ch 40–50 for smallest sizes, 50–60 for the larger sizes (or to desired length), sl st in 2nd ch from hook and ea ch back down to bonnet, sl st in bonnet to join, sc evenly across bottom of bonnet to other corner, repeat for second tie (do not fasten off). Continue with Edging.

EDGING: Switch to smaller hook (2 sizes smaller than hook used for bonnet), sc across front of bonnet (forehead), fasten off with invisible join (or sl st) in last st. (The bonnet should curve in toward the face. If it flares, use a smaller hook.) Weave in ends.

EARS (MAKE TWO)

Use the same hook as used for the Edging.

RND 1: Magic ring, ch 2, work 10 hdc in ring, join with sl st in first hdc. (10)

RND 2: ch 2, hdc in same st as ch 2, 2 hdc in ea st, join w/sl st in top of ch 2. (20)

LARGER EARS ONLY: Complete Rnd 3. (Smaller Ears: Skip to Rnd 4.)

RND 3: ch 2, hdc in same st as ch 2, hdc in next st, *2 hdc in next st, hdc in next st*, repeat between *...* to end of rnd, join with sl st in top of ch 2. (30)

RND 4: ch 1, sc in ea st to end of rnd, sk last st, join with sl st in first sc. (19, 29)

FASTEN OFF (leave 10" [25 cm] tail to fasten on bonnet with yarn needle). Attach ears before adding mane.

MANE

Cut several short pieces of brown (or red) yarn (3 to 4" [8 to 10 cm] long) and use a latch hook, or crochet hook, to attach to the bonnet (see Tip below). Attach one or two pieces at a time. Work from side to side rather than front to back. (I started by filling in between the ears, then around the ears and on the sides and kept adding until I felt it was full enough.) Trim the mane if desired (I kept mine a little shorter on the sides of the head).

NEWBORN PHOTO PROPS

The mane really only needs to look "full" from the front and it's not necessary to fill in the mane on the back of the bonnet.

OLDER KIDS: For kids that will be wearing the bonnet as a regular hat you may wish to extend the mane farther down the back of the bonnet.

BABY DIAPER COVER

Dress up this basic diaper cover pattern with an adorable lion tail to match the Lion & Lioness Baby Bonnet (page 67) or adorn it with feminine flowers. Both accessories simply button on and can be changed easily for different photography sessions. Leave it unadorned for a simple and classic look. Photographers love this prop to cover up unsightly disposable diapers that can ruin the look of newborn photos.

SKILL LEVEL:  Easy

MATERIALS

TOOLS	Measuring tape, 1–3 buttons for fastening, 1–3 buttons for optional accessories, needle & thread, latch hook (optional for lion tail)
YARN	4 oz (113 g) or less of #4 worsted weight cotton or cotton blend yarn
GAUGE	13 stitches and 9.5 rows in hdc = 4" x 4" (10 x 10 cm), or see checkpoints in pattern
HOOK SIZE	"J" hook (6 mm) or to match gauge. (I use Boye brand hooks, see notes for Bates hooks.)

ABBREVIATIONS USED

ST(S)	stitch(es)
CH	chain stitch
SC	single crochet
HDC	half double crochet
DC	double crochet
SL ST	slip stitch
SP	space
BEG	beginning
EA	each

SIZE CHART

Diaper cover measurements are larger than diaper measurements to account for the bulk of the diaper. Measure around your baby in a diaper to get the right cover measurement. "Rise" is the measurement from the top front of the cover to the top back of the cover (top-to-bottom length of the diaper cover). "Waistband" is the measurement of the back flap, not the actual circumference of the cover. "Below waistband" is the measurement across the widest part just below the waistband flap. (Diaper Cover itself is measured before adding edging.)

NEWBORN	Rise = 11" (28 cm), Waistband = 15" (38 cm), Below Waistband = 9" (23 cm)
0–6 MONTHS	Rise = 14" (36 cm), Waistband = 17.5" (44 cm), Below Waistband = 10.5" (26 cm)
6–12 MONTHS	Rise = 15" (38 cm), Waistband = 20.5" (52 cm), Below Waistband = 13" (33 cm)

NEWBORN BABY DIAPER COVER

MEASUREMENTS: *Newborn: Rise = 11" (28 cm), Waistband = 15" (38 cm), Below Waistband = 9" (23 cm)*

NOTE: *The beginning ch 2 (or ch 3) is NOT counted in the stitch count and "hdc2tog" counts as one stitch in final count.*

ROW 1: ch 52, hdc in 3rd ch from hook and each st across. (50)

ROW 2: ch 3, turn, dc in same st and each st across (this row will provide button holes by using the spaces between the stitches). (50)

ROW 3: ch 2, turn, hdc in each st across. (50)

ROW 4: ch 1, turn, sl st in next 11 sts, ch 2, hdc in next 28 sts, STOP here, do not continue to the end of the row (sl sts are not included in st count). (28)

ROW 5: ch 2, turn, hdc2tog, hdc in next 24 sts, hdc2tog. (26)

ROW 6: ch 2, turn, hdc2tog, hdc in next 22 sts, hdc2tog. (24)

ROW 7: ch 2, turn, hdc2tog, hdc in next 20 sts, hdc2tog. (22)

ROW 8: ch 2, turn, hdc2tog, hdc in next 18 sts, hdc2tog. (20)

ROW 9: ch 2, turn, hdc2tog, hdc in next 16 sts, hdc2tog. (18)

ROW 10: ch 2, turn, hdc2tog, hdc in next 14 sts, hdc2tog. (16)

ROW 11: ch 2, turn, hdc2tog, hdc in next 12 sts, hdc2tog. (14)

ROW 12: ch 2, turn, hdc in ea st to end of row. (14)

NOTE: *My testers and I have discovered that using Susan Bates hooks tends to result in a shorter vertical rise. At this point in the pattern, the rise should equal about 5 to 5.5" (13 to 14 cm). If the rise is too short, repeat Row 12 as many times as necessary to reach the correct rise.*

ROW 13: ch 2, turn, hdc2tog, hdc in next 10 sts, hdc2tog. (12)

ROWS 14–19: ch 2, turn, hdc in each st to end of row. (12)

NOTE: *At this point in the pattern, the rise should equal about 9" (23 cm). If rise is too short, repeat Row 14 as many times as necessary to reach the correct rise.*

ROW 20: ch 2, turn, 2 hdc in first st, hdc in next 10 sts, 2 hdc in last st. (14)

ROW 21: ch 2, turn, hdc in each st to end of row. (14)

ROW 22: ch 2, turn, 2 hdc in first st, hdc in next 12 sts, 2 hdc in last st. (16)

ROW 23: ch 2, turn, hdc in each st to end of row. (16)

ROW 24: ch 2, turn, 2 hdc in first st, hdc in next 14 sts, 2 hdc in last st. (18)

ROW 25: ch 2, turn, hdc in each st to end of row. (18)

NOTE: *Repeat Row 25 as many times as necessary to reach the correct rise of 11" (28 cm).*

CONTINUE with Edging Section at end of pattern (page 79).

0–6 MONTHS BABY DIAPER COVER

MEASUREMENTS: *Rise = 14" (36 cm), Waistband = 17.5" (44 cm), Below Waistband = 10.5" (26 cm)*

NOTE: *The beginning ch 2 (or ch 3) is NOT counted in the stitch count and "hdc2tog" counts as one stitch in final count.*

ROW 1: ch 58, hdc in 3rd ch from hook and each st across. (56)

ROW 2: ch 3, turn, dc in same st and each st across (this row will provide button holes by using the spaces between the stitches). (56)

ROW 3: ch 2, turn, hdc in each st across. (56)

ROW 4: ch 1, turn, sl st in next 11 sts, ch 2, hdc in next 34 sts, STOP here, do not continue to the end of the row (sl sts are not included in st count). (34)

ROW 5: ch 2, turn, hdc in ea st to end of row. (34)

ROW 6: ch 2, turn, hdc2tog, hdc in next 30 sts, hdc2tog. (32)

ROW 7: ch 2, turn, hdc in ea st to end of row. (32)

ROW 8: ch 2, turn, hdc2tog, hdc in next 28 sts, hdc2tog. (30)

ROW 9: ch 2, turn, hdc in ea st to end of row. (30)

ROW 10: ch 2, turn, hdc2tog, hdc in next 26 sts, hdc2tog. (28)

ROW 11: ch 2, turn, hdc in ea st to end of row. (28)

ROW 12: ch 2, turn, hdc2tog, hdc in next 24 sts, hdc2tog. (26)

ROW 13: ch 2, turn, hdc in ea st to end of row. (26)

ROW 14: ch 2, turn, hdc2tog, hdc in next 22 sts, hdc2tog. (24)

ROW 15: ch 2, turn, hdc in ea st to end of row. (24)

NOTE: *My testers and I have discovered that using Susan Bates hooks tends to result in a shorter vertical rise. At this point in the pattern, the rise should equal about 7" (18 cm). If the rise is too short, repeat Row 15 as many times as necessary to reach the correct rise.*

ROW 16: ch 2, turn, hdc2tog, hdc in next 20 sts, hdc2tog. (22)

ROW 17: ch 2, turn, hdc2tog, hdc in next 18 sts, hdc2tog. (20)

ROW 18: ch 2, turn, hdc2tog, hdc in next 16 sts, hdc2tog. (18)

ROW 19: ch 2, turn, hdc2tog, hdc in next 14 sts, hdc2tog. (16)

ROW 20: ch 2, turn, hdc2tog, hdc in next 12 sts, hdc2tog. (14)

ROWS 21–22: ch 2, turn, hdc in ea st to end of row. (14)

NOTE: *At this point in the pattern, the rise should equal about 10" (25 cm). If the rise is too short, repeat Row 21 as many times as necessary to reach the correct rise.*

ROW 23: ch 2, turn, 2 hdc in first st, hdc in next 12 sts, 2 hdc in last st. (16)

ROW 24: ch 2, turn, hdc in each st to end of row. (16)

ROW 25: ch 2, turn, 2 hdc in first st, hdc in next 14 sts, 2 hdc in last st. (18)

ROW 26: ch 2, turn, hdc in each st to end of row. (18)

ROW 27: ch 2, turn, 2 hdc in first st, hdc in next 16 sts, 2 hdc in last st. (20)

ROW 28: ch 2, turn, hdc in each st to end of row. (20)

ROW 29: ch 2, turn, 2 hdc in first st, hdc in next 18 sts, 2 hdc in last st. (22)

ROW 30: ch 2, turn, hdc in each st to end of row. (22)

NOTE: *Repeat Row 30 as many times as necessary to reach the correct rise of 14" (36 cm).*

CONTINUE with the Edging Section at the end of the pattern (page 79).

6–12 MONTHS BABY DIAPER COVER

MEASUREMENTS: *Rise = 15" (38 cm), Waistband = 20.5" (52 cm), Below Waistband = 13" (33 cm)*

NOTE: *The beginning ch 2 (or ch 3) is NOT counted in the stitch count and "hdc2tog" counts as one stitch in final count.*

ROW 1: ch 70, hdc in 3rd ch from hook and each st to end of row. (68)

ROW 2: ch 3, turn, dc in same st as ch 3 and each st to end of row (this row will provide button holes by using the spaces between the stitches). (68)

ROW 3: ch 2, turn, hdc in same st as ch 2 and each st to end of row. (68)

ROW 4: ch 1, turn, sl st in next 14 sts, ch 2, hdc in ea of next 40 sts, STOP here, do not continue to the end of the row (sl sts are not included in st count). (40)

ROW 5: ch 2, turn, hdc2tog, hdc in next 36 sts, hdc2tog. (38)

ROW 6: ch 2, turn, hdc2tog, hdc in next 34 sts, hdc2tog. (36)

ROW 7: ch 2, turn, hdc2tog, hdc in next 32 sts, hdc2tog. (34)

ROW 8: ch 2, turn, hdc in ea st to end of row. (34)

ROW 9: ch 2, turn, hdc2tog, hdc in next 30 sts, hdc2tog. (32)

ROW 10: ch 2, turn, hdc in ea st to end of row. (32)

ROW 11: ch 2, turn, hdc2tog, hdc in next 28 sts, hdc2tog. (30)

ROW 12: ch 2, turn, hdc in ea st to end of row. (30)

ROW 13: ch 2, turn, hdc2tog, hdc in next 26 sts, hdc2tog. (28)

ROW 14: ch 2, turn, hdc in ea st to end of row. (28)

NOTE: *My testers and I have discovered that using Susan Bates hooks tends to result in a shorter vertical rise. At this point in the pattern, the rise should equal about 6" (15 cm). If the rise is too short, repeat Row 14 as many times as necessary to reach the correct rise.*

ROW 15: ch 2, turn, hdc2tog, hdc in next 24 sts, hdc2tog. (26)

ROW 16: ch 2, turn, hdc2tog, hdc in next 22 sts, hdc2tog. (24)

ROW 17: ch 2, turn, hdc2tog, hdc in next 20 sts, hdc2tog. (22)

ROW 18: ch 2, turn, hdc2tog, hdc in next 18 sts, hdc2tog. (20)

ROW 19: ch 2, turn, hdc2tog, hdc in next 16 sts, hdc2tog. (18)

ROW 20: ch 2, turn, hdc2tog, hdc in next 14 sts, hdc2tog. (16)

ROW 21: ch 2, turn, hdc in ea st to end of row. (16)

NOTE: *At this point in the pattern, the rise should equal about 8.5" (22 cm). If the rise is too short, repeat Row 21 as many times as necessary to reach the correct rise.*

ROWS 22–25: Repeat Row 21.

ROW 26: ch 2, turn, 2 hdc in first st, hdc in next 14 sts, 2 hdc in last st. (18)

ROW 27: ch 2, turn, hdc in each st to end of row. (18)

ROW 28: ch 2, turn, 2 hdc in first st, hdc in next 16 sts, 2 hdc in last st. (20)

ROW 29: ch 2, turn, hdc in each st to end of row. (20)

ROW 30: ch 2, turn, 2 hdc in first st, hdc in next 18 sts, 2 hdc in last st. (22)

ROW 31: ch 2, turn, hdc in each st to end of row. (22)

ROWS 32–36: Repeat Row 31.

> **NOTE:** *Repeat Row 31 as many times as necessary to reach the correct rise of 15" (38 cm).*

CONTINUE with the Edging Section.

EDGING (ALL SIZES)

> **NOTE:** *It may be necessary to go down one or two hook sizes for the edging. If the diaper cover still lays flat after completing edging, try either going down 1 to 2 hook sizes or spacing the stitches farther apart. This will gather in the leg openings a little bit.*

EDGING: ch 1, turn, sc evenly around entire outer edge of the diaper cover (put 3 sc in corners of waistband flaps). On the sides of the diaper cover, place approximately one stitch in the end of each row (this will make the edges curl a little bit and that is normal). Fasten off in first sc with invisible join. Weave in ends.

CONTINUE with the Buttons (For Fastening Diaper Cover) Section.

BUTTONS (FOR FASTENING DIAPER COVER)

Sew button(s) on the front of cover about 1" (3 cm) down from the top edge (on the piece that covers the baby's belly). Flaps can be buttoned over the button(s) in various positions using the spaces between the dc stitches from row 2. The waistband is adjustable, so there can be a variety of positions with the buttons (use whatever number of buttons that you prefer). In my experience, I have found that one button works fine for the newborn size, but for older, more active babies, it is best to have three buttons or the cover will not fit as well.

LOOPY FLOWER (SELECT SIZE)

Use #4 worsted weight yarn and "J" (6 mm) hook.

> **NOTE:** *These flowers can be attached on the front of the diaper cover over the buttons used for fastening, OR buttons can be added to the back waistband (a popular pose for newborns for photographers is to have baby on their stomach).*

SMALL FLOWER

RND 1: ch 5, join with sl st in first ch to form a ring, ch 1, work 12 sc in ring, join with sl st in first sc. (12)

STOP Test the size of the buttonhole with the desired button. If the buttonhole is too small/large for the button, redo Rnd 1 and add/decrease beg number of ch sts.

RND 2: Using front loops only, ch 8, sl st in same st, *ch 8, sl st in next st*, repeat between *...* to end of rnd, join with sl st in first st. (12 loops)

RND 3: Using unused back loops from prev rnd only, ch 10, sl st in same st, *ch 10, sl st in next st*, repeat between *...* to end of rnd, fasten off with sl st in first st. (12 loops)

WEAVE in ends.

LARGE FLOWER

RND 1: ch 5, join with sl st in first ch to form a ring, ch 1, work 10 sc in ring, join with sl st in first sc. (10)

STOP Test the size of the buttonhole with the desired button. If the buttonhole is too small/large for button, redo Rnd 1 and add/decrease beg number of ch sts.

RND 2: ch 1, work 2 sc in each st to end of rnd, join with sl st in first sc. (20)

RND 3: Using front loops only, ch 8, sl st in same st, *ch 8, sl st in next st*, repeat between *...* to end of rnd, join with sl st in first st. (20 loops)

RND 4: Using unused back loops from prev rnd only, ch 10, sl st in same st, *ch 10, sl st in next st*, repeat between *...* to end of rnd, fasten off with sl st in first st. (20 loops)

WEAVE in ends.

(OPTIONAL) LION TAIL

Use #4 worsted weight yarn and "J" (6 mm) hook.

ROW 1: ch to a length of 6 to 10" (15 to 25 cm) (depending on the desired length of the lion tail), hdc in 3rd ch from hook (use back loops of ch sts) and ea ch to end of row.

ROW 2: ch 2, turn, hdc in same st as ch 2 and ea st to end of row.

ROW 3: Repeat Row 2.

Cut the yarn leaving an approximately 36" (91 cm) long tail end. Fold in half lengthwise and use a yarn needle to stitch the sides (and the opening at the end of the row) together (do not fasten off yet). The tail will curve; this is okay. Using a crochet hook again, insert the hook through one side of the closed end just finished (making sure to go under at least 2 loops), YO and pull up a loop from the tail end of the yarn, ch 5, join with sl st to other side of closed end of tail (do not fasten off yet). This creates the "button loop" that will be hooked over a button on the diaper cover. Before fastening off, be sure to test the size of the button through the loop. If needed, adjust the size of the loop by adding or decreasing chains. Fasten off.

Attach pieces of yarn (to match mane of the lion bonnet) to the other end of the tail with either a crochet hook or latch hook.

HONEYCOMB RIDGES BABY COCOON OR SWADDLE SACK

With a "honeycomb" appearance, it's easy to see how this cocoon got its name. Make it in the swaddle sack version for a newborn photography session, or make the cocoon version for an adorable snuggle sack that makes a great gift for new parents. Pair it with the coordinating Honeycomb Ridges Beanie (page 128) for a complete set.

A swaddle sack is very snug and made to fit a newborn baby. Photographers like to use swaddles to keep the baby calm for photos. A cocoon is roomier, fits longer and is generally used by parents (as well as photographers). It's great for snuggling and warmth.

SKILL LEVEL: Intermediate

MATERIALS

TOOLS	Measuring tape, yarn needle, stitch marker
YARN	14 oz (397 g) or less of #4 worsted weight yarn
GAUGE	Gauge checkpoint given in pattern after Rnd 4 for each size
HOOK SIZE	"J" (6 mm) for main portion, smaller hook may be needed for edging

SIZE CHART

NEWBORN SWADDLE SACK	16–18" (41–46 cm) circumference, 11–12" (28–30 cm) length
PREEMIE COCOON	16–18" (41–46 cm) circumference, 14" (36 cm) length
NEWBORN COCOON	18–20" (46–51 cm) circumference, 18" (46 cm) length
0–3 MONTHS COCOON	20–22" (51–56 cm) circumference, 20" (51 cm) length
3–6 MONTHS COCOON	22–24" (56–61 cm) circumference, 22" (56 cm) length

ABBREVIATIONS USED

ST(S)	stitch(es)
CH	chain stitch
SC	single crochet
DC	double crochet
FPSC	front post single crochet
FPDC	front post double crochet
BPDC	back post double crochet
SL ST	slip stitch
RND(S)	round(s)
SK	skip
SP	space
EA	each
BEG	beginning
PREV	previous
YO	Yarn Over

SPECIAL STITCHES DEFINITIONS

FRONT POST SINGLE CROCHET (FPSC): Insert hook from the front side of the work (right to left) under the post of the indicated stitch, YO and pull up a loop, YO and draw through 2 loops.

FRONT POST DOUBLE CROCHET (FPDC): Working from the front side of the work, YO and insert the hook from right to left under the post of the double crochet indicated from the previous round, YO and pull up a loop, [YO and draw through 2 loops] twice.

BACK POST DOUBLE CROCHET (BPDC): Working from the back side of the work, YO and insert the hook from right to left over the post of the double crochet indicated from the previous round, YO and pull up a loop, [YO and draw through 2 loops] twice.

SPECIAL TECHNIQUES

USING THE BEG "CH 2" AS THE FINAL DC IN THE ROUND: If there is a "ch 2" at the beginning of a round, it will stand in as the last dc in the round. This avoids having a noticeable seam. If the repeat ends on a dc at the end of the round, don't make that last dc because the "ch 2" is there and will look like a dc when you join to the top of it. If the repeat ends with 2 dc worked in one stitch, make the first dc in the same stitch as the "ch 2." This will look almost exactly the same as working 2 dc in one stitch.

JOINING IN THE "TOP" OF THE CH 2: If there is any confusion on where to join at the end of each round, use the following method: Complete the first ch 2 of the round, then add a stitch marker around the loop that is on the hook. At the end of the round, this is the stitch that will be used for joining.

NEWBORN HONEYCOMB RIDGES SWADDLE SACK AND PREEMIE HONEYCOMB RIDGES COCOON

RND 1: Magic ring, ch 2, 13 dc in ring, join with sl st in top of ch 2. (14)

OR ch 2, 14 dc in 2nd ch from hook, join with sl st in first dc. (14)

RND 2: ch 2, *fpdc around next dc, dc in top of same post just used*, repeat between *...* to end of rnd, beg ch 2 counts as last dc, join with sl st in top of ch 2. (28)

RND 3: ch 2, *fpdc around next fpdc, dc in next dc*, repeat between *...* to end of rnd, beg ch 2 counts as last dc, join with sl st in top of ch 2. (28) *This rnd intentionally does not increase.*

RND 4: ch 2, *fpdc around next fpdc, dc in next dc*, repeat between *...* to end of rnd, beg ch 2 counts as last dc, join with sl st in top of ch 2. (28) *This rnd intentionally does not increase.*

GAUGE CHECKPOINT: *Diameter of the circle should measure approximately 3.5" (9 cm) here.*

RND 5: ch 2, *fpdc around next fpdc, 2 dc in next dc*, repeat between *...* to end of rnd, beg ch 2 counts as last dc, join with sl st in top of ch 2. (42)

NOTE: *The "fpsc and ch 2" at the beginning of the following rounds creates a stitch that looks like a fpdc. Be sure to crochet the fpsc tightly around the post so it doesn't bulge at the base of the ch 2. It is correct if it looks very similar to a fpdc. Starting the round in this fashion (instead of a standard ch 2) will result in a seam that is almost completely invisible.*

RND 6: fpsc around first fpdc from prev rnd, ch 2 (serves as first fpdc), dc in ea of next 2 dc, *fpdc around next fpdc, dc in ea of next 2 dc*, repeat between *...* to end of rnd, join with sl st in top of ch 2. (42)

> **NOTE:** *Stitch marker placement in next round is for joining at the end of the round and also for guidance in the following round.*

RND 7: fpsc around first fpdc from prev rnd, ch 2 (serves as first fpdc), sk next 2 dc, fpdc around next fpdc (add stitch marker around post of st just made), ch 3, fpdc around same fpdc, *sk next 2 dc, (fpdc, ch 3, fpdc) around next fpdc*, repeat between *...* to last 2 sts, sk last 2 dc, fpdc around first fpdc from prev rnd again, ch 3, join with sl st in top of beg ch 2 (directly above post with stitch marker). (14 ch-3 sps)

> **NOTE:** *For each repeat of Rnd 8 with "3 dc in next ch-3 sp," work like this: Work first dc in ch-3 sp, work 2nd dc around both the ch 3 **and** between the 2 fpdc below, work 3rd dc in the ch-3 sp again. (This anchors them down instead of leaving a big gap between rounds. It is not critical where the 2nd dc is placed as long as it is between the 2 fpdc.)*

RND 8: fpsc around second fpdc from prev rnd (post with stitch marker), ch 2 (serves as first fpdc), 3 dc in next ch-3 sp, *fpdc around ea of next 2 fpdc, 3 dc in next ch-3 sp*, repeat between *...* to last st, fpdc around last fpdc, join with sl st in top of beg ch 2. (70)

RND 9: fpsc around post of beg ch 2 from prev rnd, ch 2 (serves as first fpdc), sk next 3 dc, fpdc around next fpdc (add stitch marker around post of st just made), ch 3, *fpdc around next fpdc, sk next 3 dc, fpdc around next fpdc, ch 3*, repeat between *...* to end of rnd, after last ch 3, join with sl st in top of beg ch 2 (directly above post with stitch marker). (14 ch-3 sps)

REPEAT Rnds 8 and 9 until the following measurement is reached (end with Rnd 8):

NB Swaddle Sack: Continue until it measures approximately 10 to 11" (25 to 28 cm) from top to bottom.

Preemie Cocoon: Continue until it measures approximately 13" (33 cm) from top to bottom.

CONTINUE with the Edging Options at the end of the pattern.

NEWBORN HONEYCOMB COCOON

RND 1: Magic ring, ch 2, 14 dc in ring, join with sl st in top of ch 2. (15)

OR ch 2, 15 dc in 2nd ch from hook, join with sl st in first dc. (15)

RND 2: ch 2, *fpdc around next dc, dc in top of same post just used*, repeat between *...* to end of rnd, beg ch 2 counts as last dc, join with sl st in top of ch 2. (30)

RND 3: ch 2, *fpdc around next fpdc, dc in next dc*, repeat between *...* to end of rnd, beg ch 2 counts as last dc, join with sl st in top of ch 2. (30) *This rnd intentionally does not increase.*

RND 4: ch 2, *fpdc around next fpdc, dc in next dc*, repeat between *...* to end of rnd, beg ch 2 counts as last dc, join with sl st in top of ch 2. (30) *This rnd intentionally does not increase.*

> **GAUGE CHECKPOINT:** *Diameter of the circle should measure approximately 4" (10 cm) here.*

RND 5: ch 2, *fpdc around next fpdc, 2 dc in next dc*, repeat between *...* to end of rnd, beg ch 2 counts as last dc, join with sl st in top of ch 2. (45)

RND 6: fpsc around first fpdc from prev rnd, ch 2 (serves as first fpdc), dc in ea of next 2 dc, *fpdc around next fpdc, dc in ea of next 2 dc*, repeat between *...* to end of rnd, join with sl st in top of ch 2. (45)

RND 7: fpsc around first fpdc from prev rnd, ch 2 (serves as first fpdc), sk next 2 dc, fpdc around next fpdc (add stitch marker around post of st just made), ch 3, fpdc around same fpdc, *sk next 2 dc, (fpdc, ch 3, fpdc) around next fpdc*, repeat between *...* to last 2 sts, sk last 2 dc, fpdc around first fpdc from prev rnd again, ch 3, join with sl st in top of beg ch 2 (directly above post with stitch marker). (15 ch-3 sps)

RND 8: fpsc around second fpdc from prev rnd (post with stitch marker), ch 2 (serves as first fpdc), 3 dc in next ch-3 sp, *fpdc around ea of next 2 fpdc, 3 dc in next ch-3 sp*, repeat between *...* to last st, fpdc around last fpdc, join with sl st in top of beg ch 2. (75)

RND 9: fpsc around post of beg ch 2 from prev rnd, ch 2 (serves as first fpdc), sk next 3 dc, fpdc around next fpdc (add stitch marker around post of st just made), ch 3, *fpdc around next fpdc, sk next 3 dc, fpdc around next fpdc, ch 3*, repeat between *...* to end of rnd, after last ch 3, join with sl st in top of beg ch 2 (directly above post with stitch marker). (15 ch-3 sps)

REPEAT Rnds 8 and 9 until the cocoon measures approximately 16 to 17" (41 to 43 cm) from top to bottom (end with Rnd 8).

CONTINUE with the Edging Options at the end of the pattern (page 88).

0–3 MONTHS HONEYCOMB RIDGES COCOON

RND 1: Magic ring, ch 2, 7 dc in ring, join with sl st in top of ch 2. (8)

OR ch 2, 8 dc in 2nd ch from hook, join with sl st in first dc. (8)

RND 2: ch 2, *fpdc around next dc, dc in top of same post just used*, repeat between *...* to end of rnd, beg ch 2 counts as last dc, join with sl st in top of ch 2. (16)

RND 3: ch 2, *fpdc around next fpdc, fpdc around next dc, dc in top of same post just used*, repeat between *...* to end of rnd, beg ch 2 counts as last dc, join with sl st in top of ch 2. (24)

RND 4: ch 2, *fpdc around next fpdc, dc in top of same post just used, fpdc around next fpdc, dc in next dc*, repeat between *...* to end of rnd, beg ch 2 counts as last dc, join with sl st in top of ch 2. (32)

RND 5: ch 2, *fpdc around next fpdc, dc in next dc, fpdc around next fpdc, 2 dc in next dc*, repeat between *...* to end of rnd, beg ch 2 counts as last dc, join with sl st in top of ch 2. (40)

RND 6: ch 2, *fpdc around next fpdc, 2 dc in next dc, fpdc around next fpdc, dc in ea of next 2 dc*, repeat between *...* to end of rnd, beg ch 2 counts as last dc, join with sl st in top of ch 2. (48)

NOTE: *The "fpsc and ch 2" at the beginning of the following rounds creates a stitch that looks like a fpdc. Be sure to crochet the fpsc tightly around the post so it doesn't bulge at the base of the ch 2. It is correct if it looks very similar to a fpdc. Starting the round in this fashion (instead of a standard ch 2) will result in a seam that is almost completely invisible. Stitch marker placement in the next round is for joining at the end of the round and also for guidance in the following round.*

RND 7: fpsc around first fpdc from prev rnd, ch 2 (serves as first fpdc), sk next 2 dc, fpdc around next fpdc (add stitch marker around post of st just made), ch 3, fpdc around same fpdc, *sk next 2 dc, (fpdc, ch 3, fpdc) around next fpdc*, repeat between *...* to last 2 sts, sk last 2 dc, fpdc around first fpdc from prev rnd again, ch 3, join with sl st in top of beg ch 2 (directly above post with stitch marker). (16 ch-3 sps)

NOTE: *For each repeat of Rnd 8 with "3 dc in next ch-3 sp," work like this: Work first dc in ch-3 sp, work 2nd dc around both the ch 3 **and** between the 2 fpdc below, work 3rd dc in the ch-3 sp again. (This anchors them down instead of leaving a big gap between rounds. It is not critical where the 2nd dc is placed as long as it is between the 2 fpdc.)*

RND 8: fpsc around second fpdc from prev rnd (post with stitch marker), ch 2 (serves as first fpdc), 3 dc in next ch-3 sp, *fpdc around ea of next 2 fpdc, 3 dc in next ch-3 sp*, repeat between *...* to last st, fpdc around last fpdc, join with sl st in top of beg ch 2. (80)

RND 9: fpsc around post of beg ch 2 from prev rnd, ch 2 (serves as first fpdc), sk next 3 dc, fpdc around next fpdc (add stitch marker around post of st just made), ch 3, *fpdc around next fpdc, sk next 3 dc, fpdc around next fpdc, ch 3*, repeat between *...* to end of rnd, after last ch 3, join with sl st in top of beg ch 2 (directly above post with stitch marker). (16 ch-3 sps)

REPEAT Rnds 8 and 9 until the cocoon measures approx. 18 to 19" (46 to 48 cm) from top to bottom (end with Rnd 8).

CONTINUE with the Edging Options at the end of the pattern (page 88).

3-6 MONTHS HONEYCOMB RIDGES COCOON

RND 1: Magic ring, ch 2, 8 dc in ring, join with sl st in top of ch 2. (9)

OR ch 2, 9 dc in 2nd ch from hook, join with sl st in first dc. (9)

RND 2: ch 2, *fpdc around next dc, dc in top of same post just used*, repeat between *...* to end of rnd, beg ch 2 counts as last dc, join with sl st in top of ch 2. (18)

RND 3: ch 2, [fpdc around next fpdc, fpdc around next dc, dc in top of same post just used] 8 times, fpdc around next fpdc, beg ch 2 counts as last dc, join with sl st in top of ch 2. (26)

RND 4: ch 2, [fpdc around next fpdc, dc in top of same post just used, fpdc around next fpdc, dc in next dc] 8 times, fpdc around next fpdc, beg ch 2 counts as last dc, join with sl st in top of ch 2. (34)

GAUGE CHECKPOINT: *Diameter of the circle should measure approximately 3.5" (9 cm) here.*

RND 5: ch 2, *fpdc around next fpdc, dc in next dc, fpdc around next fpdc, 2 dc in next dc*, repeat between *...* to last fpdc, fpdc around last fpdc, beg ch 2 counts as last dc, join with sl st in top of ch 2. (42)

RND 6: ch 2, *fpdc around next fpdc, 2 dc in next dc, fpdc around next fpdc, dc in ea of next 2 dc*, repeat between *...* to last fpdc, fpdc around last fpdc, dc in same st as beg ch 2, beg ch 2 counts as last dc, join with sl st in top of ch 2. (51)

NOTE: *The "fpsc and ch 2" at the beginning of the following rounds creates a stitch that looks like a fpdc. Be sure to crochet the fpsc tightly around the post so it doesn't bulge at the base of the ch 2. It is correct if it looks very similar to a fpdc. Starting the round in this fashion (instead of a standard ch 2) will result in a seam that is almost completely invisible. Stitch marker placement in the next round is for joining at the end of the round and also for guidance in the following round.*

RND 7: fpsc around first fpdc from prev rnd, ch 2 (serves as first fpdc), sk next 2 dc, fpdc around next fpdc (add stitch marker around post of st just made), ch 3, fpdc around same fpdc, *sk next 2 dc, (fpdc, ch 3, fpdc) around next fpdc*, repeat between *...* to last 2 sts, sk last 2 dc, fpdc around first fpdc from prev rnd again, ch 3, join with sl st in top of beg ch 2 (directly above post with stitch marker). (17 ch-3 sps)

NOTE: *For each repeat of Rnd 8 with "3 dc in next ch-3 sp," work like this: Work first dc in ch-3 sp, work 2nd dc around both the ch 3 **and** between the 2 fpdc below, work 3rd dc in the ch-3 sp again. (This anchors them down instead of leaving a big gap between rounds. It is not critical where the 2nd dc is placed as long as it is between the 2 fpdc.)*

RND 8: fpsc around second fpdc from prev rnd (post with stitch marker), ch 2 (serves as first fpdc), 3 dc in next ch-3 sp, *fpdc around ea of next 2 fpdc, 3 dc in next ch-3 sp*, repeat between *...* to last st, fpdc around last fpdc, join with sl st in top of beg ch 2. (85)

RND 9: fpsc around post of beg ch 2 from prev rnd, ch 2 (serves as first fpdc), sk next 3 dc, fpdc around next fpdc (add stitch marker around post of st just made), ch 3, *fpdc around next fpdc, sk next 3 dc, fpdc around next fpdc, ch 3*, repeat between *...* to end of rnd, after last ch 3, join with sl st in top of beg ch 2 (directly above post with stitch marker). (17 ch-3 sps)

REPEAT Rnds 8 and 9 until the cocoon measures approx. 20 to 21" (51 to 53 cm) from top to bottom (end with Rnd 8).

CONTINUE with Edging Options.

EDGING OPTIONS

Select one.

TIE OPTION

Recommended for Swaddle Sack.

> **NOTE:** *Measure the circumference after completing Rnd 1. If not within the LARGE end of the size range (page 81), redo with a smaller hook.*

RND 1: ch 1, sc in ea st to end of rnd, join with sl st in first sc. (70, 70, 75, 80, 85)

RND 2: ch 1, *sc, ch 1, sk next st*, repeat between *...* to end of rnd, join with sl st in first sc.

RND 3: ch 1, 2 sc in ea ch-1 sp to end of rnd, join with sl st (or invisible join) in first sc.

FASTEN OFF. Weave in all ends.

TIE: ch a length approximately 30 to 40" (76 to 102 cm) long, sl st in 2nd ch from hook and ea ch back down to beginning. Fasten off. Weave tie through ch-1 sps from Rnd 2. (Arrange the tie so any visible seam is at the back of the swaddle sack.)

DISCLAIMER: It's important to realize that the tie option should only be used as a photography prop under constant supervision. Never leave a baby alone with the tie.

RIBBED EDGING OPTION

> **NOTE:** *Measure after completing Rnd 1. If not within the LARGE end of the size range (page 81), redo with a smaller hook.*

RND 1: ch 2 (counts as a dc), dc in each st to end of rnd, join with sl st in top of ch 2. (70, 70, 75, 80, 85)

RND 2: ch 2, *fpdc around next st, bpdc around next st*, repeat between *...* to end of rnd, join with sl st (or invisible join) in top of ch 2 (OR this round can be repeated for a longer ribbing section). Weave in all ends.

MAKING WAVES BABY COCOON OR SWADDLE SACK

With a fabulous texture that's both fun to make and looks amazing, the Making Waves Cocoon or Swaddle Sack is one of my favorite cocoon patterns. For a perfectly coordinated set, pair it up with the matching Making Waves Beanie (page 165).

A swaddle sack is very snug and made to fit a newborn baby. Photographers like to use swaddles to keep the baby calm for photos. A cocoon is roomier, fits longer and is generally used by parents (as well as photographers). It's great for snuggling and warmth.

SKILL LEVEL: Intermediate

MATERIALS

TOOLS	Stitch marker, measuring tape, yarn needle
YARN	14 oz (397 g) or less (depending on size) of #4 worsted weight yarn
GAUGE	Gauge checkpoint given in pattern for each size after Rnd 4
HOOK SIZE	"J" (6 mm) crochet hook or to match gauge checkpoint

SIZE CHART

NEWBORN SWADDLE SACK	16–18" (41–46 cm) circumference, 11–12" (28–30 cm) length
PREEMIE COCOON	16–18" (41–46 cm) circumference, 14" (36 cm) length
NEWBORN COCOON	18–20" (46–51 cm) circumference, 18" (46 cm) length
0–3 MONTHS COCOON	20–22" (51–56 cm) circumference, 20" (51 cm) length
3–6 MONTHS COCOON	22–24" (56–61 cm) circumference, 22" (56 cm) length

ABBREVIATIONS USED

ST(S)	stitch(es)
CH	chain stitch
SC	single crochet
HDC	half double crochet
DC	double crochet
FPSC	front post single crochet
BPDC	back post double crochet
HDC2TOG	half double crochet 2 stitches together
SL ST	slip stitch
RND(S)	round(s)
SK	skip
SP	space
EA	each
BEG	beginning
PREV	previous
YO	Yarn Over

SPECIAL STITCHES DEFINITIONS

FRONT POST SINGLE CROCHET (FPSC): Insert hook from the front side of the work (right to left) under the post of the indicated stitch, YO and pull up a loop, YO and draw through 2 loops.

FRONT POST DOUBLE CROCHET (FPDC): Working from the front side of the work, YO and insert the hook from right to left under the post of the double crochet indicated from the previous round, YO and pull up a loop, [YO and draw through 2 loops] twice.

BACK POST DOUBLE CROCHET (BPDC): Working from the back side of the work, YO and insert the hook from right to left over the post of the double crochet indicated from the previous round, YO and pull up a loop, [YO and draw through 2 loops] twice.

HALF DOUBLE CROCHET IN 3RD LOOP: There are 2 main loops in a stitch—the "V" on the top—referred to as the front and back loops. With a hdc, the YO (before the hook is inserted into the next stitch) creates a 3rd loop on the back side of the stitch. In this pattern, all hdc in the 3rd loop will be worked in the BACK 3rd loop. The only difference is where the stitch is placed, not how it is worked. (See hdc2tog definition.)

HALF DOUBLE CROCHET 2 STITCHES TOGETHER (HDC2TOG): [YO, insert hook in next stitch, YO and pull up a loop] twice, YO and draw through all 5 loops on hook. (In this pattern, this stitch is always worked in the 3rd loop.)

FRONT POST DOUBLE CROCHET DECREASE (FPDC DECREASE): Work 1 fpdc around both posts of indicated stitches from previous round at the same time.

SPECIAL TECHNIQUES

USING THE BEG "CH 2" AS THE FINAL DC IN THE ROUND: If there is a "ch 2" at the beginning of a round, it will stand in as the last dc in the round. This avoids having a noticeable seam. If the repeat ends on a dc at the end of the round, don't make that last dc because the "ch 2" is there and will look like a dc when you join to the top of it. If the repeat ends with 2 dc worked in one stitch, make the first dc in the same stitch as the "ch 2". This will look almost exactly the same as working 2 dc in one stitch.

JOINING IN THE "TOP" OF THE CH 2: If there is any confusion on where to join at the end of each round, use the following method: Complete the first ch 2 of the round, then add a stitch marker around the loop that is on the hook. At the end of the round, this is the stitch that will be used for joining.

NEWBORN MAKING WAVES SWADDLE SACK AND PREEMIE MAKING WAVES COCOON

Use "J" (6 mm) hook, or match gauge checkpoint after Rnd 4.

NOTE: *The beginning ch 2 counts as the final dc or hdc in each round and is included in the stitch count for the first 2 rounds.*

RND 1: Magic ring, ch 2 (counts as dc), 13 dc in ring, join with sl st in top of ch 2. (14)

OR ch 2, 14 dc in 2nd ch from hook, join with sl st in first dc. (14)

RND 2: ch 2, *fpdc around ea of next 2 dc, dc in top of same post just used for fpdc*, repeat between *...* to end of rnd, last fpdc will be around ch 2 from prev rnd, beg ch 2 counts as last dc, join with sl st in top of ch 2. (21)

RND 5: *fpdc around next fpdc, 2 fpdc around next fpdc, fpdc around next fpdc, hdc in 3rd loop of next hdc, 2 hdc in 3rd loop of next hdc*, repeat between *...* to end of rnd, join with sl st in top of ch 2. (49)

RND 6: *fpdc around next 2 fpdc, 2 dc in top of same post just used (between 2nd and 3rd fpdc of prev round), fpdc around next 2 fpdc, hdc in 3rd loop of next hdc, hdc2tog (3rd loop) over next 2 hdc*, repeat between *...* to end of rnd, join with sl st in top of ch 2. (56)

RND 7: *fpdc around next 2 fpdc, fpdc around next dc, hdc in top of same post just used (between 2 dc of prev round), fpdc around next dc, fpdc around next 2 fpdc, hdc2tog (3rd loop) over next 2 hdc*, repeat between *...* to end of rnd, join with sl st in top of ch 2. (56)

RND 8: *fpdc around next 3 fpdc, 2 hdc (3rd loop) in next hdc, fpdc around next 3 fpdc, sk next hdc*, repeat between *...* to end of rnd, join with sl st in top of ch 2. (56)

NOTE: *A fpdc decrease is worked as follows: Work **one** fpdc around **both** middle stitches of the 6 fpdc from prev round at the same time. This method will leave less of a hole than a regular fpdc2tog. (The first time Rnd 9 is worked, the fpdc [fpsc + ch 2] decrease of the next round is worked around both the LAST fpdc [prev rnd] and the FIRST fpdc [prev rnd] at the same time. When repeated, just use the middle 2 fpdc.)*

NOTE: *From this point on, the first fpdc of EVERY round is worked as follows: fpsc around post of first fpdc from prev rnd, ch 2. The "fpsc + ch 2" creates a stitch that looks like a fpdc. Crochet the fpsc tightly around the post so it doesn't bulge at the base of the ch 2. It is correct if it looks very similar to a fpdc. Starting the round in this fashion (instead of a standard ch 2) will result in a seam that is almost completely invisible. This fpsc + ch 2 combo counts as the first fpdc of every round from this point.*

RND 3: *fpdc around ea of next 2 fpdc, fpdc around next dc, hdc in top of same post just used*, repeat between *...* to end of rnd, join with sl st in top of ch 2. (28)

RND 4: *fpdc around ea of next 3 fpdc, 2 hdc in 3rd loop of next hdc*, repeat between *...* to end of rnd, join with sl st in top of ch 2. (35)

RND 9: *fpdc decrease, fpdc around next 2 fpdc, hdc (3rd loop) in next hdc, 2 hdc (3rd loop) in next hdc, fpdc around next 2 fpdc*, repeat between *...* to end of rnd, join with sl st in top of ch 2. (56)

RND 10: *2 fpdc around next fpdc, fpdc around next 2 fpdc, hdc (3rd loop) next hdc, hdc2tog (3rd loop) over next 2 hdc, fpdc around next 2 fpdc*, repeat to end of rnd, join with sl st in top of ch 2. (56)

RND 11: *fpdc around next fpdc, hdc in top of post just used, fpdc around next 3 fpdc, hdc2tog (3rd loop) over next 2 hdc, fpdc around next 2 fpdc*, repeat to end of rnd, join with sl st in top of ch 2. (56)

RND 12: *fpdc around next fpdc, 2 hdc (3rd loop) in next hdc, fpdc around next 3 fpdc, sk next hdc, fpdc around next 2 fpdc*, repeat to end of rnd, join with sl st in top of ch 2. (56)

RND 13: *fpdc around next fpdc, hdc (3rd loop) in next hdc, 2 hdc (3rd loop) in next hdc, fpdc around next 2 fpdc, fpdc decrease, fpdc around next fpdc*, repeat to end of rnd, join with sl st in top of ch 2. (56)

RND 14: *fpdc around next fpdc, hdc (3rd loop) in next hdc, hdc2tog (3rd loop) over next 2 hdc, fpdc around next 2 fpdc, 2 fpdc around next fpdc, fpdc around next fpdc*, repeat to end of rnd, join with sl st in top of ch 2. (56)

RND 15: *fpdc around next fpdc, hdc2tog (3rd loop) over next 2 hdc, fpdc around next 3 fpdc, hdc in top of same post just used, fpdc around next 2 fpdc*, repeat to end of rnd, join with sl st in top of ch 2. (56)

RND 16: *fpdc around next fpdc, sk next hdc, fpdc around next 3 fpdc, 2 hdc (3rd loop) in next hdc, fpdc around next 2 fpdc*, repeat to end of rnd, join with sl st in top of ch 2. (56)

REPEAT RNDS 9–16 (Read Note before Rnd 9) until the following measurement is reached:

NB Swaddle Sack: Continue until it measures approx. 10 to 11" (25 to 28 cm) from top to bottom.

Preemie Cocoon: Continue until it measures approximately 13" (33 cm) from top to bottom.

CONTINUE with the Edging Options at the end of the pattern (page 98).

NEWBORN MAKING WAVES COCOON

Use "J" (6 mm) hook, or match gauge checkpoint after Rnd 4.

NOTE: *The beginning ch 2 counts as the final dc or hdc in each round and is included in the stitch count for the first 3 rounds.*

RND 1: Magic ring, ch 2 (counts as dc), 7 dc in ring, join with sl st in top of ch 2. (8)

OR ch 2, 8 dc in 2nd ch from hook, join with sl st in first dc. (8)

RND 2: ch 2, *fpdc around next dc, dc in top of same post just used for fpdc*, repeat between *...* to end of rnd, last fpdc will be around ch 2 from prev rnd, beg ch 2 counts as last dc, join with sl st in top of ch 2. (16)

RND 3: ch 2, *fpdc around next fpdc, fpdc around next dc, dc in top of same post just used*, repeat between *...* to end of rnd, last fpdc will be around ch 2 from prev rnd, beg ch 2 counts as last dc, join with sl st in top of ch 2. (24)

NOTE: *From this point on, the first fpdc of EVERY round is worked as follows: fpsc around post of first fpdc from prev rnd, ch 2. The "fpsc + ch 2" creates a stitch that looks like a fpdc. Crochet the fpsc tightly around the post so it doesn't bulge at the base of the ch 2. It is correct if it looks very similar to a fpdc. Starting the round in this fashion (instead of a standard ch 2) will result in a seam that is almost completely invisible. This fpsc + ch 2 combo counts as the first fpdc of every round from this point.*

RND 4: *fpdc around ea of next 2 fpdc, fpdc around next dc, hdc in top of same post just used*, repeat between *...* to end of rnd, join with sl st in top of ch 2. (32)

GAUGE CHECKPOINT: *Diameter of the circle should measure approximately 3.25" (8 cm) here.*

RND 5: *fpdc around ea of next 3 fpdc, 2 hdc in 3rd loop of next hdc*, repeat between *...* to end of rnd, join with sl st in top of ch 2. (40)

RND 6: *fpdc around next fpdc, 2 fpdc around next fpdc, fpdc around next fpdc, hdc in 3rd loop of next hdc, 2 hdc in 3rd loop of next hdc*, repeat between *...* to end of rnd, join with sl st in top of ch 2. (56)

RND 7: *fpdc around next 2 fpdc, 2 dc in top of same post just used (between 2nd and 3rd fpdc of prev round), fpdc around next 2 fpdc, hdc in 3rd loop of next hdc, hdc2tog (3rd loop) over next 2 hdc*, repeat between *...* to end of rnd, join with sl st in top of ch 2. (64)

RND 8: *fpdc around next 2 fpdc, fpdc around next dc, hdc in top of same post just used (between 2 dc of prev round), fpdc around next dc, fpdc around next 2 fpdc, hdc2tog (3rd loop) over next 2 hdc*, repeat between *...* to end of rnd, join with sl st in top of ch 2. (64)

RND 9: *fpdc around next 3 fpdc, 2 hdc (3rd loop) in next hdc, fpdc around next 3 fpdc, sk next hdc*, repeat between *...* to end of rnd, join with sl st in top of ch 2. (64)

NOTE: *A fpdc decrease is worked as follows: Work **one** fpdc around **both** middle stitches of the 6 fpdc from prev round at the same time. This method will leave less of a hole than a regular fpdc2tog. (The first time Rnd 10 is worked, the fpdc [fpsc + ch 2] decrease of the next round is worked around both the LAST fpdc [prev rnd] and the FIRST fpdc [prev rnd] at the same time. When repeated, just use the middle 2 fpdc.)*

RND 10: *fpdc decrease, fpdc around next 2 fpdc, hdc (3rd loop) in next hdc, 2 hdc (3rd loop) in next hdc, fpdc around next 2 fpdc*, repeat between *...* to end of rnd, join with sl st in top of ch 2. (64)

RND 11: *2 fpdc around next fpdc, fpdc around next 2 fpdc, hdc (3rd loop) next hdc, hdc2tog over next 2 hdc, fpdc around next 2 fpdc*, repeat to end of rnd, join with sl st in top of ch 2. (64)

RND 12: *fpdc around next fpdc, hdc in top of post just used, fpdc around next 3 fpdc, hdc2tog (3rd loop) over next 2 hdc, fpdc around next 2 fpdc*, repeat to end of rnd, join with sl st in top of ch 2. (64)

RND 13: *fpdc around next fpdc, 2 hdc (3rd loop) in next hdc, fpdc around next 3 fpdc, sk next hdc, fpdc around next 2 fpdc*, repeat to end of rnd, join with sl st in top of ch 2. (64)

RND 14: *fpdc around next fpdc, hdc (3rd loop) in next hdc, 2 hdc (3rd loop) in next hdc, fpdc around next 2 fpdc, fpdc decrease, fpdc around next fpdc*, repeat to end of rnd, join with sl st in top of ch 2. (64)

RND 15: *fpdc around next fpdc, hdc (3rd loop) in next hdc, hdc2tog (3rd loop) over next 2 hdc, fpdc around next 2 fpdc, 2 fpdc around next fpdc, fpdc around next fpdc*, repeat to end of rnd, join with sl st in top of ch 2. (64)

RND 16: *fpdc around next fpdc, hdc2tog (3rd loop) over next 2 hdc, fpdc around next 3 fpdc, hdc in top of same post just used, fpdc around next 2 fpdc*, repeat to end of rnd, join with sl st in top of ch 2. (64)

RND 17: *fpdc around next fpdc, sk next hdc, fpdc around next 3 fpdc, 2 hdc (3rd loop) in next hdc, fpdc around next 2 fpdc*, repeat to end of rnd, join with sl st in top of ch 2. (64)

REPEAT RNDS 10–17 (Read Note before Rnd 10) until the cocoon measures approximately 16 to 17" (41 to 43 cm) from top to bottom.

CONTINUE with the Edging Options at the end of the pattern (page 98).

0-3 MONTHS MAKING WAVES COCOON

Use "J" (6 mm) hook, or match gauge checkpoint after Rnd 4.

NOTE: *The beginning ch 2 counts as the final dc or hdc in each round and is included in the stitch count for the first 3 rounds.*

RND 1: Magic ring, ch 2 (counts as dc), 8 dc in ring, join with sl st in top of ch 2. (9)

OR ch 2, 9 dc in 2nd ch from hook, join with sl st in first dc. (9)

RND 2: ch 2, *fpdc around next dc, dc in top of same post just used for fpdc*, repeat between *...* to end of rnd, last fpdc will be around ch 2 from prev rnd, beg ch 2 counts as last dc, join with sl st in top of ch 2. (18)

RND 3: ch 2, *fpdc around next fpdc, fpdc around next dc, dc in top of same post just used*, repeat between *...* to end of rnd, last fpdc will be around ch 2 from prev rnd, beg ch 2 counts as last dc, join with sl st in top of ch 2. (27)

NOTE: *From this point on, the first fpdc of EVERY round is worked as follows: fpsc around post of first fpdc from prev rnd, ch 2. The "fpsc + ch 2" creates a stitch that looks like a fpdc. Crochet the fpsc tightly around the post so it doesn't bulge at the base of the ch 2. It is correct if it looks very similar to a fpdc. Starting the round in this fashion (instead of a standard ch 2) will result in a seam that is almost completely invisible. This fpsc + ch 2 combo counts as the first fpdc of every round from this point.*

RND 4: *fpdc around ea of next 2 fpdc, fpdc around next dc, hdc in top of same post just used*, repeat between *...* to end of rnd, join with sl st in top of ch 2. (36)

GAUGE CHECKPOINT: *Diameter of the circle should measure approximately 3.25" (8 cm) here.*

RND 5: *fpdc around ea of next 3 fpdc, 2 hdc in 3rd loop of next hdc*, repeat between *...* to end of rnd, join with sl st in top of ch 2. (45)

RND 6: *fpdc around next fpdc, 2 fpdc around next fpdc, fpdc around next fpdc, hdc in 3rd loop of next hdc, 2 hdc in 3rd loop of next hdc*, repeat between *...* to end of rnd, join with sl st in top of ch 2. (63)

RND 7: *fpdc around next 2 fpdc, 2 dc in top of same post just used (between 2nd and 3rd fpdc of prev round), fpdc around next 2 fpdc, hdc in 3rd loop of next hdc, hdc2tog (3rd loop) over next 2 hdc*, repeat between *...* to end of rnd, join with sl st in top of ch 2. (72)

RND 8: *fpdc around next 2 fpdc, fpdc around next dc, hdc in top of same post just used (between 2 dc of prev round), fpdc around next dc, fpdc around next 2 fpdc, hdc2tog (3rd loop) over next 2 hdc*, repeat between *...* to end of rnd, join with sl st in top of ch 2. (72)

RND 9: *fpdc around next 3 fpdc, 2 hdc (3rd loop) in next hdc, fpdc around next 3 fpdc, sk next hdc*, repeat between *...* to end of rnd, join with sl st in top of ch 2. (72)

NOTE: *A fpdc decrease is worked as follows: Work **one** fpdc around **both** middle stitches of the 6 fpdc from prev round at the same time. This method will leave less of a hole than a regular fpdc2tog. (The first time Rnd 10 is worked, the fpdc [fpsc + ch 2] decrease of the next round is worked around both the LAST fpdc [prev rnd] and the FIRST fpdc [prev rnd] at the same time. When repeated, just use the middle 2 fpdc.)*

RND 10: *fpdc decrease, fpdc around next 2 fpdc, hdc (3rd loop) in next hdc, 2 hdc (3rd loop) in next hdc, fpdc around next 2 fpdc*, repeat between *...* to end of rnd, join with sl st in top of ch 2. (72)

RND 11: *2 fpdc around next fpdc, fpdc around next 2 fpdc, hdc (3rd loop) next hdc, hdc2tog (3rd loop) over next 2 hdc, fpdc around next 2 fpdc*, repeat to end of rnd, join with sl st in top of ch 2. (72)

RND 12: *fpdc around next fpdc, hdc in top of post just used, fpdc around next 3 fpdc, hdc2tog (3rd loop) over next 2 hdc, fpdc around next 2 fpdc*, repeat to end of rnd, join with sl st in top of ch 2. (72)

RND 13: *fpdc around next fpdc, 2 hdc (3rd loop) in next hdc, fpdc around next 3 fpdc, sk next hdc, fpdc around next 2 fpdc*, repeat to end of rnd, join with sl st in top of ch 2. (72)

RND 14: *fpdc around next fpdc, hdc (3rd loop) in next hdc, 2 hdc (3rd loop) in next hdc, fpdc around next 2 fpdc, fpdc decrease, fpdc around next fpdc*, repeat to end of rnd, join with sl st in top of ch 2. (72)

RND 15: *fpdc around next fpdc, hdc (3rd loop) in next hdc, hdc2tog (3rd loop) over next 2 hdc, fpdc around next 2 fpdc, 2 fpdc around next fpdc, fpdc around next fpdc*, repeat to end of rnd, join with sl st in top of ch 2. (72)

RND 16: *fpdc around next fpdc, hdc2tog (3rd loop) over next 2 hdc, fpdc around next 3 fpdc, hdc in top of same post just used, fpdc around next 2 fpdc*, repeat to end of rnd, join with sl st in top of ch 2. (72)

RND 17: *fpdc around next fpdc, sk next hdc, fpdc around next 3 fpdc, 2 hdc (3rd loop) in next hdc, fpdc around next 2 fpdc*, repeat to end of rnd, join with sl st in top of ch 2. (72)

REPEAT RNDS 10–17 (Read Note before Rnd 10) until the cocoon measures approximately 18 to 19" (46 to 48 cm) from top to bottom.

CONTINUE with the Edging Options at the end of the pattern (page 98).

3–6 MONTHS MAKING WAVES COCOON

Use "J" (6 mm) hook, or match gauge checkpoint after Rnd 4.

NOTE: *The beginning ch 2 counts as the final dc or hdc in each round and is included in the stitch count for the first 3 rounds.*

RND 1: Magic ring, ch 2 (counts as dc), 9 dc in ring, join with sl st in top of ch 2. (10)

OR ch 2, 10 dc in 2nd ch from hook, join with sl st in first dc. (10)

RND 2: ch 2, *fpdc around next dc, dc in top of same post just used for fpdc*, repeat between *...* to end of rnd, last fpdc will be around ch 2 from prev rnd, beg ch 2 counts as last dc, join with sl st in top of ch 2. (20)

RND 3: ch 2, *fpdc around next fpdc, fpdc around next dc, dc in top of same post just used*, repeat between *...* to end of rnd, last fpdc will be around ch 2 from prev rnd, beg ch 2 counts as last dc, join with sl st in top of ch 2. (30)

NOTE: *From this point on, the first fpdc of EVERY round is worked as follows: fpsc around post of first fpdc from prev rnd, ch 2. The "fpsc + ch 2" creates a stitch that looks like a fpdc. Crochet the fpsc tightly around the post so it doesn't bulge at the base of the ch 2. It is correct if it looks very similar to a fpdc. Starting the round in this fashion (instead of a standard ch 2) will result in a seam that is almost completely invisible. This fpsc + ch 2 combo counts as the first fpdc of every round from this point.*

RND 4: *fpdc around ea of next 2 fpdc, fpdc around next dc, hdc in top of same post just used*, repeat between *...* to end of rnd, join with sl st in top of ch 2. (40)

> **GAUGE CHECKPOINT:** *Diameter of the circle should measure approximately 3.5" (9 cm) here.*

RND 5: *fpdc around ea of next 3 fpdc, 2 hdc in 3rd loop of next hdc*, repeat between *...* to end of rnd, join with sl st in top of ch 2. (50)

RND 6: *fpdc around next fpdc, 2 fpdc around next fpdc, fpdc around next fpdc, hdc in 3rd loop of next hdc, 2 hdc in 3rd loop of next hdc*, repeat between *...* to end of rnd, join with sl st in top of ch 2. (70)

RND 7: *fpdc around next 2 fpdc, 2 dc in top of same post just used (between 2nd and 3rd fpdc of prev round), fpdc around next 2 fpdc, hdc in 3rd loop of next hdc, hdc2tog (3rd loop) over next 2 hdc*, repeat between *...* to end of rnd, join with sl st in top of ch 2. (80)

RND 8: *fpdc around next 2 fpdc, fpdc around next dc, hdc in top of same post just used (between 2 dc of prev round), fpdc around next dc, fpdc around next 2 fpdc, hdc2tog (3rd loop) over next 2 hdc*, repeat between *...* to end of rnd, join with sl st in top of ch 2. (80)

RND 9: *fpdc around next 3 fpdc, 2 hdc (3rd loop) in next hdc, fpdc around next 3 fpdc, sk next hdc*, repeat between *...* to end of rnd, join with sl st in top of ch 2. (80)

> **NOTE:** *A fpdc decrease is worked as follows: Work **one** fpdc around **both** middle stitches of the 6 fpdc from prev round at the same time. This method will leave less of a hole than a regular fpdc2tog. (The first time Rnd 10 is worked, the fpdc [fpsc + ch 2] decrease of the next round is worked around both the LAST fpdc [prev rnd] and the FIRST fpdc [prev rnd] at the same time. When repeated, just use the middle 2 fpdc.)*

RND 10: *fpdc decrease, fpdc around next 2 fpdc, hdc (3rd loop) in next hdc, 2 hdc (3rd loop) in next hdc, fpdc around next 2 fpdc*, repeat between *...* to end of rnd, join with sl st in top of ch 2. (80)

RND 11: *2 fpdc around next fpdc, fpdc around next 2 fpdc, hdc (3rd loop) next hdc, hdc2tog (3rd loop) over next 2 hdc, fpdc around next 2 fpdc*, repeat to end of rnd, join with sl st in top of ch 2. (80)

RND 12: *fpdc around next fpdc, hdc in top of post just used, fpdc around next 3 fpdc, hdc2tog (3rd loop) over next 2 hdc, fpdc around next 2 fpdc*, repeat to end of rnd, join with sl st in top of ch 2. (80)

RND 13: *fpdc around next fpdc, 2 hdc (3rd loop) in next hdc, fpdc around next 3 fpdc, sk next hdc, fpdc around next 2 fpdc*, repeat to end of rnd, join with sl st in top of ch 2. (80)

RND 14: *fpdc around next fpdc, hdc (3rd loop) in next hdc, 2 hdc (3rd loop) in next hdc, fpdc around next 2 fpdc, fpdc decrease, fpdc around next fpdc*, repeat to end of rnd, join with sl st in top of ch 2. (80)

RND 15: *fpdc around next fpdc, hdc (3rd loop) in next hdc, hdc2tog (3rd loop) over next 2 hdc, fpdc around next 2 fpdc, 2 fpdc around next fpdc, fpdc around next fpdc*, repeat to end of rnd, join with sl st in top of ch 2. (80)

RND 16: *fpdc around next fpdc, hdc2tog (3rd loop) over next 2 hdc, fpdc around next 3 fpdc, hdc in top of same post just used, fpdc around next 2 fpdc*, repeat to end of rnd, join with sl st in top of ch 2. (80)

RND 17: *fpdc around next fpdc, sk next hdc, fpdc around next 3 fpdc, 2 hdc (3rd loop) in next hdc, fpdc around next 2 fpdc*, repeat to end of rnd, join with sl st in top of ch 2. (80)

REPEAT RNDS 10–17 (Read Note before Rnd 10) until the cocoon measures approximately 20 to 21" (51 to 53 cm) from top to bottom.

CONTINUE with the Edging Options.

EDGING OPTIONS

Select one.

TIE OPTION

Recommended for Swaddle Sack.

NOTE: *Measure after completing Rnd 1. If not within the LARGE end of the size range (see page 89), redo with a smaller hook.*

RND 1: ch 1, sc in ea st to end of rnd, join with sl st in first sc. (56, 56, 64, 72, 80)

RND 2: ch 1, *sc, ch 1, sk next st*, repeat between *…* to end of rnd, join with sl st in first sc.

RND 3: ch 1, 2 sc in ea ch-1 sp to end of rnd, join with sl st (or invisible join) in first sc.

FASTEN OFF. Weave in all ends.

TIE: ch a length approximately 30 to 40" (76 to 102 cm) long, sl st in 2nd ch from hook and ea ch back down to beginning. Fasten off. Weave tie through ch-1 sps from Rnd 2.

DISCLAIMER: It's important to realize that the tie option should only be used as a photography prop under constant supervision. Never leave a baby alone with the tie.

RIBBED EDGING OPTION

NOTE: *Measure circumference after completing Rnd 1. If not within the LARGE end of the size range (see page 89), redo with a smaller hook.*

RND 1: ch 2 (counts as a dc), dc in each st to end of rnd, join with sl st in top of ch 2. (56, 56, 64, 72, 80)

RND 2: ch 2, *fpdc around next st, bpdc around next st*, repeat between *…* to end of rnd, join with sl st (or invisible join) in top of ch 2. (OR this rnd can be repeated for a longer ribbing section.) Fasten off. Weave in all ends.

HARLEQUIN BABY PANTS, ROMPER OR OVERALLS

Available in sizes from newborn to 24 months, the Harlequin Baby Pants, Romper or Overalls pattern has multiple options for photographers and parents alike. Make this pattern for a newborn session and then make it again for baby's one-year photo session! With two different top options and three different options for the bottom, there are lots of possible combinations for both boys and girls!

SKILL LEVEL: ⬤▬▭ Intermediate

MATERIALS

TOOLS	Measuring tape, yarn needle, buttons (optional), needle and thread (optional)
YARN	10 oz (283 g) or less of #4 worsted weight yarn. This pattern was designed and tested with cotton or cotton blend yarns. You may have different results with other fibers.
GAUGE	14 stitches and 10 rows in hdc = 4" x 4" (10 x 10 cm) with 5.5 mm hook
HOOK SIZE	"G" (4 mm) for waistband/cuffs, "I" (5.5 mm) for pants/bib

SIZE CHART

NEWBORN	12–13" (30–33 cm) waist circumference
0–3 MONTHS	12–13" (30–33 cm) waist circumference
3–6 MONTHS	12–13" (30–33 cm) waist circumference
6–12 MONTHS	12–13" (30–33 cm) waist circumference
12–18 MONTHS	12–13" (30–33 cm) waist circumference
18–24 MONTHS	12–13" (30–33 cm) waist circumference

ABBREVIATIONS USED

ST(S)	stitch(es)
CH	chain stitch
SC	single crochet
HDC	half double crochet
DC	double crochet
SL ST	slip stitch
FDC	Foundationless Double Crochet
FPSC	front post single crochet
FPDC	front post double crochet
BPDC	back post double crochet
FPTR	front post treble crochet
HDC2TOG	half double crochet 2 stitches together
RND(S)	round(s)
SK	skip
EA	each
BEG	beginning
PREV	previous
YO	Yarn Over

SPECIAL STITCHES DEFINITIONS

FRONT POST SINGLE CROCHET (FPSC): Insert hook from the front side of the work (right to left) under the post of the indicated stitch, YO and pull up a loop, YO and draw through 2 loops.

FRONT POST DOUBLE CROCHET (FPDC): Working from the front side of the work, YO and insert the hook from right to left under the post of the double crochet indicated from the previous round, YO and pull up a loop, [YO and draw through 2 loops] twice.

BACK POST DOUBLE CROCHET (BPDC): Working from the back side of the work, YO and insert the hook from right to left over the post of the double crochet indicated from the previous round, YO and pull up a loop, [YO and draw through 2 loops] twice.

FRONT POST TREBLE CROCHET (FPTR): YO hook twice, insert hook from right to left under the post of the stitch indicated, YO and pull up loop, [YO and draw through 2 loops] 3 times.

HALF DOUBLE CROCHET 2 STITCHES TOGETHER (HDC2TOG): YO and insert hook in stitch indicated, YO and draw up a loop, YO and insert hook in next st, YO and draw up another loop. YO again and draw through all 5 loops on hook.

BABY PANTS, ROMPER OR OVERALLS WAISTBAND (ALL SIZES)

Start with "G" (4 mm) hook. The beginning ch 3 (or ch 2) is included in the stitch count. Leave 8" (20 cm) long tail at beginning to sew the gap closed at the join. See Note after Rnd 1. (The Foundationless Double Crochet method is listed first with the traditional chain method as an alternative option listed second.)

RND 1: ch 3, (47, 55, 55, 63, 71, 79) FDC, join with sl st in top of beg ch 3 to form a circle. (48, 56, 56, 64, 72, 80)

OR ch (50, 58, 58, 66, 74, 82), dc in 4th ch from hook and ea ch to end of row, join with sl st in first dc to form a circle. (48, 56, 56, 64, 72, 80)

GAUGE CHECKPOINT: *Chain should be the following approximate measurement before joining (see Note below).*

NEWBORN	12.5–13" (32–33 cm)
0–3 MONTHS	15" (38 cm)
3–6 MONTHS	15" (38 cm)
6–12 MONTHS	17–18" (43–46 cm)
12–18 MONTHS	19–20" (48–51 cm)
18–24 MONTHS	20–21" (51–53 cm)

NOTE: *Be sure not to twist the waistband when joining into a circle. There will be a little bit of a gap where it was joined. This will be closed up with the tail end as it is woven in.*

RND 2: ch 2, *fpdc around next st, bpdc around next st*, repeat between *...* to end of rnd, beg ch 2 serves as last bpdc, join with sl st in top of ch 2. (48, 56, 56, 64, 72, 80)

RND 3: ch 2, *fpdc around next fpdc, bpdc around next bpdc*, repeat between *...* to end of rnd, join with sl st in top of ch 2. (48, 56, 56, 64, 72, 80)

GAUGE CHECKPOINT: *Waistband should be approximately (6" [15 cm], 7.5 to 8" [19 to 20 cm], 7.5 to 8" [19 to 20 cm], 8" [20 cm], 9" [23 cm], 10" [25 cm]) wide. The next section will be slightly wider.*

Switch to "I" (5.5 mm) hook (or two hook sizes larger than gauge).

NOTE: *The "fpsc + ch 2" (or "fpsc + ch 3") combo at the beginning of the following rounds creates a stitch that looks like a fpdc/fptr (and it also counts as the first fpdc/fptr). Be sure to crochet the fpsc tightly around the post so it doesn't bulge at the base of the ch 2. It is correct if it looks very similar to a fpdc/fptr. Starting the round in this fashion (instead of a standard ch 2) will result in a seam that is almost completely invisible.*

RND 4: fpsc around post of first fpdc from prev rnd, ch 3 (serves as first fptr), now working **over** fptr, go back 2 sts into prev rnd just completed (skip ch 2) and work a fptr around last fpdc ("x" completed), now moving forward again (past "x" just created), work 2 dc in top of next bpdc, *sk next fpdc and next bpdc, fptr around next fpdc, now working **over** fptr just made, work fptr around skipped fpdc, now moving forward again (past "x" just created) work 2 dc in top of next bpdc*, repeat between *...* to end of rnd, join with sl st in top of ch 3. (48, 56, 56, 64, 72, 80)

NOTE: *The (fpsc + ch 2) or (fpsc + ch 3) combo at the beginning of each round counts as the **first** fpdc/fptr for the **next** rnd (see Note above).*

RND 5: fpsc around post of first fptr from prev rnd (bottom of twist), ch 2 (serves as first fpdc), dc in sp between first 2 fptr from prev rnd, fpdc around next fptr, dc in sp between next 2 dc, *fpdc around next fptr (the post on the bottom), dc in sp between the 2 fptr, fpdc around next fptr, dc in sp between next 2 dc*, repeat between *...* to end of rnd, join with sl st in top of ch 2. (48, 56, 56, 64, 72, 80)

RND 6: fpsc around post of first fpdc from prev rnd, ch 3 (serves as first fptr), now working **under** fptr, go back 2 sts into prev rnd just completed (skip dc) and work a fptr around last fpdc ("x" completed), now moving forward again (past "x" just created), work 2 dc in next dc, *sk next fpdc and next dc, fptr around next fpdc, now working **under** fptr just made, work fptr around skipped fpdc, now moving forward again (past "x" just created) work 2 dc in next dc*, repeat between *...* to end of rnd, join with sl st in top of ch 3. (48, 56, 56, 64, 72, 80)

RND 7: fpsc around post of first fptr from prev rnd (top of twist), ch 2 (serves as first fpdc), dc in sp between first 2 fptr from prev rnd, fpdc around next fptr, dc in sp between next 2 dc, *fpdc around next fptr (the post on top), dc in sp between the 2 fptr, fpdc around next fptr, dc in sp between next 2 dc*, repeat between *...* to end of rnd, join with sl st in top of ch 2. (48, 56, 56, 64, 72, 80)

RND 8: fpsc around post of first fpdc from prev rnd, ch 3 (serves as first fptr), now working **over** fptr, go back 2 sts into prev rnd just completed (skip dc) and work a fptr around last fpdc ("x" completed), now moving forward again (past "x" just created), work 2 dc in next dc, *sk next fpdc and next dc, fptr around next fpdc, now working **over** fptr just made, work fptr around skipped fpdc, now moving forward again (past "x" just created) work 2 dc in next dc*, repeat between *...* to end of rnd, join with sl st in top of ch 3. (48, 56, 56, 64, 72, 80)

REPEAT RNDS 5–8 until the pants reach the following measurement from top to bottom (end with either Rnd 5 or 7). (Then continue with first leg.)

NEWBORN	5.5" (14 cm) from top to bottom
0–3 MONTHS	5.5–6.5" (14–17 cm) from top to bottom
3–6 MONTHS	6.5–7" (17–18 cm) from top to bottom
6–12 MONTHS	6.5–7.5" (17–19 cm) from top to bottom
12–18 MONTHS	7–7.5" (18–19 cm) from top to bottom
18–24 MONTHS	7.5–8" (19–20 cm) from top to bottom

FIRST LEG (ALL SIZES)

Use "I" (5.5 mm) hook.

NOTE: *The pattern will continue to alternate the "under" or "over" pattern of Rnds 5–8 for each leg. However, the circle will now be divided in half (to form each leg). The last slip stitch of Rnd 1 will span both sides of the circle to create the first leg.*

RND 1 OF FIRST LEG: Repeat Rnd 6 or 8 (if the last section ended with Rnd 7, start with Rnd 8, etc.) for the first (24, 28, 28, 32, 36, 40) sts (half the rnd). After completing last 2 dc, reach across the circle and join with a sl st in the beg ch 3. (24, 28, 28, 32, 36, 40)

RND 2 OF FIRST LEG: fpsc around post of first fptr from prev rnd, ch 2 (serves as first fpdc), dc in sp between first 2 fptr from prev rnd, fpdc around next fptr, dc in sp between next 2 dc, *fpdc around next fptr, dc in sp between the 2 fptr, fpdc around next fptr, dc in sp between next 2 dc*, repeat between *...* to end of rnd, join with sl st in top of ch 2. (24, 28, 28, 32, 36, 40)

ROMPER (ANY SIZE)

REPEAT RNDS 5-8 (working in order from last rnd above) for a total of 1–3 times for each leg (your preference), then work one rnd of sc, fasten off with invisible join (skip Cuff section). (24, 28, 28, 32, 36, 40)

PANTS/OVERALLS

REPEAT RNDS 5-8 (working in order from last rnd above [24, 28, 28, 32, 36, 40]) until pants reach the following measurement:

NEWBORN	10″ (25 cm) from top of waistband to end of leg
0-3 MONTHS	11–12″ (28–30 cm) from top of waistband to end of leg
3-6 MONTHS	12–13″ (30–33 cm) from top of waistband to end of leg
6-12 MONTHS	13–14″ (33–36 cm) from top of waistband to end of leg
12-18 MONTHS	14–15″ (36–38 cm) from top of waistband to end of leg
18-24 MONTHS	16–17″ (41–43 cm) from top of waistband to end of leg

DO NOT FASTEN OFF. Continue with Cuff.

SHORT PANTS OR "SHORTIES"

Subtract 2″ (5 cm) from any size to the left, then work one rnd of sc, fasten off with invisible join (skip Cuff section).

CUFF (ALL SIZES)

Use "G" (4 mm) hook.

RND 1: ch 1, sc in first st and next st, sc2tog, *sc in next 2 sts, sc2tog*, repeat to end of rnd, join with sl st in first sc. (18, 21, 21, 24, 27, 30)

RND 2: ch 1, sc in first st and ea st to end of rnd, join with sl st in first sc. (18, 21, 21, 24, 27, 30)

RND 3: Repeat Rnd 2, fasten off with invisible join in first sc. (18, 21, 21, 24, 27, 30)

SECOND LEG (ALL SIZES)

Use "I" (5.5 mm) hook.

> **NOTE:** *Leave an 18" (46-cm) tail end when attaching the yarn. This will be used to sew up the gap between the two legs.*

REPEAT steps for the first leg, starting with the stitch you would have continued with if you hadn't reached across the circle to make the first leg. (Start with the (fpsc, ch 3) around the 2nd fptr, then go back and work around the skipped fptr.) Continue with Cuff (same as first cuff). Use a yarn needle and the tail ends of the yarn to close up gaps at the waistband and crotch of the pants.

ROMPER OR OVERALLS BIB (OPTIONAL)

Use "I" (5.5 mm) hook.

ROW 1: (All sizes) Lay the pants flat with the middle exactly centered (front side up). Attach the yarn on the right-hand side, two stitches in from edge, ch 2 (does not count as a st), work (20, 24, 24, 28, 32, 36) hdc across the waistband. (If centered properly, there will be 2 extra sts on each side of this row.) Continue with the section for the size you are making. (Do not count ch 2 as a st.)

CONTINUE with the Top Edging Section on page 106.

NEWBORN BIB

ROW 2: ch 2, turn, hdc in ea st to end of row. (20)

ROWS 3–4: Repeat Row 2.

ROW 5: ch 2, turn, hdc2tog, hdc in next 16 sts, hdc2tog. (18)

ROW 6: ch 2, turn, hdc2tog, hdc in next 14 sts, hdc2tog. (16)

ROW 7: ch 2, turn, hdc2tog, hdc in next 12 sts, hdc2tog. (14)

ROW 8: ch 2, turn, hdc2tog, hdc in next 10 sts, hdc2tog. (12)

ROW 9: ch 2, turn, hdc2tog, hdc in next 8 sts, hdc2tog. (10)

CONTINUE with the Top Edging Section on page 106.

0–3 MONTHS BIB

ROW 2: ch 2, turn, hdc in ea st to end of row. (24)

ROWS 3–4: Repeat Row 2.

ROW 5: ch 2, turn, hdc2tog, hdc in next 20 sts, hdc2tog. (22)

ROW 6: ch 2, turn, hdc2tog, hdc in next 18 sts, hdc2tog. (20)

ROW 7: ch 2, turn, hdc2tog, hdc in next 16 sts, hdc2tog. (18)

ROW 8: ch 2, turn, hdc2tog, hdc in next 14 sts, hdc2tog. (16)

ROW 9: ch 2, turn, hdc2tog, hdc in next 12 sts, hdc2tog. (14)

ROW 10: ch 2, turn, hdc2tog, hdc in next 10 sts, hdc2tog. (12)

ROW 11: ch 2, turn, hdc2tog, hdc in next 8 sts, hdc2tog. (10)

CONTINUE with the Top Edging Section on page 106.

3–6 MONTHS BIB

ROW 2: ch 2, turn, hdc in ea st to end of row. (24)

ROWS 3–4: Repeat Row 2.

ROW 5: ch 2, turn, hdc2tog, hdc in next 20 sts, hdc2tog. (22)

ROW 6: ch 2, turn, hdc2tog, hdc in next 18 sts, hdc2tog. (20)

ROW 7: ch 2, turn, hdc2tog, hdc in next 16 sts, hdc2tog. (18)

ROW 8: ch 2, turn, hdc2tog, hdc in next 14 sts, hdc2tog. (16)

ROW 9: ch 2, turn, hdc2tog, hdc in next 12 sts, hdc2tog. (14)

ROW 10: ch 2, turn, hdc2tog, hdc in next 10 sts, hdc2tog. (12)

ROW 11: ch 2, turn, hdc2tog, hdc in next 8 sts, hdc2tog. (10)

CONTINUE with the Top Edging Section on page 106.

6–12 MONTHS BIB

ROW 2: ch 2, turn, hdc in ea st to end of row. (28)

ROWS 3–4: Repeat Row 2.

ROW 5: ch 2, turn, hdc2tog, hdc in next 24 sts, hdc2tog. (26)

ROW 6: ch 2, turn, hdc in ea st to end of row. (26)

ROW 7: ch 2, turn, hdc2tog, hdc in next 22 sts, hdc2tog. (24)

ROW 8: ch 2, turn, hdc2tog, hdc in next 20 sts, hdc2tog. (22)

ROW 9: ch 2, turn, hdc2tog, hdc in next 18 sts, hdc2tog. (20)

ROW 10: ch 2, turn, hdc2tog, hdc in next 16 sts, hdc2tog. (18)

ROW 11: ch 2, turn, hdc2tog, hdc in next 14 sts, hdc2tog. (16)

ROW 12: ch 2, turn, hdc2tog, hdc in next 12 sts, hdc2tog. (14)

ROW 13: ch 2, turn, hdc2tog, hdc in next 10 sts, hdc2tog. (12)

CONTINUE with the Top Edging Section on page 106.

12–18 MONTHS BIB

ROW 2: ch 2, turn, hdc in ea st to end of row. (32)

ROWS 3–4: Repeat Row 2.

ROW 5: ch 2, turn, hdc2tog, hdc in next 28 sts, hdc2tog. (30)

ROW 6: ch 2, turn, hdc in ea st to end of row. (30)

ROW 7: ch 2, turn, hdc2tog, hdc in next 26 sts, hdc2tog. (28)

ROW 8: ch 2, turn, hdc2tog, hdc in next 24 sts, hdc2tog. (26)

ROW 9: ch 2, turn, hdc2tog, hdc in next 22 sts, hdc2tog. (24)

ROW 10: ch 2, turn, hdc2tog, hdc in next 20 sts, hdc2tog. (22)

ROW 11: ch 2, turn, hdc2tog, hdc in next 18 sts, hdc2tog. (20)

ROW 12: ch 2, turn, hdc2tog, hdc in next 16 sts, hdc2tog. (18)

ROW 13: ch 2, turn, hdc2tog, hdc in next 14 sts, hdc2tog. (16)

CONTINUE with the Top Edging Section on page 106.

18–24 MONTHS BIB

ROW 2: ch 2, turn, hdc in ea st to end of row. (36)

ROWS 3–5: Repeat Row 2.

ROW 6: ch 2, turn, hdc2tog, hdc in next 32 sts, hdc2tog. (34)

ROW 7: ch 2, turn, hdc in ea st to end of row. (34)

ROW 8: ch 2, turn, hdc2tog, hdc in next 30 sts, hdc2tog. (32)

ROW 9: ch 2, turn, hdc2tog, hdc in next 28 sts, hdc2tog. (30)

ROW 10: ch 2, turn, hdc2tog, hdc in next 26 sts, hdc2tog. (28)

ROW 11: ch 2, turn, hdc2tog, hdc in next 24 sts, hdc2tog. (26)

ROW 12: ch 2, turn, hdc2tog, hdc in next 22 sts, hdc2tog. (24)

ROW 13: ch 2, turn, hdc2tog, hdc in next 20 sts, hdc2tog. (22)

ROW 14: ch 2, turn, hdc2tog, hdc in next 18 sts, hdc2tog. (20)

ROW 15: ch 2, turn, hdc2tog, hdc in next 16 sts, hdc2tog. (18)

CONTINUE with the Top Edging Section on page 106.

TOP EDGING SECTION (ALL SIZES)

Use "I" (5.5 mm) hook.

Select a version below:

EDGING WITH CROCHETED TIES (ROMPER)

With right side facing, ch 1, rotate so you are working down side, sc evenly along side edge of overall bib, around back of waistband and back up other side. Once you reach the top again, ch (60, 65, 70, 75, 80, 85), sl st in second ch from hook and ea ch back down to overall bib, sk next st, sc in next st and ea st across top edge up to the second to last st, repeat steps for second tie, fasten off with invisible join in last st. Weave in ends.

EDGING WITH STRAPS (OVERALLS)

With right side facing, ch 1, rotate so you are working down side, sc evenly along side edge of overall bib, around back of waistband and back up other side, 2 sc in top corner, sc across top, fasten off with invisible join in first sc. Weave in ends. Continue with Overall Straps.

OVERALL STRAPS (MAKE TWO)

Use "I" (5.5 mm) hook.

> **NOTE:** *Leave a 6" (15 cm) long tail (see Alternate Option below first).*

NEWBORN	ch 25, dc in 4th ch from hook and ea ch back down to beg. Fasten off.
0-3 MONTHS	ch 30, dc in 4th ch from hook and ea ch back down to beg. Fasten off.
3-6 MONTHS	ch 35, dc in 4th ch from hook and ea ch back down to beg. Fasten off.
6-12 MONTHS	ch 40, dc in 4th ch from hook and ea ch back down to beg. Fasten off.
12-18 MONTHS	ch 45, dc in 4th ch from hook and ea ch back down to beg. Fasten off.
18-24 MONTHS	ch 50, dc in 4th ch from hook and ea ch back down to beg. Fasten off.

Using a yarn needle and the tail end of the yarn, attach straps on the back of the waistband (arrange so they will crisscross before going over the shoulders). The other end will button over the button on the front of the overalls. (Be sure to test the button size with the strap to make sure it fits between the dc stitches.)

Sew a button (or see below) on each top corner of the overall bib (after testing the size on the strap).

> **ALTERNATE OPTION:** *If you'd like to use a larger button in front (that won't fit through the stitches), this method can also be used: Sew the straps and larger buttons on the front. In the back, determine where the straps will go after they cross, then sew the smaller correct size buttons (that will fit through the stitches) on the inside of the waistband. This allows each strap to still be adjustable (in the back) but there won't be any excess strap hanging down in front (on the bib).*

TEMPEST BABY BONNET

An interesting arrangement of chain stitches forms geometric shapes in this darling baby bonnet. It looks great in traditional yarns, and it's especially beautiful in mohair yarn.

SKILL LEVEL: Intermediate

MATERIALS

TOOLS	Stitch marker, measuring tape, yarn needle
YARN	2 oz (57 g) or less of #4 worsted weight yarn or 1.5 oz (43 g) or less of #2 fine weight (mohair blend yarn such as "Patons Lace") with 2 strands held together
GAUGE	Diameter of circle after Rnd 5 should measure approximately 4" (10 cm)
HOOK SIZE	"I" (5.5 mm) for #4 worsted weight or "K" (6.5 mm) for #2 fine weight mohair (1–2 strands)

BONNET SIZE CHART

PREEMIE/DOLL	10–12" (25–30 cm) circumference, finished bonnet approximately 4.5" x 4.5" (11 x 11 cm)
NEWBORN	12–13" (30–33 cm) circumference, finished bonnet approximately 5" x 5" (13 x 13 cm)
0–3 MONTHS	13–14" (33–36 cm) circumference, finished bonnet approximately 5.5" x 5.5" (14 x 14 cm)
3–6 MONTHS	14–16" (36–41 cm) circumference, finished bonnet approximately 6.5" x 6.5" (17 x 17 cm)
6–12 MONTHS	16–18" (41–46 cm) circumference, finished bonnet approximately 7" x 7" (18 x 18 cm)
TODDLER	18–20" (46–51 cm) circumference, finished bonnet approximately 7.5" x 7.5" (19 x 19 cm)

ABBREVIATIONS USED

ST(S)	stitch(es)
CH	chain stitch
SC	single crochet
HDC	half double crochet
TR	treble crochet
SL ST	slip stitch
RND(S)	round(s)
SK	skip
SP	space
EA	each
PREV	previous
YO	Yarn Over

SPECIAL STITCH DEFINITION

TREBLE CROCHET (TR): YO hook twice, insert hook in indicated st and pull up a loop (4 loops on hook), YO and draw through 2 loops (3 loops on hook), YO hook and draw through 2 loops (2 loops on hook), YO hook and draw through last 2 loops.

PREEMIE/DOLL TEMPEST BABY BONNET

NOTE: *The beginning of this bonnet is worked in continuous rounds. Do not join after Rnd 2. Add a stitch marker around loop on hook and move after each round.*

RND 1: Magic ring, ch 2, work 8 hdc in ring, join with sl st in first hdc. (8)

OR ch 2, 8 hdc in 2nd ch from hook, join with sl st in first hdc. (8)

RND 2: (sc, hdc) in first st, work 2 hdc in ea remaining st to end of rnd, do not join. (16)

RND 3: *hdc in next st, 2 hdc in next st*, repeat between *...* to end of rnd. (24)

RND 4: *hdc ea of next 2 sts, 2 hdc next st*, repeat between *...* to end of rnd. (32)

RND 5: *hdc ea of next 7 sts, 2 hdc next st*, repeat between *...* to end of rnd. (36)

GAUGE CHECKPOINT: *Diameter of the circle should measure approximately 4" (10 cm) here.*

NOTE: *Pattern is now worked back and forth in rows instead of rounds.*

ROW 1: sc in next st, sl st in next st, *ch 3, sk next st, tr in next st, ch 3, sk next st, sc in next st*, repeat between *...* to last 7 sts (do not count the sl st where the ch 3 begins), ch 3, sk next st, tr in next st, leave remaining 5 sts unworked.

ROW 2: ch 1, turn, sk first tr, *ch 2, sk 3 ch, tr in next sc, ch 2, sk 3 ch, sc in next tr*, repeat between *...* to end of row.

ROW 3: ch 7, turn, sk first sc and 2 ch, *sc in next tr, ch 3, sk 2 ch**, tr in next sc, ch 3, sk 2 ch*, repeat between *...* to end of row, end last repeat at **, tr in top of turning ch.

ROW 4: ch 1, turn, sk first tr, *ch 2, sk 3 ch, tr in next sc, ch 2, sk 3 ch, sc in next tr*, repeat between *...* to end of row, end last repeat with sc in 4th ch of turning ch.

REPEAT ROWS 3 AND 4 until the bonnet measures approximately 4 to 4.5" (10 to 11 cm) (end with Row 4).

EDGING AND TIES: ch 1, turn, sc in first sc, work 2 sc in ea ch-2 sp to end of row, sc in top of turning ch, *ch 35, sl st in 2nd ch from hook and in ea ch back down to bonnet*, sc evenly across bottom of bonnet, repeat between *...* for second tie, fasten off with invisible join (or sl st) in bonnet. Weave in ends.

NEWBORN TEMPEST BABY BONNET

NOTE: *The beginning of this bonnet is worked in continuous rounds. Do not join after Rnd 2. Add a stitch marker around loop on hook and move after each round.*

RND 1: Magic ring, ch 2, work 8 hdc in ring, join with sl st in first hdc. (8)

OR ch 2, 8 hdc in 2nd ch from hook, join with sl st in first hdc. (8)

RND 2: (sc, hdc) in first st, work 2 hdc in ea remaining st to end of rnd, do not join. (16)

RND 3: *hdc in next st, 2 hdc in next st*, repeat between *...* to end of rnd. (24)

RND 4: *hdc ea of next 2 sts, 2 hdc next st*, repeat between *...* to end of rnd. (32)

RND 5: *hdc ea of next 3 sts, 2 hdc next st*, repeat between *...* to end of rnd. (40)

GAUGE CHECKPOINT: *Diameter of the circle should measure approximately 4" (10 cm) here.*

NOTE: *Pattern is now worked back and forth in rows instead of rounds.*

ROW 1: sc in next st, sl st in next st, *ch 3, sk next st, tr in next st, ch 3, sk next st, sc in next st*, repeat between *...* to last 7 sts (do not count the sl st where the ch 3 begins), ch 3, sk next st, tr in next st, leave remaining 5 sts unworked.

ROW 2: ch 1, turn, sk first tr, *ch 2, sk 3 ch, tr in next sc, ch 2, sk 3 ch, sc in next tr*, repeat between *...* to end of row.

ROW 3: ch 7, turn, sk first sc and 2 ch, *sc in next tr, ch 3, sk 2 ch**, tr in next sc, ch 3, sk 2 ch*, repeat between *...* to end of row, end last repeat at **, tr in top of turning ch.

ROW 4: ch 1, turn, sk first tr, *ch 2, sk 3 ch, tr in next sc, ch 2, sk 3 ch, sc in next tr*, repeat between *...* to end of row, end last repeat with sc in 4th ch of turning ch.

REPEAT ROWS 3 AND 4 until the bonnet measures approximately 5" (13 cm) (end with Row 4) from the center of the magic ring to the edge of the bonnet.

EDGING AND TIES: ch 1, turn, sc in first sc, work 2 sc in ea ch-2 sp to end of row, sc in top of turning ch, *ch 40, sl st in 2nd ch from hook and in ea ch back down to bonnet*, sc evenly across bottom of bonnet, repeat between *...* for second tie, fasten off with invisible join (or sl st) in bonnet. Weave in ends.

0–3 MONTHS TEMPEST BABY BONNET

NOTE: *The beginning of this bonnet is worked in continuous rounds. Do not join after Rnd 2. Add a stitch marker around loop on hook and move after each round.*

RND 1: Magic ring, ch 2, work 8 hdc in ring, join with sl st in first hdc. (8)

OR ch 2, 8 hdc in 2nd ch from hook, join with sl st in first hdc. (8)

RND 2: (sc, hdc) in first st, work 2 hdc in ea remaining st to end of rnd, do not join. (16)

RND 3: *hdc in next st, 2 hdc in next st*, repeat between *...* to end of rnd. (24)

RND 4: *hdc ea of next 2 sts, 2 hdc next st*, repeat between *...* to end of rnd. (32)

RND 5: *hdc ea of next 3 sts, 2 hdc next st*, repeat between *...* to end of rnd. (40)

> **GAUGE CHECKPOINT:** *Diameter of the circle should measure approximately 4" (10 cm) here.*

RND 6: *hdc ea of next 9 sts, 2 hdc next st*, repeat between *...* to end of rnd. (44)

> **NOTE:** *Pattern is now worked back and forth in rows instead of rounds.*

ROW 1: sc in next st, sl st in next st, *ch 3, sk next st, tr in next st, ch 3, sk next st, sc in next st*, repeat between *...* to last 7 sts (do not count the sl st where the ch 3 begins), ch 3, sk next st, tr in next st, leave remaining 5 sts unworked.

ROW 2: ch 1, turn, sk first tr, *ch 2, sk 3 ch, tr in next sc, ch 2, sk 3 ch, sc in next tr*, repeat between *...* to end of row.

ROW 3: ch 7, turn, sk first sc and 2 ch, *sc in next tr, ch 3, sk 2 ch**, tr in next sc, ch 3, sk 2 ch*, repeat between *...* to end of row, end last repeat at **, tr in top of turning ch.

ROW 4: ch 1, turn, sk first tr, *ch 2, sk 3 ch, tr in next sc, ch 2, sk 3 ch, sc in next tr*, repeat between *...* to end of row, end last repeat with sc in 4th ch of turning ch.

REPEAT ROWS 3 AND 4 until the bonnet measures approximately 5.5" (14 cm) (end with Row 4) from the center of the magic ring to the edge of bonnet.

EDGING AND TIES: ch 1, turn, sc in first sc, work 2 sc in ea ch-2 sp to end of row, sc in top of turning ch, *ch 45, sl st in 2nd ch from hook and in ea ch back down to bonnet*, sc evenly across bottom of bonnet, repeat between *...* for second tie, fasten off with invisible join (or sl st) in bonnet. Weave in ends.

3-6 MONTHS TEMPEST BABY BONNET

> **NOTE:** *The beginning of this bonnet is worked in continuous rounds. Do not join after Rnd 2. Add a stitch marker around loop on hook and move after each round.*

RND 1: Magic ring, ch 2, work 8 hdc in ring, join with sl st in first hdc. (8)

OR ch 2, 8 hdc in 2nd ch from hook, join with sl st in first hdc. (8)

RND 2: (sc, hdc) in first st, work 2 hdc in ea remaining st to end of rnd, do not join. (16)

RND 3: *hdc in next st, 2 hdc in next st*, repeat between *...* to end of rnd. (24)

RND 4: *hdc ea of next 2 sts, 2 hdc next st*, repeat between *...* to end of rnd. (32)

RND 5: *hdc ea of next 3 sts, 2 hdc next st*, repeat between *...* to end of rnd. (40)

> **GAUGE CHECKPOINT:** *Diameter of the circle should measure approximately 4" (10 cm) here.*

RND 6: *hdc in ea of next 4 sts, 2 hdc next st*, repeat between *...* to end of rnd. (48)

> **NOTE:** *Pattern is now worked back and forth in rows instead of rounds.*

ROW 1: sc in next st, sl st in next st, *ch 3, sk next st, tr in next st, ch 3, sk next st, sc in next st*, repeat between *...* to last 7 sts (do not count the sl st where the ch 3 begins), ch 3, sk next st, tr in next st, leave remaining 5 sts unworked.

ROW 2: ch 1, turn, sk first tr, *ch 2, sk 3 ch, tr in next sc, ch 2, sk 3 ch, sc in next tr*, repeat between *...* to end of row.

ROW 3: ch 7, turn, sk first sc and 2 ch, *sc in next tr, ch 3, sk 2 ch**, tr in next sc, ch 3, sk 2 ch*, repeat between *...* to end of row, end last repeat at **, tr in top of turning ch.

ROW 4: ch 1, turn, sk first tr, *ch 2, sk 3 ch, tr in next sc, ch 2, sk 3 ch, sc in next tr*, repeat between *...* to end of row, end last repeat with sc in 4th ch of turning ch.

REPEAT ROWS 3 AND 4 until the bonnet measures approximately 6" (15 cm) (end with Row 4) from the center of the magic ring to edge of the bonnet.

EDGING AND TIES: ch 1, turn, sc in first sc, work 2 sc in ea ch-2 sp to end of row, sc in top of turning ch, *ch 50, sl st in 2nd ch from hook and in ea ch back down to bonnet*, sc evenly across bottom of bonnet, repeat between *...* for second tie, fasten off with invisible join (or sl st) in bonnet. Weave in ends.

6–12 MONTHS TEMPEST BABY BONNET

NOTE: *The beginning of this bonnet is worked in continuous rounds. Do not join after Rnd 2. Add a stitch marker around loop on hook and move after each round.*

RND 1: Magic ring, ch 2, work 8 hdc in ring, join with sl st in first hdc. (8)

OR ch 2, 8 hdc in 2nd ch from hook, join with sl st in first hdc. (8)

RND 2: (sc, hdc) in first st, work 2 hdc in ea remaining st to end of rnd, do not join. (16)

RND 3: *hdc in next st, 2 hdc in next st*, repeat between *...* to end of rnd. (24)

RND 4: *hdc ea of next 2 sts, 2 hdc next st*, repeat between *...* to end of rnd. (32)

RND 5: *hdc ea of next 3 sts, 2 hdc next st*, repeat between *...* to end of rnd. (40)

GAUGE CHECKPOINT: *Diameter of the circle should measure approximately 4" (10 cm) here.*

RND 6: *hdc ea of next 4 sts, 2 hdc next st*, repeat between *...* to end of rnd. (48)

RND 7: *hdc ea of next 11 sts, 2 hdc next st*, repeat between *...* to end of rnd. (52)

NOTE: *Pattern is now worked back and forth in rows instead of rounds.*

ROW 1: sc in next st, sl st in next st, *ch 3, sk next st, tr in next st, ch 3, sk next st, sc in next st*, repeat between *...* to last 7 sts (do not count the sl st where the ch 3 begins), ch 3, sk next st, tr in next st, leave remaining 5 sts unworked.

ROW 2: ch 1, turn, sk first tr, *ch 2, sk 3 ch, tr in next sc, ch 2, sk 3 ch, sc in next tr*, repeat between *...* to end of row.

ROW 3: ch 7, turn, sk first sc and 2 ch, *sc in next tr, ch 3, sk 2 ch**, tr in next sc, ch 3, sk 2 ch*, repeat between *...* to end of row, end last repeat at **, tr in top of turning ch.

ROW 4: ch 1, turn, sk first tr, *ch 2, sk 3 ch, tr in next sc, ch 2, sk 3 ch, sc in next tr*, repeat between *...* to end of row, end last repeat with sc in 4th ch of turning ch.

REPEAT ROWS 3 AND 4 until the bonnet measures approximately 6.5″ (17 cm) (end with Row 4) from the center of the magic ring to the edge of the bonnet.

EDGING AND TIES: ch 1, turn, sc in first sc, work 2 sc in ea ch-2 sp to end of row, sc in top of turning ch, *ch 55, sl st in 2nd ch from hook and in ea ch back down to bonnet*, sc evenly across bottom of bonnet, repeat between *...* for second tie, fasten off with invisible join (or sl st) in bonnet. Weave in ends.

TODDLER TEMPEST BABY BONNET

NOTE: *The beginning of this bonnet is worked in continuous rounds. Do not join after Rnd 2. Add a stitch marker around loop on hook and move after each round.*

RND 1: Magic ring, ch 2, work 8 hdc in ring, join with sl st in first hdc. (8)

OR ch 2, 8 hdc in 2nd ch from hook, join with sl st in first hdc. (8)

RND 2: (sc, hdc) in first st, work 2 hdc in ea remaining st to end of rnd, do not join. (16)

RND 3: *hdc in next st, 2 hdc in next st*, repeat between *...* to end of rnd. (24)

RND 4: *hdc ea of next 2 sts, 2 hdc next st*, repeat between *...* to end of rnd. (32)

RND 5: *hdc ea of next 3 sts, 2 hdc next st*, repeat between *...* to end of rnd. (40)

GAUGE CHECKPOINT: *Diameter of the circle should measure approximately 4″ (10 cm) here.*

RND 6: *hdc ea of next 4 sts, 2 hdc next st*, repeat between *...* to end of rnd. (48)

RND 7: *hdc ea of next 5 sts, 2 hdc next st*, repeat between *...* to end of rnd. (56)

NOTE: *Pattern is now worked back and forth in rows instead of rounds.*

ROW 1: sc in next st, sl st in next st, *ch 3, sk next st, tr in next st, ch 3, sk next st, sc in next st*, repeat between *...* to last 7 sts (do not count the sl st where the ch 3 begins), ch 3, sk next st, tr in next st, leave remaining 5 sts unworked.

ROW 2: ch 1, turn, sk first tr, *ch 2, sk 3 ch, tr in next sc, ch 2, sk 3 ch, sc in next tr*, repeat between *...* to end of row.

ROW 3: ch 7, turn, sk first sc and 2 ch, *sc in next tr, ch 3, sk 2 ch**, tr in next sc, ch 3, sk 2 ch*, repeat between *...* to end of row, end last repeat at **, tr in top of turning ch.

ROW 4: ch 1, turn, sk first tr, *ch 2, sk 3 ch, tr in next sc, ch 2, sk 3 ch, sc in next tr*, repeat between *...* to end of row, end last repeat with sc in 4th ch of turning ch.

REPEAT ROWS 3 AND 4 until the bonnet measures approximately 7″ (18 cm) (end with Row 4) from the center of the magic ring to the edge of the bonnet.

EDGING AND TIES: ch 1, turn, sc in first sc, work 2 sc in ea ch-2 sp to end of row, sc in top of turning ch, *ch 60, sl st in 2nd ch from hook and in ea ch back down to bonnet*, sc evenly across bottom of bonnet, repeat between *...* for second tie, fasten off with invisible join (or sl st) in bonnet. Weave in ends.

TEMPEST WRAP OR LAYERING BLANKET

A delicate looking accessory wrap or blanket that coordinates perfectly with the Tempest Baby Bonnet (page 107), photographers will love this one.

SKILL LEVEL: Intermediate

MATERIALS

TOOLS	Measuring tape, yarn needle
YARN	6–12 oz (170–340 g) (depending on size) of any #4 worsted weight yarn or 2–4 oz (57–113 g) of #2 fine weight (mohair blend yarn such as Patons Lace) with 2 strands held together
HOOK SIZE	"I" (5.5 mm) for #4 worsted weight or "K" (6.5 mm) for #2 fine weight mohair (1–2 strands)

SIZE CHART (SUGGESTED SIZES)

20" x 20" (51 x 51 cm) (chain 91)

22" x 22" (56 x 56 cm) (chain 97)

24" x 24" (61 x 61 cm) (chain 109)

26" x 26" (66 x 66 cm) (chain 115)

28" x 28" (71 x 71 cm) (chain 127)

ABBREVIATIONS USED

ST(S)	stitch(es)
CH	chain stitch
SC	single crochet
TR	treble crochet
SK	skip
YO	Yarn Over

SPECIAL STITCH DEFINITION

TREBLE CROCHET (TR): YO hook twice, insert hook in indicated st and pull up a loop (4 loops on hook), YO and draw through 2 loops (3 loops on hook), YO hook and draw through 2 loops (2 loops on hook), YO hook and draw through last 2 loops.

TEMPEST WRAP OR BLANKET

TIP: *To adjust the size, chain any multiple of 6, plus 7 for turning. This pattern can be made in any yarn weight or hook size. The beginning chain will shrink up by a few inches after the first few rows, so make the foundation chain a few inches longer than your desired final size.*

NOTE: *Instructions below are for a wrap that is approximately 24" (61 cm) wide, made with #4 worsted weight yarn and an "I" (5.5 mm) hook. (To make other sizes, see the size chart at beginning of the pattern, or follow the Tip above to adjust the beginning chain.)*

ROW 1: ch 109, sc in 10th ch from hook, *ch 3, sk 2 ch, tr in next ch, ch 3, sk 2 ch, sc in next ch*, repeat between *...* to last 3 ch, ch 3, sk 2 ch, tr in last ch.

ROW 2: ch 1, turn, sk first tr, *ch 2, sk 3 ch, tr in next sc, ch 2, sk 3 ch, sc in next tr*, repeat between *...* to end of row, end last repeat with sc in 4th ch of turning ch.

ROW 3: ch 7, turn, sk next sc and 2 ch, *sc in next tr, ch 3, sk 2 ch**, tr in next sc, ch 3, sk 2 ch*, repeat between *...* to end of row, end last repeat at **, tr in top of turning ch.

REPEAT ROWS 2 AND 3 until the wrap/blanket reaches desired size, end with Row 2. Fasten off. Weave in ends.

ZIGZAG WEAVE BLANKET

With a zigzag texture reminiscent of the Thunderstruck Beanie (page 141), this blanket works up soft and squishy in super bulky yarn. Need a last-minute gift idea? The smaller sizes of this pattern work up easily in one evening!

SKILL LEVEL: ◼ Intermediate

MATERIALS

TOOLS	Measuring tape, large yarn needle (for weaving in ends)
YARN	Bernat Blanket yarn (baby or regular) or any super bulky (#6 weight) yarn. (This pattern can also be used with any other weight yarn but you'll have to figure out how much yarn you need.) Suggested amounts for average sizes made with #6 super bulky yarn are given below: **PHOTOGRAPHY PROP SIZE** (20" x 20" [51 x 51 cm]): One skein of Bernat Blanket 10.5 oz (300 g) each (or 258 yds total) **BABY BLANKET SIZE** (30" x 46" [76 x 117 cm]): Four skeins of Bernat Blanket 10.5 oz (300 g) each (or 1032 yds total) **THROW SIZE** (60" x 90" [152 x 229 cm]): Fifteen skeins of Bernat Blanket 10.5 oz (300 g) each (or 3,870 yds total) **KING SIZE** (100" x 108" [254 x 274 cm]): Thirty skeins of Bernat Blanket 10.5 oz (300 g) each (or 7,740 yds total)
GAUGE	8 stitches and 5 rows in pattern = 4" x 4" (10 x 10 cm)
HOOK SIZE	"P" (10 mm) Boye hook. Other brands may vary in size; be sure to match mm size.

SIZE CHART (COMMON BLANKET SIZES)

This is by no means a comprehensive list (common sizes may vary). Sizes given are only suggestions.

BABY THROUGH TEEN SIZES	
LOVEY	10" x 10" (25 x 25 cm)
SECURITY	14" x 17" (36 x 43 cm)
LAYERING BLANKET	12" x 12" (30 x 30 cm) to 15" x 15" (38 x 38 cm)
PROP BLANKET	18" x 18" (46 x 46 cm) up to 20" x 20" (51 x 51 cm)
STROLLER	30" x 40" (76 X 102 cm)
BASSINET	16" x 36" (41 x 91 cm)
CRADLE	20" x 36" (51 x 91 cm)
PACK 'N PLAY	26" x 36" (66 x 91 cm)
CRIB	30" x 36" (76 x 91 cm) up to 45" x 60" (114 x 152 cm)
RECEIVING	24" x 24" (61 x 61 cm) up to 36" x 36" (91 x 91 cm)
INFANT	24" x 30" (61 x 76 cm) up to 36" x 48" (91 x 122 cm)
TODDLER	36" x 48" (91 x 122 cm)
CHILD	42" x 48" (107 x 122 cm)
TEEN	48" x 60" (122 x 152 cm)

SIZE CHART (CONTINUED)

ADULT SIZES	
LAPGHAN	36" x 48" (91 x 122 cm) (often used in nursing homes and wheelchairs)
ADULT	50" x 70" (127 x 178 cm)
THROW	50" x 60" (127 x 152 cm)
TWIN	60" x 90" (152 x 228 cm)
EXTRA LONG TWIN	66" x 95" (168 x 241 cm)
FULL	80" x 90" (203 x 228 cm)
QUEEN	90" x 100" (228 x 254 cm)
KING	100" x 108" (254 x 274 cm)
CALIFORNIA KING	104" x 108" (264 x 274 cm)

ABBREVIATIONS USED

ST(S)	stitch(es)
CH	chain stitch
SC	single crochet
DC	double crochet
FPDC	front post double crochet
BPDC	back post double crochet
SL ST	slip stitch
SK	skip
EA	each
YO	Yarn Over
WS	Wrong Side
RS	Right Side

SPECIAL STITCHES DEFINITIONS

FRONT POST DOUBLE CROCHET (FPDC): Working from the front side of the work, YO and insert the hook from right to left **under** the post of the double crochet indicated from the previous round, YO and pull up a loop [YO and draw through 2 loops], twice.

BACK POST DOUBLE CROCHET (BPDC): Working from the back side of the work, YO and insert the hook from right to left **over** the post of the double crochet indicated from the previous round, YO and pull up a loop [YO and draw through 2 loops], twice.

ZIGZAG WEAVE BLANKET

> **NOTE:** *This pattern is written for a blanket that is approximately 30" x 46" (76 x 102 cm) and uses 4 skeins of Bernat Blanket yarn (10.5 oz [300 g] each or 1032 yds total). To adjust size/gauge, start with any multiple of 8 for the Foundation Row.*

FOUNDATION ROW: (WS) ch 60, dc in 4th ch from hook (counts as first dc) and ea ch to end of row. (58)

ROW 1: (RS) ch 2 (counts as dc), turn, sk base of ch 2, *fpdc around ea of next 2 sts, bpdc around ea of next 2 sts*, repeat between *...* to end of row, dc in top of turning ch.

ROW 2: ch 2 (counts as dc), turn, sk base of ch 2, bpdc around next st, *fpdc around ea of next 2 sts, bpdc around ea of next 2 sts*, repeat between *...* to last 2 sts, bpdc around next st, dc in top of turning ch.

ROW 3: ch 2 (counts as dc), turn, sk base of ch 2, *bpdc around ea of next 2 sts, fpdc around ea of next 2 sts*, repeat between *...* to end of row, dc in top of turning ch.

ROW 4: ch 2 (counts as dc), turn, sk base of ch 2, fpdc around next st, *bpdc around ea of next 2 sts, fpdc around ea of next 2 sts*, repeat between *...* to last 2 sts, fpdc around next st, dc in top of turning ch.

ROW 5: Repeat Row 3.

ROW 6: Repeat Row 2.

ROW 7: Repeat Row 1.

ROW 8: Repeat Row 4.

REPEAT ROWS 1–8 until the blanket reaches desired length. Fasten off. Weave in ends.

OPTIONAL EDGING

Ch 1, turn, with RS facing, sc evenly (3 sc in corners) around entire blanket. Fasten off with invisible join (or sl st). Weave in ends.

3

BIG KIDS &
COLD WEATHER
ACCESSORIES

This chapter includes several warm accessory patterns with sizes ranging from baby to adult. Make coordinating winter accessories for the whole family! Try feminine styles such as the Snow Flurry Slouch (page 125) or Snow Bunny Hat (page 197), or choose a unisex design such as the Making Waves Beanie (page 165) or Thunderstruck Beanie (page 141). No matter which you choose, you'll have a wide range of stylish options for your entire family.

SNOW FLURRY SLOUCH

The Snow Flurry Slouch is perfect for every female in the family, with sizes from newborn to large adult. Create matching hats for mother and daughter, or use contrasting colors for sisters. With a "knit" look ribbing and an intricate combination of puff stitches and chains, this slouch has an elegant and dressy appearance that is sure to please everyone. With the coordinating Snow Flurry Baby Bonnet (page 17), even the youngest members of the family can match!

SKILL LEVEL: ◖ ▮ ▯ **INTERMEDIATE**

MATERIALS

TOOLS	Stitch marker (optional), measuring tape, yarn needle
YARN	5 oz (142 g) or less of #4 worsted weight cotton or cotton blend yarn. This pattern was designed and tested with cotton or 50/50 cotton/acrylic blend yarns. You may have different results with other fibers.
GAUGE	15 stitches and 7 rows in dc = 4" x 4" (10 x 10 cm)
HOOK SIZE	"I" (5.5 mm) for ribbing, "J" (6 mm) for main portion of hat

HAT SIZE CHART

0-3 MONTHS	12-14" (30-36 cm) circumference, approximately 5.5" (14 cm) from crown to brim
3-6 MONTHS	14-16" (36-41 cm) circumference, approximately 5.5-6" (14-15 cm) from crown to brim
6-12 MONTHS	16-18" (41-46 cm) circumference, approximately 6.5-7" (17-18 cm) from crown to brim
TODDLER/CHILD	18-20" (46-51 cm) circumference, approximately 7.5-8" (19-20 cm) from crown to brim
TEEN/ADULT	20-22" (51-56 cm) circumference, approximately 8-8.5" (20-22 cm) from crown to brim
LARGE ADULT	22-24" (56-61 cm) circumference, approximately 8.5-9" (22-23 cm) from crown to brim

ABBREVIATIONS USED

ST(S)	stitch(es)
CH	chain stitch
SC	single crochet
DC	double crochet
SC2TOG	single crochet 2 stitches together
PUFF ST	puff stitch
PUFF ST SHELL	puff stitch shell
V-ST	v-stitch
SL ST	slip stitch
RND(S)	round(s)
SK	skip
SP	space
EA	each
BEG	beginning
BLO	Back Loop Only
YO	Yarn Over

SPECIAL STITCHES DEFINITIONS

PUFF STITCH (PUFF ST): [YO, insert hook in indicated stitch, YO, draw up loop] 3 times in same stitch, YO, draw through all 7 loops on hook.

PUFF STITCH SHELL (PUFF ST SHELL): [(puff st, ch 3) twice, puff st] in indicated stitch or space.

V-STITCH (V-ST): (dc, ch 1, dc) in indicated stitch or space.

SINGLE CROCHET 2 STITCHES TOGETHER (SC2TOG): Insert hook in stitch indicated, YO and draw up a loop, insert hook in next st, YO and draw up another loop. YO again and draw through all 3 loops on hook.

SNOW FLURRY SLOUCH (ALL SIZES)

Use #4 worsted weight yarn and an "I" (5.5 mm) hook.

NOTE: *This slouch is worked from the bottom up. The beginning chain determines the "height" of the bottom ribbing and can be adjusted to any size desired. The number of times Row 2 is repeated determines the circumference of the hat (once joined).*

ROW 1: (ch 7–9 for smaller sizes) ch 12, sl st in 2nd ch from hook (use back loops) and in ea ch to end of row. (6–8, 11)

ROW 2: ch 1, turn, sl st in BLO of ea st to end of row. (6–8, 11)

REPEAT ROW 2 until the following measurement is reached (measure lightly stretched). The sl st ribbing is very stretchy. If not sure on size, go with the smaller measurement.

0–3 MONTHS	11–12" (28–30 cm)
3–6 MONTHS	12–13" (30–33 cm)
6–12 MONTHS	14–15" (36–38 cm)
TODDLER/CHILD	15–17" (38–43 cm)
TEEN/ADULT	18–19" (46–48 cm)
LARGE ADULT	19–20" (48–51 cm)

SEAM: ch 1, turn and sl st the short ends of the ribbing together (using 1 loop from each end) to form a circle. Turn right side out. The pattern is now worked in rounds instead of rows.

NOTE: *If you crochet loosely, stick with the "I" (5.5 mm) hook, otherwise switch to a "J" (6 mm) hook here.*

FOUNDATION RND: ch 1, work (40, 48, 56, 64, 72, 80) sc evenly around ribbing, join with sl st in top of first sc. (40, 48, 56, 64, 72, 80)

RND 1: ch 4 (counts as dc + ch 1), dc in same st as ch 4, sk next 3 sc, puff st shell in next sc, ch 1, *sk next 3 sc, v-st in next sc, sk next 3 sc, puff st shell in next sc, ch 1*, repeat between *...* to end of rnd, join with sl st in 3rd ch of beg ch-4. (5, 6, 7, 8, 9, 10 v-st and puff st shell combos)

RND 2: sl st in ch-1 sp of first v-st directly below, pull up a longer loop on hook, (puff st, ch 3, puff st) in same ch-1 sp, ch 1, v-st in center puff st of next puff st shell, *puff st shell in next v-st ch-1 sp, ch 1, v-st in center puff st of next puff st shell*, repeat between *...* to end of rnd, work (puff st, ch 3) in first ch-1 sp of the rnd to complete the first puff st shell, join with sl st in top of first puff st. (5, 6, 7, 8, 9, 10 v-st and puff st shell combos)

RND 3: ch 4 (counts as dc + ch 1), dc in same st as ch 4, puff st shell in next v-st ch-1 sp, ch 1, *v-st in center puff st of next puff st shell, puff st shell in next v-st ch-1 sp, ch 1*, repeat between *...* to end of rnd, join with sl st in 3rd ch of beg ch-4. (5, 6, 7, 8, 9, 10 v-st and puff st shell combos)

REPEAT RNDS 2 AND 3 until the hat reaches the following measurement from top to bottom (**end with Rnd 3**). The amount of slouch can vary by which measurement is chosen.

0–3 MONTHS	5–5.5" (13–14 cm)
3–6 MONTHS	5.5–6.5" (14–17 cm)
6–12 MONTHS	6–7" (15–18 cm)
TODDLER/CHILD	7–8" (18–20 cm)
TEEN/ADULT	8–9" (20–23 cm)
LARGE ADULT	9–10" (23–25 cm)

DECREASING ROUNDS

DECREASING RND 1: sl st in ch-1 sp of first v-st directly below, ch 2, sc in next ch-3 sp, ch 1, sc in next ch-3 sp, *ch 2, sc in next v-st ch-1 sp, ch 2, sc in next ch-3 sp, ch 1, sc in next ch-3 sp*, repeat between *...* to end of rnd, ch 2, join with sl st in base of ch 2.

DECREASING RND 2: ch 1, sc in next ch-1 sp between next 2 sc, ch 1, *sc in next sc (the one made in the v-st ch-1 sp), ch 1, sc in next ch-1 sp between next 2 sc, ch 1*, repeat between *...* to end of rnd, join with sl st in beg ch 1.

DECREASING RND 3: ch 1, sc in ea ch-1 sp to end of rnd, join with sl st in first sc.

DECREASING RND 4: do not ch, sc in ea sc to end of rnd, do not join at end of rnd.

DECREASING RND 5: do not ch, work sc2tog over next 2 sts until there are only a few sts remaining in rnd. Use a yarn needle to close remaining sts. Fasten off. Weave in ends.

HONEYCOMB RIDGES BEANIE

Including sizes from premature baby (or 18" [46 cm] doll) all the way up to large adult, this uniquely textured beanie can be made for everyone in the family, including your daughter's favorite doll. Little girls will love being able to match their doll with this stylish beanie.

SKILL LEVEL: ◼️◻️ **INTERMEDIATE**

MATERIALS

TOOLS	Measuring tape, yarn needle, stitch marker
YARN	4 oz (113 g) or less of #4 worsted weight yarn
GAUGE	Gauge checkpoint given in pattern after Rnd 4 for each size
HOOK SIZE	"J" (6 mm) for main portion of hat, "H" (5 mm) for edging

ABBREVIATIONS USED

ST(S)	stitch(es)
CH	chain stitch
SC	single crochet
DC	double crochet
FPSC	front post single crochet
FPDC	front post double crochet
SL ST	slip stitch
RND(S)	round(s)
SK	skip
SP	space
EA	each
BEG	beginning
PREV	previous
YO	Yarn Over

BEANIE SIZE CHART

PREEMIE/DOLL	10–12" (25–30 cm) circumference, approximately 4.5" (11 cm) from crown to brim
NEWBORN	12–13" (30–33 cm) circumference, approximately 5" (13 cm) from crown to brim
0–3 MONTHS	13–14" (33–36 cm) circumference, approximately 5.5" (14 cm) from crown to brim
3–6 MONTHS	14–16" (36–41 cm) circumference, approximately 5.5–6" (14–15 cm) from crown to brim
6–12 MONTHS	16–18" (41–46 cm) circumference, approximately 6.5–7" (17–18 cm) from crown to brim
TODDLER	17–19" (43–48 cm) circumference, approximately 7–7.5" (18–19 cm) from crown to brim
CHILD	18–20" (46–51 cm) circumference, approximately 7.5–8" (19–20 cm) from crown to brim
TEEN/ADULT	20–22" (51–56 cm) circumference, approximately 8–8.5" (20–22 cm) from crown to brim
LARGE ADULT	22–24" (56–61 cm) circumference, approximately 8.5–9" (22–23 cm) from crown to brim

SPECIAL STITCHES DEFINITIONS

FRONT POST SINGLE CROCHET (FPSC): Insert hook from the front side of the work (right to left) under the post of the indicated stitch, YO and pull up a loop, YO and draw through 2 loops.

FRONT POST DOUBLE CROCHET (FPDC): Working from the front side of the work, YO and insert the hook from right to left under the post of the double crochet indicated from the previous round, YO and pull up a loop, [YO and draw through 2 loops] twice.

SPECIAL TECHNIQUES

USING THE BEG "CH 2" AS THE FINAL DC IN THE RND: If there is a "ch 2" at the beginning of a round, it will stand in as the last dc in the round. This avoids having a noticeable seam. If the repeat ends on a dc at the end of the round, don't make that last dc because the "ch 2" is there and will look like a dc when you join to the top of it. If the repeat ends with 2 dc worked in one stitch, make the first dc in the same stitch as the "ch 2." This will look almost exactly the same as working 2 dc in one stitch.

JOINING IN THE "TOP" OF THE CH 2: If there is any confusion on where to join at the end of each rnd, use the following method: Complete the first ch 2 of the round, then add a stitch marker around the loop that is on the hook. At the end of the round, this is the stitch that will be used for joining.

PREEMIE/DOLL HONEYCOMB RIDGES BEANIE

RND 1: Magic ring, ch 2, 8 dc in ring, join with sl st in top of ch 2. (9)

OR ch 2, 9 dc in 2nd ch from hook, join with sl st in first dc. (9)

RND 2: ch 2, *fpdc around next dc, dc in top of same post just used*, repeat between *...* to end of rnd, beg ch 2 counts as last dc, join with sl st in top of ch 2. (18)

RND 3: ch 2, *fpdc around next fpdc, 2 dc in next dc*, repeat between *...* to end of rnd, beg ch 2 counts as last dc, join with sl st in top of ch 2. (27)

NOTE: *The "fpsc and ch 2" at the beginning of the following rounds creates a stitch that looks like a fpdc. Be sure to crochet the fpsc tightly around the post so it doesn't bulge at the base of the ch 2. It is correct if it looks very similar to a fpdc. Starting the round in this fashion (instead of a standard ch 2) will result in a seam that is almost completely invisible. Stitch marker placement in the next round is for joining at the end of the round and also for guidance in the following round.*

RND 4: fpsc around first fpdc from prev rnd, ch 2 (serves as first fpdc), sk next 2 dc, fpdc around next fpdc (add stitch marker around post of st just made), ch 3, fpdc around same fpdc, *sk next 2 dc, (fpdc, ch 3, fpdc) around next fpdc*, repeat between *...* to last 2 sts, sk last 2 dc, fpdc around first fpdc from prev rnd again, ch 3, join with sl st in top of beg ch 2 (directly above post with stitch marker). (9 ch-3 sps)

GAUGE CHECKPOINT: *Diameter of the circle should measure approximately 3.25 to 3.5" (8 to 9 cm) here.*

NOTE: *For each repeat of Rnd 5 with "3 dc in next ch-3 sp," work like this: Work first dc in ch-3 sp, work 2nd dc around both the ch 3 **and** between the 2 fpdc below, work 3rd dc in the ch-3 sp again. (This anchors them down instead of leaving a big gap between rounds. It is not critical where the 2nd dc is placed as long as it is between the 2 fpdc.)*

RND 5: fpsc around second fpdc from prev rnd (post with stitch marker), ch 2 (serves as first fpdc), 3 dc in next ch-3 sp, *fpdc around ea of next 2 fpdc, 3 dc in next ch-3 sp*, repeat between *...* to last st, fpdc around last fpdc, join with sl st in top of beg ch 2. (45)

RND 6: fpsc around post of beg ch 2 from prev rnd, ch 2 (serves as first fpdc), sk next 3 dc, fpdc around next fpdc (add stitch marker around post of st just made), ch 3, *fpdc around next fpdc, sk next 3 dc, fpdc around next fpdc, ch 3*, repeat between *...* to end of rnd, after last ch 3, join with sl st in top of beg ch 2 (directly above post with stitch marker). (9 ch-3 sps)

REPEAT RNDS 5 AND 6 until the beanie measures approximately 4.5" (11 cm) from top to bottom, end with Rnd 5.

CONTINUE with the Edging on page 139.

NEWBORN HONEYCOMB RIDGES BEANIE

RND 1: Magic ring, ch 2, 9 dc in ring, join with sl st in top of ch 2. (10)

OR, ch 2, 10 dc in 2nd ch from hook, join with sl st in first dc. (10)

RND 2: ch 2, *fpdc around next dc, dc in top of same post just used*, repeat between *...* to end of rnd, beg ch 2 counts as last dc, join with sl st in top of ch 2. (20)

RND 3: ch 2, *fpdc around next fpdc, 2 dc in next dc*, repeat between *...* to end of rnd, beg ch 2 counts as last dc, join with sl st in top of ch 2. (30)

NOTE: *The "fpsc and ch 2" at the beginning of the following rounds creates a stitch that looks like a fpdc. Be sure to crochet the fpsc tightly around the post so it doesn't bulge at the base of the ch 2. It is correct if it looks very similar to a fpdc. Starting the round in this fashion (instead of a standard ch 2) will result in a seam that is almost completely invisible. Stitch marker placement in next round is for joining at end of round and also for guidance in the following round.*

RND 4: fpsc around first fpdc from prev rnd, ch 2 (serves as first fpdc), sk next 2 dc, fpdc around next fpdc (add stitch marker around post of st just made), ch 3, fpdc around same fpdc, *sk next 2 dc, (fpdc, ch 3, fpdc) around next fpdc*, repeat between *...* to last 2 sts, sk last 2 dc, fpdc around first fpdc from prev rnd again, ch 3, join with sl st in top of beg ch 2 (directly above post with stitch marker). (10 ch-3 sps)

GAUGE CHECKPOINT: *Diameter of the circle should measure approximately 3.5" (9 cm) here.*

NOTE: *For each repeat of Rnd 5 with "3 dc in next ch-3 sp," work like this: Work first dc in ch-3 sp, work 2nd dc around both the ch 3 **and** between the 2 fpdc below, work 3rd dc in the ch-3 sp again. (This anchors them down instead of leaving a big gap between rounds. It is not critical where the 2nd dc is placed as long as it is between the 2 fpdc.)*

RND 5: fpsc around second fpdc from prev rnd (post with stitch marker), ch 2 (serves as first fpdc), 3 dc in next ch-3 sp, *fpdc around ea of next 2 fpdc, 3 dc in next ch-3 sp*, repeat between *...* to last st, fpdc around last fpdc, join with sl st in top of beg ch 2. (50)

RND 6: fpsc around post of beg ch 2 from prev rnd, ch 2 (serves as first fpdc), sk next 3 dc, fpdc around next fpdc (add stitch marker around post of st just made), ch 3, *fpdc around next fpdc, sk next 3 dc, fpdc around next fpdc, ch 3*, repeat between *...* to end of rnd, after last ch 3, join with sl st in top of beg ch 2 (directly above post with stitch marker). (10 ch-3 sps)

REPEAT RNDS 5 AND 6 until the beanie measures approximately 5" (13 cm) from top to bottom, end with Rnd 5.

CONTINUE with the Edging on page 139.

0-3 MONTHS HONEYCOMB RIDGES BEANIE

RND 1: Magic ring, ch 2, 10 dc in ring, join with sl st in top of ch 2. (11)

OR ch 2, 11 dc in 2nd ch from hook, join with sl st in first dc. (11)

RND 2: ch 2, *fpdc around next dc, dc in top of same post just used*, repeat between *...* to end of rnd, beg ch 2 counts as last dc, join with sl st in top of ch 2. (22)

RND 3: ch 2, *fpdc around next fpdc, dc in next dc*, repeat between *...* to end of rnd, beg ch 2 counts as last dc, join with sl st in top of ch 2. (22) *This rnd intentionally does not increase.*

RND 4: ch 2, *fpdc around next fpdc, 2 dc in next dc*, repeat between *...* to end of rnd, beg ch 2 counts as last dc, join with sl st in top of ch 2. (33)

GAUGE CHECKPOINT: *Diameter of the circle should measure approximately 3.5" (9 cm) here.*

NOTE: *The "fpsc and ch 2" at the beginning of the following rounds creates a stitch that looks like a fpdc. Be sure to crochet the fpsc tightly around the post so it doesn't bulge at the base of the ch 2. It is correct if it looks very similar to a fpdc. Starting the round in this fashion (instead of a standard ch 2) will result in a seam that is almost completely invisible. Stitch marker placement in next round is for joining at end of round and also for guidance in the following round.*

RND 5: fpsc around first fpdc from prev rnd, ch 2 (serves as first fpdc), sk next 2 dc, fpdc around next fpdc (add stitch marker around post of st just made), ch 3, fpdc around same fpdc, *sk next 2 dc, (fpdc, ch 3, fpdc) around next fpdc*, repeat between *...* to last 2 sts, sk last 2 dc, fpdc around first fpdc from prev rnd again, ch 3, join with sl st in top of beg ch 2 (directly above post with stitch marker). (11 ch-3 sps)

NOTE: *For each repeat of Rnd 6 with "3 dc in next ch-3 sp," work like this: Work first dc in ch-3 sp, work 2nd dc around both the ch 3 **and** between the 2 fpdc below, work 3rd dc in the ch-3 sp again. (This anchors them down instead of leaving a big gap between rounds. It is not critical where the 2nd dc is placed as long as it is between the 2 fpdc.)*

RND 6: fpsc around second fpdc from prev rnd (post with stitch marker), ch 2 (serves as first fpdc), 3 dc in next ch-3 sp, *fpdc around ea of next 2 fpdc, 3 dc in next ch-3 sp*, repeat between *...* to last st, fpdc around last fpdc, join with sl st in top of beg ch 2. (55)

RND 7: fpsc around post of beg ch 2 from prev rnd, ch 2 (serves as first fpdc), sk next 3 dc, fpdc around next fpdc (add stitch marker around post of st just made), ch 3, *fpdc around next fpdc, sk next 3 dc, fpdc around next fpdc, ch 3*, repeat between *...* to end of rnd, after last ch 3, join with sl st in top of beg ch 2 (directly above post with stitch marker). (11 ch-3 sps)

REPEAT RNDS 6 AND 7 until the beanie measures approximately 5.5" (14 cm) from top to bottom, end with Rnd 6.

CONTINUE with the Edging on page 139.

3-6 MONTHS HONEYCOMB RIDGES BEANIE

RND 1: Magic ring, ch 2, 11 dc in ring, join with sl st in top of ch 2. (12)

OR, ch 2, 12 dc in 2nd ch from hook, join with sl st in first dc. (12)

RND 2: ch 2, *fpdc around next dc, dc in top of same post just used*, repeat between *...* to end of rnd, beg ch 2 counts as last dc, join with sl st in top of ch 2. (24)

RND 3: ch 2, *fpdc around next fpdc, dc in next dc*, repeat between *...* to end of rnd, beg ch 2 counts as last dc, join with sl st in top of ch 2. (24) *This rnd intentionally does not increase.*

RND 4: ch 2, *fpdc around next fpdc, 2 dc in next dc*, repeat between *...* to end of rnd, beg ch 2 counts as last dc, join with sl st in top of ch 2. (36)

> **GAUGE CHECKPOINT:** *Diameter of the circle should measure approximately 4" (10 cm) here.*

> **NOTE:** *The "fpsc and ch 2" at the beginning of the following rounds creates a stitch that looks like a fpdc. Be sure to crochet the fpsc tightly around the post so it doesn't bulge at the base of the ch 2. It is correct if it looks very similar to a fpdc. Starting the round in this fashion (instead of a standard ch 2) will result in a seam that is almost completely invisible. Stitch marker placement in next round is for joining at end of round and also for guidance in the following round.*

RND 5: fpsc around first fpdc from prev rnd, ch 2 (serves as first fpdc), sk next 2 dc, fpdc around next fpdc (add stitch marker around post of st just made), ch 3, fpdc around same fpdc, *sk next 2 dc, (fpdc, ch 3, fpdc) around next fpdc*, repeat between *...* to last 2 sts, sk last 2 dc, fpdc around first fpdc from prev rnd again, ch 3, join with sl st in top of beg ch 2 (directly above post with stitch marker). (12 ch-3 sps)

> **NOTE:** *For each repeat of Rnd 6 with "3 dc in next ch-3 sp," work like this: Work first dc in ch-3 sp, work 2nd dc around both the ch 3 **and** between the 2 fpdc below, work 3rd dc in the ch-3 sp again. (This anchors them down instead of leaving a big gap between rounds. It is not critical where the 2nd dc is placed as long as it is between the 2 fpdc.)*

RND 6: fpsc around second fpdc from prev rnd (post with stitch marker), ch 2 (serves as first fpdc), 3 dc in next ch-3 sp, *fpdc around ea of next 2 fpdc, 3 dc in next ch-3 sp*, repeat between *...* to last st, fpdc around last fpdc, join with sl st in top of beg ch 2. (60)

RND 7: fpsc around post of beg ch 2 from prev rnd, ch 2 (serves as first fpdc), sk next 3 dc, fpdc around next fpdc (add stitch marker around post of st just made), ch 3, *fpdc around next fpdc, sk next 3 dc, fpdc around next fpdc, ch 3*, repeat between *...* to end of rnd, after last ch 3, join with sl st in top of beg ch 2 (directly above post with stitch marker). (12 ch-3 sps)

REPEAT RNDS 6 AND 7 until the beanie measures approximately 5.5 to 6" (14 to 15 cm) from top to bottom, end with Rnd 6.

CONTINUE with the Edging on page 139.

6–12 MONTHS HONEYCOMB RIDGES BEANIE

RND 1: Magic ring, ch 2, 12 dc in ring, join with sl st in top of ch 2. (13)

OR ch 2, 13 dc in 2nd ch from hook, join with sl st in first dc. (13)

RND 2: ch 2, *fpdc around next dc, dc in top of same post just used*, repeat between *…* to end of rnd, beg ch 2 counts as last dc, join with sl st in top of ch 2. (26)

RND 3: ch 2, *fpdc around next fpdc, dc in next dc*, repeat between *…* to end of rnd, beg ch 2 counts as last dc, join with sl st in top of ch 2. (26) *This rnd intentionally does not increase.*

RND 4: ch 2, *fpdc around next fpdc, 2 dc in next dc*, repeat between *…* to end of rnd, beg ch 2 counts as last dc, join with sl st in top of ch 2. (39)

GAUGE CHECKPOINT: *Diameter of the circle should measure approximately 4" (10 cm) here.*

NOTE: *The "fpsc and ch 2" at the beginning of the following rounds creates a stitch that looks like a fpdc. Be sure to crochet the fpsc tightly around the post so it doesn't bulge at the base of the ch 2. It is correct if it looks very similar to a fpdc. Starting the round in this fashion (instead of a standard ch 2) will result in a seam that is almost completely invisible. Stitch marker placement in next round is for joining at end of round and also for guidance in the following round.*

RND 5: fpsc around first fpdc from prev rnd, ch 2 (serves as first fpdc), sk next 2 dc, fpdc around next fpdc (add stitch marker around post of st just made), ch 3, fpdc around same fpdc, *sk next 2 dc, (fpdc, ch 3, fpdc) around next fpdc*, repeat between *…* to last 2 sts, sk last 2 dc, fpdc around first fpdc from prev rnd again, ch 3, join with sl st in top of beg ch 2 (directly above post with stitch marker). (13 ch-3 sps)

NOTE: *For each repeat of Rnd 6 with "3 dc in next ch-3 sp," work like this: Work first dc in ch-3 sp, work 2nd dc around both the ch 3 **and** between the 2 fpdc below, work 3rd dc in the ch-3 sp again. (This anchors them down instead of leaving a big gap between rounds. It is not critical where the 2nd dc is placed as long as it is between the 2 fpdc.)*

RND 6: fpsc around second fpdc from prev rnd (post with stitch marker), ch 2 (serves as first fpdc), 3 dc in next ch-3 sp, *fpdc around ea of next 2 fpdc, 3 dc in next ch-3 sp*, repeat between *…* to last st, fpdc around last fpdc, join with sl st in top of beg ch 2. (65)

RND 7: fpsc around post of beg ch 2 from prev rnd, ch 2 (serves as first fpdc), sk next 3 dc, fpdc around next fpdc (add stitch marker around post of st just made), ch 3, *fpdc around next fpdc, sk next 3 dc, fpdc around next fpdc, ch 3*, repeat between *…* to end of rnd, after last ch 3, join with sl st in top of beg ch 2 (directly above post with stitch marker). (13 ch-3 sps)

REPEAT RNDS 6 AND 7 until the beanie measures approximately 6.5 to 7" (17 to 18 cm) from top to bottom, end with Rnd 6.

CONTINUE with the Edging on page 139.

TODDLER HONEYCOMB RIDGES BEANIE

RND 1: Magic ring, ch 2, 13 dc in ring, join with sl st in top of ch 2. (14)

OR ch 2, 14 dc in 2nd ch from hook, join with sl st in first dc. (14)

RND 2: ch 2, *fpdc around next dc, dc in top of same post just used*, repeat between *...* to end of rnd, beg ch 2 counts as last dc, join with sl st in top of ch 2. (28)

RND 3: ch 2, *fpdc around next fpdc, dc in next dc*, repeat between *...* to end of rnd, beg ch 2 counts as last dc, join with sl st in top of ch 2. (28) *This rnd intentionally does not increase.*

RND 4: ch 2, *fpdc around next fpdc, dc in next dc*, repeat between *...* to end of rnd, beg ch 2 counts as last dc, join with sl st in top of ch 2. (28) *This rnd intentionally does not increase.*

GAUGE CHECKPOINT: *Diameter of the circle should measure approximately 3.5" (9 cm) here.*

RND 5: ch 2, *fpdc around next fpdc, 2 dc in next dc*, repeat between *...* to end of rnd, beg ch 2 counts as last dc, join with sl st in top of ch 2. (42)

NOTE: *The "fpsc and ch 2" at the beginning of the following rounds creates a stitch that looks like a fpdc. Be sure to crochet the fpsc tightly around the post so it doesn't bulge at the base of the ch 2. It is correct if it looks very similar to a fpdc. Starting the round in this fashion (instead of a standard ch 2) will result in a seam that is almost completely invisible.*

RND 6: fpsc around first fpdc from prev rnd, ch 2 (serves as first fpdc), dc in ea of next 2 dc, *fpdc around next fpdc, dc in ea of next 2 dc*, repeat between *...* to end of rnd, join with sl st in top of ch 2. (42)

NOTE: *Stitch marker placement in the next round is for joining at the end of the round and also for guidance in the following round.*

RND 7: fpsc around first fpdc from prev rnd, ch 2 (serves as first fpdc), sk next 2 dc, fpdc around next fpdc (add stitch marker around post of st just made), ch 3, fpdc around same fpdc, *sk next 2 dc, (fpdc, ch 3, fpdc) around next fpdc*, repeat between *...* to last 2 sts, sk last 2 dc, fpdc around first fpdc from prev rnd again, ch 3, join with sl st in top of beg ch 2 (directly above post with stitch marker). (14 ch-3 sps)

NOTE: *For each repeat of Rnd 8 with "3 dc in next ch-3 sp," work like this: Work first dc in ch-3 sp, work 2nd dc around both the ch 3 **and** between the 2 fpdc below, work 3rd dc in the ch-3 sp again. (This anchors them down instead of leaving a big gap between rounds. It is not critical where the 2nd dc is placed as long as it is between the 2 fpdc.)*

RND 8: fpsc around second fpdc from prev rnd (post with stitch marker), ch 2 (serves as first fpdc), 3 dc in next ch-3 sp, *fpdc around ea of next 2 fpdc, 3 dc in next ch-3 sp*, repeat between *...* to last st, fpdc around last fpdc, join with sl st in top of beg ch 2. (70)

RND 9: fpsc around post of beg ch 2 from prev rnd, ch 2 (serves as first fpdc), sk next 3 dc, fpdc around next fpdc (add stitch marker around post of st just made), ch 3, *fpdc around next fpdc, sk next 3 dc, fpdc around next fpdc, ch 3*, repeat between *...* to end of rnd, after last ch 3, join with sl st in top of beg ch 2 (directly above post with stitch marker). (14 ch-3 sps)

REPEAT RNDS 8 AND 9 until the beanie measures approximately 7 to 7.5" (18 to 19 cm) from top to bottom, end with Rnd 8.

CONTINUE with the Edging on page 139.

CHILD HONEYCOMB RIDGES BEANIE

RND 1: Magic ring, ch 2, 14 dc in ring, join with sl st in top of ch 2. (15)

OR ch 2, 15 dc in 2nd ch from hook, join with sl st in first dc. (15)

RND 2: ch 2, *fpdc around next dc, dc in top of same post just used*, repeat between *...* to end of rnd, beg ch 2 counts as last dc, join with sl st in top of ch 2. (30)

RND 3: ch 2, *fpdc around next fpdc, dc in next dc*, repeat between *...* to end of rnd, beg ch 2 counts as last dc, join with sl st in top of ch 2. (30) *This rnd intentionally does not increase.*

RND 4: ch 2, *fpdc around next fpdc, dc in next dc*, repeat between *...* to end of rnd, beg ch 2 counts as last dc, join with sl st in top of ch 2. (30) *This rnd intentionally does not increase.*

GAUGE CHECKPOINT: *Diameter of the circle should measure approximately 4" (10 cm) here.*

RND 5: ch 2, *fpdc around next fpdc, 2 dc in next dc*, repeat between *...* to end of rnd, beg ch 2 counts as last dc, join with sl st in top of ch 2. (45)

NOTE: *The "fpsc and ch 2" at the beginning of the following rounds creates a stitch that looks like a fpdc. Be sure to crochet the fpsc tightly around the post so it doesn't bulge at the base of the ch 2. It is correct if it looks very similar to a fpdc. Starting the round in this fashion (instead of a standard ch 2) will result in a seam that is almost completely invisible.*

RND 6: fpsc around first fpdc from prev rnd, ch 2 (serves as first fpdc), dc in ea of next 2 dc, *fpdc around next fpdc, dc in ea of next 2 dc*, repeat between *...* to end of rnd, join with sl st in top of ch 2. (45)

NOTE: *Stitch marker placement in the next round is for joining at the end of the round and also for guidance in the following round.*

RND 7: fpsc around first fpdc, ch 2 (serves as first fpdc), sk next 2 dc, fpdc around next fpdc (add stitch marker around post of st just made), ch 3, fpdc around same fpdc, *sk next 2 dc, (fpdc, ch 3, fpdc) around next fpdc*, repeat between *...* to last 2 sts, sk last 2 dc, fpdc around first fpdc from prev rnd again, ch 3, join with sl st in top of beg ch 2 (directly above post with stitch marker). (15 ch-3 sps)

NOTE: *For each repeat of Rnd 8 with "3 dc in next ch-3 sp," work like this: Work first dc in ch-3 sp, work 2nd dc around both the ch 3 **and** between the 2 fpdc below, work 3rd dc in the ch-3 sp again. (This anchors them down instead of leaving a big gap between rounds. It is not critical where the 2nd dc is placed as long as it is between the 2 fpdc.)*

RND 8: fpsc around second fpdc from prev rnd (post with stitch marker), ch 2 (serves as first fpdc), 3 dc in next ch-3 sp, *fpdc around ea of next 2 fpdc, 3 dc in next ch-3 sp*, repeat between *...* to last st, fpdc around last fpdc, join with sl st in top of beg ch 2. (75)

RND 9: fpsc around post of beg ch 2 from prev rnd, ch 2 (serves as first fpdc), sk next 3 dc, fpdc around next fpdc (add stitch marker around post of st just made), ch 3, *fpdc around next fpdc, sk next 3 dc, fpdc around next fpdc, ch 3*, repeat between *...* to end of rnd, after last ch 3, join with sl st in top of beg ch 2 (directly above post with stitch marker). (15 ch-3 sps)

REPEAT RNDS 8 AND 9 until the beanie measures approximately 7.5 to 8" (19 to 20 cm) from top to bottom, end with Rnd 8.

CONTINUE with the Edging on page 139.

TEEN/ADULT HONEYCOMB RIDGES BEANIE

RND 1: Magic ring, ch 2, 7 dc in ring, join with sl st in top of ch 2. (8)

OR ch 2, 8 dc in 2nd ch from hook, join with sl st in first dc. (8)

RND 2: ch 2, *fpdc around next dc, dc in top of same post just used*, repeat between *...* to end of rnd, beg ch 2 counts as last dc, join with sl st in top of ch 2. (16)

RND 3: ch 2, *fpdc around next fpdc, fpdc around next dc, dc in top of same post just used*, repeat between *...* to end of rnd, beg ch 2 counts as last dc, join with sl st in top of ch 2. (24)

RND 4: ch 2, *fpdc around next fpdc, dc in top of same post just used, fpdc around next fpdc, dc in next dc*, repeat between *...* to end of rnd, beg ch 2 counts as last dc, join with sl st in top of ch 2. (32)

> **GAUGE CHECKPOINT:** *Diameter of the circle should measure approximately 3.5" (9 cm) here.*

RND 5: ch 2, *fpdc around next fpdc, dc in next dc, fpdc around next fpdc, 2 dc in next dc*, repeat between *...* to end of rnd, beg ch 2 counts as last dc, join with sl st in top of ch 2. (40)

RND 6: ch 2, *fpdc around next fpdc, 2 dc in next dc, fpdc around next fpdc, dc in ea of next 2 dc*, repeat between *...* to end of rnd, beg ch 2 counts as last dc, join with sl st in top of ch 2. (48)

> **NOTE:** *The "fpsc and ch 2" at the beginning of the following rounds creates a stitch that looks like a fpdc. Be sure to crochet the fpsc tightly around the post so it doesn't bulge at the base of the ch 2. It is correct if it looks very similar to a fpdc. Starting the round in this fashion (instead of a standard ch 2) will result in a seam that is almost completely invisible. Stitch marker placement in next round is for joining at end of round and also for guidance in the following round.*

RND 7: fpsc around first fpdc from prev rnd, ch 2 (serves as first fpdc), sk next 2 dc, fpdc around next fpdc (add stitch marker around post of st just made), ch 3, fpdc around same fpdc, *sk next 2 dc, (fpdc, ch 3, fpdc) around next fpdc*, repeat between *...* to last 2 sts, sk last 2 dc, fpdc around first fpdc from prev rnd again, ch 3, join with sl st in top of beg ch 2 (directly above post with stitch marker). (16 ch-3 sps)

NOTE: *For each repeat of Rnd 8 with "3 dc in next ch-3 sp," work like this: Work first dc in ch-3 sp, work 2nd dc around both the ch 3 **and** between the 2 fpdc below, work 3rd dc in the ch-3 sp again. (This anchors them down instead of leaving a big gap between rounds. It is not critical where the 2nd dc is placed as long as it is between the 2 fpdc.)*

RND 8: fpsc around second fpdc from prev rnd (post with stitch marker), ch 2 (serves as first fpdc), 3 dc in next ch-3 sp, *fpdc around ea of next 2 fpdc, 3 dc in next ch-3 sp*, repeat between *...* to last st, fpdc around last fpdc, join with sl st in top of beg ch 2. (80)

RND 9: fpsc around post of beg ch 2 from prev rnd, ch 2 (serves as first fpdc), sk next 3 dc, fpdc around next fpdc (add stitch marker around post of st just made), ch 3, *fpdc around next fpdc, sk next 3 dc, fpdc around next fpdc, ch 3*, repeat between *...* to end of rnd, after last ch 3, join with sl st in top of beg ch 2 (directly above post with stitch marker). (16 ch-3 sps)

REPEAT RNDS 8 AND 9 until the beanie measures approximately 8 to 8.5" (20 to 22 cm) from top to bottom, end with Rnd 8.

CONTINUE with the Edging on page 139.

LARGE ADULT HONEYCOMB RIDGES BEANIE

RND 1: Magic ring, ch 2, 8 dc in ring, join with sl st in top of ch 2. (9)

OR ch 2, 9 dc in 2nd ch from hook, join with sl st in first dc. (9)

RND 2: ch 2, *fpdc around next dc, dc in top of same post just used*, repeat between *...* to end of rnd, beg ch 2 counts as last dc, join with sl st in top of ch 2. (18)

RND 3: ch 2, [fpdc around next fpdc, fpdc around next dc, dc in top of same post just used] 8 times, fpdc around next fpdc, beg ch 2 counts as last dc, join with sl st in top of ch 2. (26)

RND 4: ch 2, [fpdc around next fpdc, dc in top of same post just used, fpdc around next fpdc, dc in next dc] 8 times, fpdc around next fpdc, beg ch 2 counts as last dc, join with sl st in top of ch 2. (34)

GAUGE CHECKPOINT: *Diameter of circle should measure approximately 3.5" (9 cm) here.*

RND 5: ch 2, *fpdc around next fpdc, dc in next dc, fpdc around next fpdc, 2 dc in next dc*, repeat between *...* to last fpdc, fpdc around last fpdc, beg ch 2 counts as last dc, join with sl st in top of ch 2. (42)

RND 6: ch 2, *fpdc around next fpdc, 2 dc in next dc, fpdc around next fpdc, dc in ea of next 2 dc*, repeat between *...* to last fpdc, fpdc around last fpdc, dc in same st as beg ch 2, beg ch 2 counts as last dc, join with sl st in top of ch 2. (51)

NOTE: *The "fpsc and ch 2" at the beginning of the following rounds creates a stitch that looks like a fpdc. Be sure to crochet the fpsc tightly around the post so it doesn't bulge at the base of the ch 2. It is correct if it looks very similar to a fpdc. Starting the round in this fashion (instead of a standard ch 2) will result in a seam that is almost completely invisible. Stitch marker placement in next round is for joining at end of round and also for guidance in the following round.*

RND 7: fpsc around first fpdc from prev rnd, ch 2 (serves as first fpdc), sk next 2 dc, fpdc around next fpdc (add stitch marker around post of st just made), ch 3, fpdc around same fpdc, *sk next 2 dc, (fpdc, ch 3, fpdc) around next fpdc*, repeat between *...* to last 2 sts, sk last 2 dc, fpdc around first fpdc from prev rnd again, ch 3, join with sl st in top of beg ch 2 (directly above post with stitch marker). (17 ch-3 sps)

> **NOTE:** *For each repeat of Rnd 8 with "3 dc in next ch-3 sp," work like this: Work first dc in ch-3 sp, work 2nd dc around both the ch 3 **and** between the 2 fpdc below, work 3rd dc in the ch-3 sp again. (This anchors them down instead of leaving a big gap between rounds. It is not critical where the 2nd dc is placed as long as it is between the 2 fpdc.)*

RND 8: fpsc around second fpdc from prev rnd (post with stitch marker), ch 2 (serves as first fpdc), 3 dc in next ch-3 sp, *fpdc around ea of next 2 fpdc, 3 dc in next ch-3 sp*, repeat between *...* to last st, fpdc around last fpdc, join with sl st in top of beg ch 2. (85)

RND 9: fpsc around post of beg ch 2 from prev rnd, ch 2 (serves as first fpdc), sk next 3 dc, fpdc around next fpdc (add stitch marker around post of st just made), ch 3, *fpdc around next fpdc, sk next 3 dc, fpdc around next fpdc, ch 3*, repeat between *...* to end of rnd, after last ch 3, join with sl st in top of beg ch 2 (directly above post with stitch marker). (17 ch-3 sps)

REPEAT RNDS 8 AND 9 until the beanie measures approximately 8.5 to 9" (22 to 23 cm) from top to bottom, end with Rnd 8.

CONTINUE with the Edging.

EDGING (ALL SIZES)

> **NOTE:** *Switch to "H" (5 mm) hook (or 2 hook sizes smaller than gauge). Measure the circumference after the Edging round to make sure it is within the range listed in the Size Chart on page 128. If it is larger than the size range listed, go down as many hook sizes as needed to match the circumference and redo.*

EDGING: ch 1, sc in same st as ch 1 and ea st to end of rnd, fasten off with invisible join (or sl st) in first sc. (45, 50, 55, 60, 65, 70, 75, 80, 85)

WEAVE in ends.

THUNDERSTRUCK BEANIE

Designed with a zigzag "lightning" texture, this unisex beanie pattern is a great way for Dad to match his kids . . . and it's one of my favorite hat designs for men!

SKILL LEVEL: **INTERMEDIATE**

MATERIALS

TOOLS	Measuring tape, yarn needle, stitch marker (optional)
YARN	7 oz (198 g) or less of #4 worsted weight cotton or 50/50 cotton/acrylic blend yarn. This pattern was designed and tested with cotton or cotton blend yarns. You may have different results with other fibers.
GAUGE	Gauge checkpoint is listed in pattern for each size after Rnd 4
HOOK SIZE	"J" (6 mm) for main portion of hat, smaller hook may be needed for edging

BEANIE SIZE CHART

Bonus instructions included for slouch version.

0-3 MONTHS	12–14" (30–36 cm) circumference, approximately 5.5" (14 cm) from crown to brim
3-6 MONTHS	14–16" (36–41 cm) circumference, approximately 5.5–6" (14–15 cm) from crown to brim
6-12 MONTHS	16–18" (41–46 cm) circumference, approximately 6.5–7" (17–18 cm) from crown to brim
TODDLER/CHILD	18–20" (46–51 cm) circumference, approximately 7.5–8" (19–20 cm) from crown to brim
TEEN/ADULT	20–22" (51–56 cm) circumference, approximately 8" (20 cm) from crown to brim
LARGE ADULT	22–24" (56–61 cm) circumference, approximately 8.5" (22 cm) from crown to brim

ABBREVIATIONS USED

ST(S)	stitch(es)
CH	chain stitch
SC	single crochet
DC	double crochet
FPSC	front post single crochet
FPDC	front post double crochet
BPDC	back post double crochet
SL ST	slip stitch
RND(S)	round(s)
EA	each
BEG	beginning
PREV	previous
YO	Yarn Over

SPECIAL STITCHES DEFINITIONS

FRONT POST DOUBLE CROCHET (FPDC): Working from the front side of the work, YO and insert the hook from right to left under the post of the double crochet indicated from the previous round, YO and pull up a loop, [YO and draw through 2 loops] twice.

BACK POST DOUBLE CROCHET (BPDC): Working from the back side of the work, YO and insert the hook from right to left over the post of the double crochet indicated from the previous round, YO and pull up a loop, [YO and draw through 2 loops] twice.

FRONT POST SINGLE CROCHET (FPSC): Insert hook from the front side of the work (right to left) under the post of the indicated stitch, YO and pull up a loop, YO and draw through 2 loops.

SPECIAL TECHNIQUES

USING THE BEG "CH 2" AS THE FINAL DC IN THE ROUND: If there is a "ch 2" at the beg of a round, it will stand in as the last dc in the round. This avoids having a noticeable seam. If the repeat ends on a dc at the end of the round, don't make that last dc because the "ch 2" is there and will look like a dc when you join to the top of it. If the repeat ends with 2 dc worked in one stitch, make the first dc in the same stitch as the "ch 2." This will look almost exactly the same as working 2 dc in one stitch.

JOINING IN THE "TOP" OF THE CH 2: If there is any confusion on where to join at the end of each round, use the following method: Complete the first ch 2 of the round, then add a stitch marker around the loop that is on the hook. At the end of the round, this is the stitch that will be used for joining.

0–3 MONTHS THUNDERSTRUCK BEANIE

Use "J" (6 mm) hook, or match gauge checkpoint after Rnd 4.

NOTE: *The beginning ch 2 counts as the final dc in each round and is included in the stitch count. In this pattern, a dc following a fpdc will always be made in the top of the same post that was just used for the fpdc.*

RND 1: Magic ring, ch 2 (counts as dc), 9 dc in ring, join with sl st in top of ch 2. (10)

OR ch 2, 10 dc in 2nd ch from hook, join with sl st in first dc. (10)

RND 2: ch 2, *fpdc around next dc, dc in top of same post just used for fpdc*, repeat between *...* to end of rnd, last fpdc will be around ch 2 from prev rnd, beg ch 2 counts as last dc, join with sl st in top of ch 2. (20)

RND 3: ch 2, *(fpdc around next fpdc, fpdc around next dc) twice, dc in top of same post just used*, repeat between *...* to end of rnd, last fpdc will be around ch 2 from prev rnd, beg ch 2 counts as last dc, join with sl st in top of ch 2. (25)

NOTE: *The "fpsc and ch 2" at the beginning of the following rounds creates a stitch that looks like a fpdc. Be sure to crochet the fpsc tightly around the post so it doesn't bulge at the base of the ch 2. It is correct if it looks very similar to a fpdc. Starting the round in this fashion (instead of a standard ch 2) will result in a seam that is almost completely invisible.*

RND 4: fpsc around first fpdc from prev rnd, ch 2 (serves as first fpdc), fpdc around ea of next 3 sts, 2 bpdc around next dc, *fpdc around next 4 sts, 2 bpdc around next dc*, repeat between *...* to end of rnd, join with sl st in top of ch 2. (30)

GAUGE CHECKPOINT: *Diameter of the circle should measure approximately 3.5 to 3.75" (9 to 10 cm) here.*

RND 5: fpsc around first fpdc from prev rnd, ch 2 (serves as first fpdc), fpdc around ea of next 3 sts, bpdc around next bpdc, 2 bpdc around next bpdc, *fpdc around next 4 sts, bpdc around next bpdc, 2 bpdc around next bpdc*, repeat between *...* to end of rnd, join with sl st in top of ch 2. (35)

RND 6: fpsc around first fpdc from prev rnd, ch 2 (serves as first fpdc), fpdc around ea of next 3 sts, bpdc around ea of next 2 bpdc, 2 bpdc around next bpdc, *fpdc around next 4 sts, bpdc around ea of next 2 bpdc, 2 bpdc around next bpdc*, repeat between *...* to end of rnd, join with sl st in top of ch 2. (40)

> **NOTE:** *The next round uses the same stitch pattern, but is offset by one stitch, which creates the "chevron" effect.*

RND 7: fpsc around **2nd fpdc** from prev rnd, ch 2 (serves as first fpdc), fpdc around ea of next 3 sts, bpdc around next 4 sts, *fpdc around next 4 sts, bpdc around next 4 sts*, repeat between *...* to end of rnd, last bpdc will be made around the first skipped fpdc of the prev rnd, join with sl st in top of ch 2. (40)

RNDS 8–9: Repeat Rnd 7.

RND 10: sl st in ea of next 6 sts, fpsc around **4th bpdc** from prev rnd, ch 2 (serves as first fpdc), fpdc around ea of next 3 fpdc, bpdc around ea of next 4 sts, *fpdc around next 4 sts, bpdc around next 4 sts*, repeat between *...* to end of rnd, join with sl st in top of ch 2. (40)

RNDS 11–12: Repeat Rnd 10.

REPEAT RND 7 (3 times) and Rnd 10 (3 times) until the hat reaches the following measurement (measure from the center of the magic ring to the edge of the hat; for best appearance, try to end with the 3rd repeat of either rnd):

BEANIE	5 to 5.5" (13 to 14 cm) from crown to brim
SLOUCH	5.5 to 6" (14 to 15 cm) from crown to brim

> **NOTE:** *Measure the circumference before completing the Edging. If not within size range listed in the beginning of the pattern, adjust the hook size as necessary.*

CONTINUE with Edging at end of pattern (page 149).

3–6 MONTHS THUNDERSTRUCK BEANIE

Use "J" (6 mm) hook, or match gauge checkpoint after Rnd 4.

> **NOTE:** *The beginning ch 2 counts as the final dc in each round and is included in the stitch count. In this pattern, a dc following a fpdc will always be made in the top of the same post that was just used for the fpdc.*

RND 1: Magic ring, ch 2 (counts as dc), 11 dc in ring, join with sl st in top of ch 2. (12)

OR ch 2, 12 dc in 2nd ch from hook, join with sl st in first dc. (12)

RND 2: ch 2, *fpdc around next dc, dc in top of same post just used for fpdc*, repeat between *...* to end of rnd, last fpdc will be around ch 2 from prev rnd, beg ch 2 counts as last dc, join with sl st in top of ch 2. (24)

RND 3: ch 2, *(fpdc around next fpdc, fpdc around next dc) twice, dc in top of same post just used*, repeat between *...* to end of rnd, last fpdc will be around ch 2 from prev rnd, beg ch 2 counts as last dc, join with sl st in top of ch 2. (30)

> **NOTE:** *The "fpsc and ch 2" at the beginning of the following rounds creates a stitch that looks like a fpdc. Be sure to crochet the fpsc tightly around the post so it doesn't bulge at the base of the ch 2. It is correct if it looks very similar to a fpdc. Starting the round in this fashion (instead of a standard ch 2) will result in a seam that is almost completely invisible.*

RND 4: fpsc around first fpdc from prev rnd, ch 2 (serves as first fpdc), fpdc around ea of next 3 sts, 2 bpdc around next dc, *fpdc around next 4 sts, 2 bpdc around next dc*, repeat between *...* to end of rnd, join with sl st in top of ch 2. (36)

> **GAUGE CHECKPOINT:** *Diameter of the circle should measure approximately 3.75 to 4" (9 to 10 cm) here.*

RND 5: fpsc around first fpdc from prev rnd, ch 2 (serves as first fpdc), fpdc around ea of next 3 sts, bpdc around next bpdc, 2 bpdc around next bpdc, *fpdc around next 4 sts, bpdc around next bpdc, 2 bpdc around next bpdc*, repeat between *...* to end of rnd, join with sl st in top of ch 2. (42)

RND 6: fpsc around first fpdc from prev rnd, ch 2 (serves as first fpdc), fpdc around ea of next 3 sts, bpdc around ea of next 2 bpdc, 2 bpdc around next bpdc, *fpdc around next 4 sts, bpdc around ea of next 2 bpdc, 2 bpdc around next bpdc*, repeat between *...* to end of rnd, join with sl st in top of ch 2. (48)

> **NOTE:** *The next round uses the same stitch pattern, but is offset by one stitch, which creates the "chevron" effect.*

RND 7: fpsc around **2nd fpdc** from prev rnd, ch 2 (serves as first fpdc), fpdc around ea of next 3 sts, bpdc around next 4 sts, *fpdc around next 4 sts, bpdc around next 4 sts*, repeat between *...* to end of rnd, last bpdc will be made around the first skipped fpdc of the prev rnd, join with sl st in top of ch 2. (48)

RNDS 8–9: Repeat Rnd 7.

RND 10: sl st in ea of next 6 sts, fpsc around **4th bpdc** from prev rnd, ch 2 (serves as first fpdc), fpdc around ea of next 3 fpdc, bpdc around ea of next 4 sts, *fpdc around next 4 sts, bpdc around next 4 sts*, repeat between *...* to end of rnd, join with sl st in top of ch 2. (48)

RNDS 11–12: Repeat Rnd 10.

REPEAT RND 7 (3 times) and Rnd 10 (3 times) until the hat reaches the following measurement (measure from the center of the magic ring to the edge of the hat; for best appearance, try to end with the 3rd repeat of either rnd):

BEANIE	6 to 6.5" (15 to 17 cm) from crown to brim
SLOUCH	6.5 to 7" (17 to 18 cm) from crown to brim

> **NOTE:** *Measure the circumference before completing the Edging. If not within the size range listed on page 141, adjust the hook size as necessary.*

CONTINUE with Edging at end of pattern (page 149).

6–12 MONTHS THUNDERSTRUCK BEANIE

Use "J" (6 mm) hook, or match gauge checkpoint after Rnd 4.

> **NOTE:** *The beginning ch 2 counts as the final dc in each round and is included in the stitch count. In this pattern, a dc following a fpdc will always be made in the top of the same post that was just used for the fpdc.*

RND 1: Magic ring, ch 2 (counts as dc), 13 dc in ring, join with sl st in top of ch 2. (14)

OR ch 2, 14 dc in 2nd ch from hook, join with sl st in first dc. (14)

RND 2: ch 2, *fpdc around ea of next 2 dc, dc in top of same post just used for fpdc*, repeat between *...* to end of rnd, last fpdc will be around ch 2 from prev rnd, beg ch 2 counts as last dc, join with sl st in top of ch 2. (21)

RND 3: ch 2, *fpdc around ea of next 2 fpdc, fpdc around next dc, dc in top of same post just used*, repeat between *...* to end of rnd, last fpdc will be around ch 2 from prev rnd, beg ch 2 counts as last dc, join with sl st in top of ch 2. (28)

RND 4: ch 2, *fpdc around ea of next 3 fpdc, fpdc around next dc, dc in top of same post just used*, repeat between *...* to end of rnd, last fpdc will be around ch 2 from prev rnd, beg ch 2 counts as last dc, join with sl st in top of ch 2. (35)

> **GAUGE CHECKPOINT:** *Diameter of the circle should measure approximately 3.5" (9 cm) here.*

RND 5: fpsc around first fpdc from prev rnd, ch 2 (serves as first fpdc), fpdc around ea of next 3 sts, 2 bpdc around next dc, *fpdc around next 4 sts, 2 bpdc around next dc*, repeat between *...* to end of rnd, join with sl st in top of ch 2. (42)

RND 6: fpsc around first fpdc from prev rnd, ch 2 (serves as first fpdc), fpdc around ea of next 3 sts, bpdc around next bpdc, 2 bpdc around next bpdc, *fpdc around next 4 sts, bpdc around next bpdc, 2 bpdc around next bpdc*, repeat between *...* to end of rnd, join with sl st in top of ch 2. (49)

RND 7: fpsc around first fpdc from prev rnd, ch 2 (serves as first fpdc), fpdc around ea of next 3 sts, bpdc around ea of next 2 bpdc, 2 bpdc around next bpdc, *fpdc around next 4 sts, bpdc around ea of next 2 bpdc, 2 bpdc around next bpdc*, repeat between *...* to end of rnd, join with sl st in top of ch 2. (56)

RND 8: fpsc around **2nd fpdc** from prev rnd, ch 2 (serves as first fpdc), fpdc around ea of next 3 sts, bpdc around next 4 sts, *fpdc around next 4 sts, bpdc around next 4 sts*, repeat between *...* to end of rnd, last bpdc will be made around the first skipped fpdc of the prev rnd, join with sl st in top of ch 2. (56)

RNDS 9–10: Repeat Rnd 8.

RND 11: sl st in ea of next 6 sts, fpsc around **4th bpdc** from prev rnd, ch 2 (serves as first fpdc), fpdc around ea of next 3 fpdc, bpdc around ea of next 4 sts, *fpdc around next 4 sts, bpdc around next 4 sts*, repeat between *...* to end of rnd, join with sl st in top of ch 2. (56)

RNDS 12–13: Repeat Rnd 11.

REPEAT RND 8 (3 times) and Rnd 11 (3 times) until the hat reaches the following measurement (measure from the center of the magic ring to the edge of the hat; for best appearance, try to end with the 3rd repeat of either rnd):

BEANIE	6.5 to 7" (17 to 18 cm) from crown to brim
SLOUCH	7 to 7.5" (18 to 19 cm) from crown to brim

CONTINUE with Edging at end of pattern (page 149).

TODDLER/CHILD THUNDERSTRUCK BEANIE

Use "J" (6 mm) hook, or match gauge checkpoint after Rnd 4.

NOTE: *The beginning ch 2 counts as the final dc in each round and is included in the stitch count. In this pattern, a dc following a fpdc will always be made in the top of the same post that was just used for the fpdc.*

RND 1: Magic ring, ch 2 (counts as dc), 15 dc in ring, join with sl st in top of ch 2. (16)

OR ch 2, 16 dc in 2nd ch from hook, join with sl st in first dc. (16)

RND 2: ch 2, *fpdc around ea of next 2 dc, dc in top of same post just used for fpdc*, repeat between *...* to end of rnd, last fpdc will be around ch 2 from prev rnd, beg ch 2 counts as last dc, join with sl st in top of ch 2. (24)

RND 3: ch 2, *fpdc around ea of next 2 fpdc, fpdc around next dc, dc in top of same post just used*, repeat between *...* to end of rnd, last fpdc will be around ch 2 from prev rnd, beg ch 2 counts as last dc, join with sl st in top of ch 2. (32)

RND 4: ch 2, *fpdc around ea of next 3 fpdc, fpdc around next dc, dc in top of same post just used*, repeat between *...* to end of rnd, last fpdc will be around ch 2 from prev rnd, beg ch 2 counts as last dc, join with sl st in top of ch 2. (40)

GAUGE CHECKPOINT: *Diameter of the circle should measure approximately 4 to 4.25" (10 to 11 cm) here.*

NOTE: *The "fpsc and ch 2" at the beginning of the following rounds creates a stitch that looks like a fpdc. Be sure to crochet the fpsc tightly around the post so it doesn't bulge at the base of the ch 2. It is correct if it looks very similar to a fpdc. Starting the round in this fashion (instead of a standard ch 2) will result in a seam that is almost completely invisible.*

RND 5: fpsc around first fpdc from prev rnd, ch 2 (serves as first fpdc), fpdc around ea of next 3 sts, 2 bpdc around next dc, *fpdc around next 4 sts, 2 bpdc around next dc*, repeat between *...* to end of rnd, join with sl st in top of ch 2. (48)

RND 6: fpsc around first fpdc from prev rnd, ch 2 (serves as first fpdc), fpdc around ea of next 3 sts, bpdc around next bpdc, 2 bpdc around next bpdc, *fpdc around next 4 sts, bpdc around next bpdc, 2 bpdc around next bpdc*, repeat between *...* to end of rnd, join with sl st in top of ch 2. (56)

RND 7: fpsc around first fpdc from prev rnd, ch 2 (serves as first fpdc), fpdc around ea of next 3 sts, bpdc around ea of next 2 bpdc, 2 bpdc around next bpdc, *fpdc around next 4 sts, bpdc around ea of next 2 bpdc, 2 bpdc around next bpdc*, repeat between *...* to end of rnd, join with sl st in top of ch 2. (64)

NOTE: *The next round uses the same stitch pattern, but is offset by one stitch, which creates the "chevron" effect.*

RND 8: fpsc around **2nd fpdc** from prev rnd, ch 2 (serves as first fpdc), fpdc around ea of next 3 sts, bpdc around next 4 sts, *fpdc around next 4 sts, bpdc around next 4 sts*, repeat between *...* to end of rnd, last bpdc will be made around the first skipped fpdc of the prev rnd, join with sl st in top of ch 2. (64)

RNDS 9–11: Repeat Rnd 8.

RND 12: sl st in ea of next 6 sts, fpsc around **4th bpdc** from prev rnd, ch 2 (serves as first fpdc), fpdc around ea of next 3 fpdc, bpdc around ea of next 4 sts, *fpdc around next 4 sts, bpdc around next 4 sts*, repeat between *...* to end of rnd, join with sl st in top of ch 2. (64)

RNDS 13–15: Repeat Rnd 12.

REPEAT RND 8 (4 times) and Rnd 12 (4 times) until the hat reaches the following measurement (measure from the center of the magic ring to the edge of the hat; for best appearance, try to end with the 4th repeat of either rnd):

TODDLER BEANIE	7 to 7.5″ (18 to 19 cm)
TODDLER SLOUCH	7.5 to 8″ (19 to 20 cm)
CHILD BEANIE	7.5 to 8″ (19 to 20 cm)
CHILD SLOUCH	8 to 8.5″ (20 to 22 cm)

CONTINUE with Edging at end of pattern (page 149).

TEEN/ADULT THUNDERSTRUCK BEANIE

Use "J" (6 mm) hook, or match gauge checkpoint after Rnd 4.

NOTE: *The beginning ch 2 counts as the final dc in each round and is included in the stitch count. In this pattern, a dc following a fpdc will always be made in the top of the same post that was just used for the fpdc.*

RND 1: Magic ring, ch 2 (counts as dc), 8 dc in ring, join with sl st in top of ch 2. (9)

OR ch 2, 9 dc in 2nd ch from hook, join with sl st in first dc. (9)

RND 2: ch 2, *fpdc around next dc, dc in top of same post just used for fpdc*, repeat between *...* to end of rnd, last fpdc will be around ch 2 from prev rnd, beg ch 2 counts as last dc, join with sl st in top of ch 2. (18)

RND 3: ch 2, *fpdc around next fpdc, fpdc around next dc, dc in top of same post just used for fpdc*, repeat between *...* to end of rnd, last fpdc will be around ch 2 from prev rnd, beg ch 2 counts as last dc, join with sl st in top of ch 2. (27)

RND 4: ch 2, *fpdc around ea of next 2 fpdc, fpdc around next dc, dc in top of same post just used*, repeat between *...* to end of rnd, last fpdc will be around ch 2 from prev rnd, beg ch 2 counts as last dc, join with sl st in top of ch 2. (36)

GAUGE CHECKPOINT: *Diameter of the circle should measure approximately 3.75 to 4″ (9 to 10 cm) here.*

RND 5: ch 2, *fpdc around ea of next 3 fpdc, fpdc around next dc, dc in top of same post just used*, repeat between *...* to end of rnd, last fpdc will be around ch 2 from prev rnd, beg ch 2 counts as last dc, join with sl st in top of ch 2. (45)

NOTE: *The "fpsc and ch 2" at the beginning of the following rounds creates a stitch that looks like a fpdc. Be sure to crochet the fpsc tightly around the post so it doesn't bulge at the base of the ch 2. It is correct if it looks very similar to a fpdc. Starting the round in this fashion (instead of a standard ch 2) will result in a seam that is almost completely invisible.*

RND 6: fpsc around first fpdc from prev rnd, ch 2 (serves as first fpdc), fpdc around ea of next 3 sts, 2 bpdc around next dc, *fpdc around next 4 sts, 2 bpdc around next dc*, repeat between *...* to end of rnd, join with sl st in top of ch 2. (54)

RND 7: fpsc around first fpdc from prev rnd, ch 2 (serves as first fpdc), fpdc around ea of next 3 sts, bpdc around next bpdc, 2 bpdc around next bpdc, *fpdc around next 4 sts, bpdc around next bpdc, 2 bpdc around next bpdc*, repeat between *...* to end of rnd, join with sl st in top of ch 2. (63)

RND 8: fpsc around first fpdc from prev rnd, ch 2 (serves as first fpdc), fpdc around ea of next 3 sts, bpdc around ea of next 2 bpdc, 2 bpdc around next bpdc, *fpdc around next 4 sts, bpdc around ea of next 2 bpdc, 2 bpdc around next bpdc*, repeat between *...* to end of rnd, join with sl st in top of ch 2. (72)

NOTE: *The next round uses the same stitch pattern, but is offset by one stitch, which creates the "chevron" effect.*

RND 9: fpsc around **2nd fpdc** from prev rnd, ch 2 (serves as first fpdc), fpdc around ea of next 3 sts, bpdc around next 4 sts, *fpdc around next 4 sts, bpdc around next 4 sts*, repeat between *...* to end of rnd, last bpdc will be made around the first skipped fpdc of the prev rnd, join with sl st in top of ch 2. (72)

RNDS 10-12: Repeat Rnd 9.

RND 13: sl st in ea of next 6 sts, fpsc around **4th bpdc** from prev rnd, ch 2 (serves as first fpdc), fpdc around ea of next 3 fpdc, bpdc around ea of next 4 sts, *fpdc around next 4 sts, bpdc around next 4 sts*, repeat between *...* to end of rnd, join with sl st in top of ch 2. (72)

RNDS 14-16: Repeat Rnd 13.

REPEAT RND 9 (4 times) and Rnd 13 (4 times) until the hat reaches the following measurement (measure from the center of the magic ring to the edge of the hat; for best appearance, try to end with the 4th repeat of either rnd):

BEANIE	8 to 8.5″ (20 to 22 cm) from crown to brim
SLOUCH	9 to 9.5″ (23 to 24 cm) from crown to brim

CONTINUE with Edging at end of pattern (page 149).

LARGE ADULT THUNDERSTRUCK BEANIE

Use "J" (6 mm) hook, or match gauge checkpoint after Rnd 4.

NOTE: *The beginning ch 2 counts as the final dc in each round and is included in the stitch count. In this pattern, a dc following a fpdc will always be made in the top of the same post that was just used for the fpdc.*

RND 1: Magic ring, ch 2 (counts as dc), 9 dc in ring, join with sl st in top of ch 2. (10)

OR ch 2, 10 dc in 2nd ch from hook, join with sl st in first dc. (10)

RND 2: ch 2, *fpdc around next dc, dc in top of same post just used for fpdc*, repeat between *...* to end of rnd, last fpdc will be around ch 2 from prev rnd, beg ch 2 counts as last dc, join with sl st in top of ch 2. (20)

RND 3: ch 2, *fpdc around next fpdc, fpdc around next dc, dc in top of same post just used for fpdc*, repeat between *...* to end of rnd, last fpdc will be around ch 2 from prev rnd, beg ch 2 counts as last dc, join with sl st in top of ch 2. (30)

RND 4: ch 2, *fpdc around ea of next 2 fpdc, fpdc around next dc, dc in top of same post just used*, repeat between *...* to end of rnd, last fpdc will be around ch 2 from prev rnd, beg ch 2 counts as last dc, join with sl st in top of ch 2. (40)

> **GAUGE CHECKPOINT:** *Diameter of the circle should measure approximately 3.5 to 3.75" (9 to 10 cm) here.*

RND 5: ch 2, *fpdc around ea of next 3 fpdc, fpdc around next dc, dc in top of same post just used*, repeat between *...* to end of rnd, last fpdc will be around ch 2 from prev rnd, beg ch 2 counts as last dc, join with sl st in top of ch 2. (50)

> **NOTE:** *The "fpsc and ch 2" at the beginning of the following rounds creates a stitch that looks like a fpdc. Be sure to crochet the fpsc tightly around the post so it doesn't bulge at the base of the ch 2. It is correct if it looks very similar to a fpdc. Starting the round in this fashion (instead of a standard ch 2) will result in a seam that is almost completely invisible.*

RND 6: fpsc around first fpdc from prev rnd, ch 2 (serves as first fpdc), fpdc around ea of next 3 sts, 2 bpdc around next dc, *fpdc around next 4 sts, 2 bpdc around next dc*, repeat between *...* to end of rnd, join with sl st in top of ch 2. (60)

RND 7: fpsc around first fpdc from prev rnd, ch 2 (serves as first fpdc), fpdc around ea of next 3 sts, bpdc around next bpdc, 2 bpdc around next bpdc, *fpdc around next 4 sts, bpdc around next bpdc, 2 bpdc around next bpdc*, repeat between *...* to end of rnd, join with sl st in top of ch 2. (70)

RND 8: fpsc around first fpdc from prev rnd, ch 2 (serves as first fpdc), fpdc around ea of next 3 sts, bpdc around ea of next 2 bpdc, 2 bpdc around next bpdc, *fpdc around next 4 sts, bpdc around ea of next 2 bpdc, 2 bpdc around next bpdc*, repeat between *...* to end of rnd, join with sl st in top of ch 2. (80)

> **NOTE:** *The next round uses the same stitch pattern, but is offset by one stitch, which creates the "chevron" effect.*

RND 9: fpsc around **2nd fpdc** from prev rnd, ch 2 (serves as first fpdc), fpdc around ea of next 3 sts, bpdc around next 4 sts, *fpdc around next 4 sts, bpdc around next 4 sts*, repeat between *...* to end of rnd, last bpdc will be made around the first skipped fpdc of the prev rnd, join with sl st in top of ch 2. (80)

RNDS 10-12: Repeat Rnd 9.

RND 13: sl st in ea of next 6 sts, fpsc around **4th bpdc** from prev rnd, ch 2 (serves as first fpdc), fpdc around ea of next 3 fpdc, bpdc around ea of next 4 sts, *fpdc around next 4 sts, bpdc around next 4 sts*, repeat between *...* to end of rnd, join with sl st in top of ch 2. (80)

RNDS 14-16: Repeat Rnd 13.

REPEAT RND 9 (4 times) and Rnd 13 (4 times) until the hat reaches the following measurement (measure from center of the magic ring to the edge of the hat; for best appearance, try to end with the 4th repeat of either rnd):

BEANIE	8.5–9" (22 to 23 cm) from crown to brim
SLOUCH	9.5–10" (24 to 25 cm) from crown to brim

EDGING (ALL SIZES)

Ch 1, sc in same st as ch 1 and ea st to end of rnd, fasten off with invisible join (or sl st, if repeating this rnd) in first sc. (40, 48, 56, 64, 72, 80)

REPEAT EDGING for Slouch version (2–5 times, or as desired). Weave in ends.

EMBOSSED HEART BEANIE

Incorporating a subtle heart pattern that looks "embossed," this pattern comes in sizes for the whole family. It is a great choice for "mommy and me" or hats for sisters. A great hat for Valentine's Day as well!

SKILL LEVEL: ▮▮◻️◻️◻️ **INTERMEDIATE**

MATERIALS

TOOLS	Stitch marker (optional), measuring tape, yarn needle
YARN	4 oz (113 g) or less of #4 worsted weight yarn
GAUGE	Gauge checkpoint given in pattern after Rnd 5 for each size
HOOK SIZE	"J" (6 mm) hook, or to match gauge checkpoint

BEANIE SIZE CHART

0-3 MONTHS	12-14" (30-36 cm) circumference, approximately 5.5" (14 cm) from crown to brim
3-6 MONTHS	14-16" (36-41 cm) circumference, approximately 5.5-6" (14-15 cm) from crown to brim
6-12 MONTHS	16-18" (41-46 cm) circumference, approximately 6.5-7" (17-18 cm) from crown to brim
TODDLER	17-19" (43-48 cm) circumference, approximately 7-7.5" (18-19 cm) from crown to brim
CHILD	18-20" (46-51 cm) circumference, approximately 7.5-8" (19-20 cm) from crown to brim
TEEN/ADULT	20-22" (51-56 cm) circumference, approximately 8-8.5" (20-22 cm) from crown to brim
LARGE ADULT	22-24" (56-61 cm) circumference, approximately 8.5-9" (22-23 cm) from crown to brim

ABBREVIATIONS USED

ST(S)	stitch(es)
CH	chain stitch
SC	single crochet
DC	double crochet
FPSC	front post single crochet
FPDC	front post double crochet
BPDC	back post double crochet
SL ST	slip stitch
RND(S)	round(s)
SK	skip
EA	each
BEG	beginning
PREV	previous
YO	Yarn Over

SPECIAL STITCHES DEFINITIONS

FRONT POST SINGLE CROCHET (FPSC): Insert hook from the front side of the work (right to left) under the post of the indicated stitch, YO and pull up a loop, YO and draw through 2 loops.

FRONT POST DOUBLE CROCHET (FPDC): Working from the front side of the work, YO and insert the hook from right to left under the post of the double crochet indicated from the previous round, YO and pull up a loop, [YO and draw through 2 loops] twice.

BACK POST DOUBLE CROCHET (BPDC): Working from the back side of the work, YO and insert the hook from right to left over the post of the double crochet indicated from the previous round, YO and pull up a loop, [YO and draw through 2 loops] twice.

SPECIAL TECHNIQUES

USING THE BEG "CH 2" AS THE FINAL DC IN THE RND: If there is a "ch 2" at the beg of a rnd, it will stand in as the last dc in the rnd. This avoids having a noticeable seam. If the repeat ends on a dc at the end of the rnd, don't make that last dc because the "ch 2" is there and will look like a dc when you join to the top of it. If the repeat ends with 2 dc worked in one stitch, make the first dc in the same st as the "ch 2." This will look almost exactly the same as working 2 dc in one stitch.

JOINING IN THE "TOP" OF THE CH 2: If there is any confusion on where to join at the end of each rnd, use the following method: Complete the first ch 2 of the rnd, then add a stitch marker around the loop that is on the hook. At the end of the rnd, this is the stitch that will be used for joining.

0–3 MONTH EMBOSSED HEART BEANIE

Use "J" (6 mm) hook, or match gauge checkpoint after Rnd 5.

NOTE: *The beginning ch 2 counts as the final dc in each round and is included in the stitch count. In this pattern, a dc following a fpdc will always be made in the top of the same post that was just used for the fpdc.*

RND 1: Magic ring, ch 2 (counts as dc), 15 dc in ring, join with sl st in top of ch 2. (16)

OR ch 2, 16 dc in 2nd ch from hook, join with sl st in first dc. (16)

RND 2: ch 2, *fpdc around ea of next 2 dc, dc in top of same post just used for fpdc*, repeat between *…* to end of rnd, last fpdc will be around ch 2 from prev rnd, beg ch 2 counts as last dc, join with sl st in top of ch 2. (24)

RND 3: ch 2, *fpdc around ea of next 2 fpdc, fpdc around next dc, dc in top of same post just used*, repeat between *…* to end of rnd, last fpdc will be around ch 2 from prev rnd, beg ch 2 counts as last dc, join with sl st in top of ch 2. (32)

RND 4: ch 2, *fpdc around ea of next 3 fpdc, fpdc around next dc, dc in top of same post just used*, repeat between *…* to end of rnd, last fpdc will be around ch 2 from prev rnd, beg ch 2 counts as last dc, join with sl st in top of ch 2. (40)

RND 5: ch 2, *[fpdc around ea of next 4 fpdc, fpdc around next dc] twice, dc in top of same post just used*, repeat between *…* to end of rnd, last fpdc will be around ch 2 from prev rnd, beg ch 2 counts as last dc, join with sl st in top of ch 2. (44)

NOTE: *The "fpsc and ch 2" at the beginnings of the following rounds creates a stitch that looks like a fpdc. Be sure to crochet the fpsc tightly around the post so it doesn't bulge at the base of the ch 2. It is correct if it looks very similar to a fpdc. Starting the round in this fashion (instead of a standard ch 2) will result in a seam that is almost completely invisible. This fpsc + ch 2 combo counts as the first fpdc of every round from this point.*

RND 6: fpsc around first fpdc from prev rnd, ch 2 (serves as first fpdc), fpdc around ea st to end of rnd, last fpdc will be around beg ch 2 from prev rnd, join with sl st in top of ch 2. (44)

RND 7: fpsc around first fpdc from prev rnd, ch 2 (serves as first fpdc), fpdc around ea of next 19 sts, bpdc around next 2 sts, fpdc around next 3 sts, bpdc around next 2 sts, fpdc around ea of remaining sts to end of rnd, join with sl st in top of ch 2. (44)

RND 8: fpsc around first fpdc from prev rnd, ch 2 (serves as first fpdc), fpdc around ea of next 18 sts, bpdc around next 4 sts, fpdc around next st, bpdc around next 4 sts, fpdc around ea of remaining sts to end of rnd, join with sl st in top of ch 2. (44)

RND 9: fpsc around first fpdc from prev rnd, ch 2 (serves as first fpdc), fpdc around ea of next 17 sts, bpdc around next 11 sts, fpdc around ea of remaining sts to end of rnd, join with sl st in top of ch 2. (44)

RND 10: Repeat Rnd 9.

RND 11: fpsc around first fpdc from prev rnd, ch 2 (serves as first fpdc), fpdc around ea of next 18 sts, bpdc around next 9 sts, fpdc around ea of remaining sts to end of rnd, join with sl st in top of ch 2. (44)

RND 12: fpsc around first fpdc from prev rnd, ch 2 (serves as first fpdc), fpdc around ea of next 19 sts, bpdc around next 7 sts, fpdc around ea of remaining sts to end of rnd, join with sl st in top of ch 2. (44)

RND 13: fpsc around first fpdc from prev rnd, ch 2 (serves as first fpdc), fpdc around ea of next 20 sts, bpdc around next 5 sts, fpdc around ea of remaining sts to end of rnd, join with sl st in top of ch 2. (44)

RND 14: fpsc around first fpdc from prev rnd, ch 2 (serves as first fpdc), fpdc around ea of next 21 sts, bpdc around next 3 sts, fpdc around ea of remaining sts to end of rnd, join with sl st in top of ch 2. (44)

RND 15: fpsc around first fpdc from prev rnd, ch 2 (serves as first fpdc), fpdc around ea of next 22 sts, bpdc around next st, fpdc around ea of remaining sts to end of rnd, join with sl st in top of ch 2. (44)

RND 16: fpsc around first fpdc from prev rnd, ch 2 (serves as first fpdc), fpdc around ea st to end of rnd, join with sl st in top of ch 2. (44)

REPEAT RND 16 until the hat measures approximately 5 to 5.25" (13 cm) from crown to brim (center of the magic ring to the edge of the hat).

CONTINUE with Edging at end of pattern (page 163).

3-6 MONTH EMBOSSED HEART BEANIE

Use "J" (6 mm) hook, or match gauge checkpoint after Rnd 5.

NOTE: *The beginning ch 2 counts as the final dc in each round and is included in the stitch count. In this pattern, a dc following a fpdc will always be made in the top of the same post that was just used for the fpdc.*

RND 1: Magic ring, ch 2 (counts as dc), 15 dc in ring, join with sl st in top of ch 2. (16)

OR ch 2, 16 dc in 2nd ch from hook, join with sl st in first dc. (16)

RND 2: ch 2, *fpdc around ea of next 2 dc, dc in top of same post just used for fpdc*, repeat between *...* to end of rnd, last fpdc will be around ch 2 from prev rnd, beg ch 2 counts as last dc, join with sl st in top of ch 2. (24)

RND 3: ch 2, *fpdc around ea of next 2 fpdc, fpdc around next dc, dc in top of same post just used*, repeat between *...* to end of rnd, last fpdc will be around ch 2 from prev rnd, beg ch 2 counts as last dc, join with sl st in top of ch 2. (32)

RND 4: ch 2, *fpdc around ea of next 3 fpdc, fpdc around next dc, dc in top of same post just used*, repeat between *...* to end of rnd, last fpdc will be around ch 2 from prev rnd, beg ch 2 counts as last dc, join with sl st in top of ch 2. (40)

RND 5: ch 2, *fpdc around ea of next 4 fpdc, fpdc around next dc, dc in top of same post just used*, repeat between *...* to end of rnd, last fpdc will be around ch 2 from prev rnd, beg ch 2 counts as last dc, join with sl st in top of ch 2. (48)

GAUGE CHECKPOINT: *Diameter of the circle should measure approximately 4.5" (11 cm) here.*

NOTE: *The "fpsc and ch 2" at the beginnings of the following rounds creates a stitch that looks like a fpdc. Be sure to crochet the fpsc tightly around the post so it doesn't bulge at the base of the ch 2. It is correct if it looks very similar to a fpdc. Starting the round in this fashion (instead of a standard ch 2) will result in a seam that is almost completely invisible. This fpsc + ch 2 combo counts as the first fpdc of every round from this point.*

RND 6: fpsc around first fpdc from prev rnd, ch 2 (serves as first fpdc), fpdc around ea st to end of rnd, last fpdc will be around beg ch 2 from prev rnd, join with sl st in top of ch 2. (48)

RND 7: fpsc around first fpdc from prev rnd, ch 2 (serves as first fpdc), fpdc around ea of next 20 sts, bpdc around next 2 sts, fpdc around next 3 sts, bpdc around next 2 sts, fpdc around ea of remaining sts to end of rnd, join with sl st in top of ch 2. (48)

RND 8: fpsc around first fpdc from prev rnd, ch 2 (serves as first fpdc), fpdc around ea of next 19 sts, bpdc around next 4 sts, fpdc around next st, bpdc around next 4 sts, fpdc around ea of remaining sts to end of rnd, join with sl st in top of ch 2. (48)

RND 9: fpsc around first fpdc from prev rnd, ch 2 (serves as first fpdc), fpdc around ea of next 18 sts, bpdc around next 11 sts, fpdc around ea of remaining sts to end of rnd, join with sl st in top of ch 2. (48)

RNDS 10-11: Repeat Rnd 9.

RND 12: fpsc around first fpdc from prev rnd, ch 2 (serves as first fpdc), fpdc around ea of next 19 sts, bpdc around next 9 sts, fpdc around ea of remaining sts to end of rnd, join with sl st in top of ch 2. (48)

RND 13: fpsc around first fpdc from prev rnd, ch 2 (serves as first fpdc), fpdc around ea of next 20 sts, bpdc around next 7 sts, fpdc around ea of remaining sts to end of rnd, join with sl st in top of ch 2. (48)

RND 14: fpsc around first fpdc from prev rnd, ch 2 (serves as first fpdc), fpdc around ea of next 21 sts, bpdc around next 5 sts, fpdc around ea of remaining sts to end of rnd, join with sl st in top of ch 2. (48)

RND 15: fpsc around first fpdc from prev rnd, ch 2 (serves as first fpdc), fpdc around ea of next 22 sts, bpdc around next 3 sts, fpdc around ea of remaining sts to end of rnd, join with sl st in top of ch 2. (48)

RND 16: fpsc around first fpdc from prev rnd, ch 2 (serves as first fpdc), fpdc around ea of next 23 sts, bpdc around next st, fpdc around ea of remaining sts to end of rnd, join with sl st in top of ch 2. (48)

RND 17: fpsc around first fpdc from prev rnd, ch 2 (serves as first fpdc), fpdc around ea st to end of rnd, join with sl st in top of ch 2. (48)

REPEAT RND 17 until the hat measures approximately 5.5″ (14 cm) from crown to brim (center of the magic ring to the edge of the hat).

CONTINUE with Edging at end of pattern (page 163).

6-12 MONTH EMBOSSED HEART BEANIE

Use "J" (6 mm) hook, or match gauge checkpoint after Rnd 5.

NOTE: *The beginning ch 2 counts as the final dc in each round and is included in the stitch count. In this pattern, a dc following a fpdc will always be made in the top of the same post that was just used for the fpdc.*

RND 1: Magic ring, ch 2 (counts as dc), 15 dc in ring, join with sl st in top of ch 2. (16)

OR ch 2, 16 dc in 2nd ch from hook, join with sl st in first dc. (16)

RND 2: ch 2, *fpdc around ea of next 2 dc, dc in top of same post just used for fpdc*, repeat between *...* to end of rnd, last fpdc will be around ch 2 from prev rnd, beg ch 2 counts as last dc, join with sl st in top of ch 2. (24)

RND 3: ch 2, *fpdc around ea of next 2 fpdc, fpdc around next dc, dc in top of same post just used*, repeat between *...* to end of rnd, last fpdc will be around ch 2 from prev rnd, beg ch 2 counts as last dc, join with sl st in top of ch 2. (32)

RND 4: ch 2, *fpdc around ea of next 3 fpdc, fpdc around next dc, dc in top of same post just used*, repeat between *...* to end of rnd, last fpdc will be around ch 2 from prev rnd, beg ch 2 counts as last dc, join with sl st in top of ch 2. (40)

RND 5: ch 2, *fpdc around ea of next 4 fpdc, fpdc around next dc, dc in top of same post just used*, repeat between *...* to end of rnd, last fpdc will be around ch 2 from prev rnd, beg ch 2 counts as last dc, join with sl st in top of ch 2. (48)

GAUGE CHECKPOINT: *Diameter of the circle should measure approximately 4.5″ (11 cm) here.*

RND 6: ch 2, *fpdc around ea of next 5 fpdc, fpdc around next dc, dc in top of same post just used*, repeat between *...* to end of rnd, last fpdc will be around ch 2 from prev rnd, beg ch 2 counts as last dc, join with sl st in top of ch 2. (56)

NOTE: *The "fpsc and ch 2" at the beginnings of the following rounds creates a stitch that looks like a fpdc. Be sure to crochet the fpsc tightly around the post so it doesn't bulge at the base of the ch 2. It is correct if it looks very similar to a fpdc. Starting the round in this fashion (instead of a standard ch 2) will result in a seam that is almost completely invisible. This fpsc + ch 2 combo counts as the first fpdc of every round from this point.*

RND 7: fpsc around first fpdc from prev rnd, ch 2 (serves as first fpdc), fpdc around ea st to end of rnd, last fpdc will be around beg ch 2 from prev rnd, join with sl st in top of ch 2. (56)

RND 8: fpsc around first fpdc from prev rnd, ch 2 (serves as first fpdc), fpdc around ea of next 24 sts, bpdc around next 2 sts, fpdc around next 3 sts, bpdc around next 2 sts, fpdc around ea of remaining sts to end of rnd, join with sl st in top of ch 2. (56)

RND 9: fpsc around first fpdc from prev rnd, ch 2 (serves as first fpdc), fpdc around ea of next 23 sts, bpdc around next 4 sts, fpdc around next st, bpdc around next 4 sts, fpdc around ea of remaining sts to end of rnd, join with sl st in top of ch 2. (56)

RND 10: fpsc around first fpdc from prev rnd, ch 2 (serves as first fpdc), fpdc around ea of next 22 sts, bpdc around next 11 sts, fpdc around ea of remaining sts to end of rnd, join with sl st in top of ch 2. (56)

RNDS 11–12: Repeat Rnd 10.

RND 13: fpsc around first fpdc from prev rnd, ch 2 (serves as first fpdc), fpdc around ea of next 23 sts, bpdc around next 9 sts, fpdc around ea of remaining sts to end of rnd, join with sl st in top of ch 2. (56)

RND 14: fpsc around first fpdc from prev rnd, ch 2 (serves as first fpdc), fpdc around ea of next 24 sts, bpdc around next 7 sts, fpdc around ea of remaining sts to end of rnd, join with sl st in top of ch 2. (56)

RND 15: fpsc around first fpdc from prev rnd, ch 2 (serves as first fpdc), fpdc around ea of next 25 sts, bpdc around next 5 sts, fpdc around ea of remaining sts to end of rnd, join with sl st in top of ch 2. (56)

RND 16: fpsc around first fpdc from prev rnd, ch 2 (serves as first fpdc), fpdc around ea of next 26 sts, bpdc around next 3 sts, fpdc around ea of remaining sts to end of rnd, join with sl st in top of ch 2. (56)

RND 17: fpsc around first fpdc from prev rnd, ch 2 (serves as first fpdc), fpdc around ea of next 27 sts, bpdc around next st, fpdc around ea of remaining sts to end of rnd, join with sl st in top of ch 2. (56)

RND 18: fpsc around first fpdc from prev rnd, ch 2 (serves as first fpdc), fpdc around ea st to end of rnd, join with sl st in top of ch 2. (56)

REPEAT RND 18 until the hat measures approximately 6.5″ (17 cm) from crown to brim (center of the magic ring to the edge of the hat).

CONTINUE with Edging at end of pattern (page 163).

TODDLER EMBOSSED HEART BEANIE

Use "J" (6 mm) hook, or match gauge checkpoint after Rnd 5.

NOTE: *The beginning ch 2 counts as the final dc in each round and is included in the stitch count. In this pattern, a dc following a fpdc will always be made in the top of the same post that was just used for the fpdc.*

RND 1: Magic ring, ch 2 (counts as dc), 15 dc in ring, join with sl st in top of ch 2. (16)

OR ch 2, 16 dc in 2nd ch from hook, join with sl st in first dc. (16)

RND 2: ch 2, *fpdc around ea of next 2 dc, dc in top of same post just used for fpdc*, repeat between *...* to end of rnd, last fpdc will be around ch 2 from prev rnd, beg ch 2 counts as last dc, join with sl st in top of ch 2. (24)

RND 3: ch 2, *fpdc around ea of next 2 fpdc, fpdc around next dc, dc in top of same post just used*, repeat between *...* to end of rnd, last fpdc will be around ch 2 from prev rnd, beg ch 2 counts as last dc, join with sl st in top of ch 2. (32)

RND 4: ch 2, *fpdc around ea of next 3 fpdc, fpdc around next dc, dc in top of same post just used*, repeat between *...* to end of rnd, last fpdc will be around ch 2 from prev rnd, beg ch 2 counts as last dc, join with sl st in top of ch 2. (40)

RND 5: ch 2, *fpdc around ea of next 4 fpdc, fpdc around next dc, dc in top of same post just used*, repeat between *...* to end of rnd, last fpdc will be around ch 2 from prev rnd, beg ch 2 counts as last dc, join with sl st in top of ch 2. (48)

> **GAUGE CHECKPOINT:** *Diameter of the circle should measure approximately 4.5" (11 cm) here.*

RND 6: ch 2, *fpdc around ea of next 5 fpdc, fpdc around next dc, dc in top of same post just used*, repeat between *...* to end of rnd, last fpdc will be around ch 2 from prev rnd, beg ch 2 counts as last dc, join with sl st in top of ch 2. (56)

RND 7: ch 2, *fpdc around ea of next 6 fpdc, fpdc around next dc, dc in top of same post just used*, repeat between *...* to end of rnd, last fpdc will be around ch 2 from prev rnd, beg ch 2 counts as last dc, join with sl st in top of ch 2. (64)

> **NOTE:** *The "fpsc and ch 2" at the beginnings of the following rounds creates a stitch that looks like a fpdc. Be sure to crochet the fpsc tightly around the post so it doesn't bulge at the base of the ch 2. It is correct if it looks very similar to a fpdc. Starting the round in this fashion (instead of a standard ch 2) will result in a seam that is almost completely invisible. This fpsc + ch 2 combo counts as the first fpdc of every round from this point.*

RND 8: fpsc around first fpdc from prev rnd, ch 2 (serves as first fpdc), fpdc around ea st to end of rnd, last fpdc will be around beg ch 2 from prev rnd, join with sl st in top of ch 2. (64)

RND 9: fpsc around first fpdc from prev rnd, ch 2 (serves as first fpdc), fpdc around ea of next 27 sts, bpdc around next 3 sts, fpdc around next 3 sts, bpdc around next 3 sts, fpdc around ea of remaining sts to end of rnd, join with sl st in top of ch 2. (64)

RND 10: fpsc around first fpdc from prev rnd, ch 2 (serves as first fpdc), fpdc around ea of next 26 sts, bpdc around next 5 sts, fpdc around next st, bpdc around next 5 sts, fpdc around ea of remaining sts to end of rnd, join with sl st in top of ch 2. (64)

RND 11: fpsc around first fpdc from prev rnd, ch 2 (serves as first fpdc), fpdc around ea of next 25 sts, bpdc around next 13 sts, fpdc around ea of remaining sts to end of rnd, join with sl st in top of ch 2. (64)

RNDS 12–13: Repeat Rnd 11.

RND 14: fpsc around first fpdc from prev rnd, ch 2 (serves as first fpdc), fpdc around ea of next 26 sts, bpdc around next 11 sts, fpdc around ea of remaining sts to end of rnd, join with sl st in top of ch 2. (64)

RND 15: fpsc around first fpdc from prev rnd, ch 2 (serves as first fpdc), fpdc around ea of next 27 sts, bpdc around next 9 sts, fpdc around ea of remaining sts to end of rnd, join with sl st in top of ch 2. (64)

RND 16: fpsc around first fpdc from prev rnd, ch 2 (serves as first fpdc), fpdc around ea of next 28 sts, bpdc around next 7 sts, fpdc around ea of remaining sts to end of rnd, join with sl st in top of ch 2. (64)

RND 17: fpsc around first fpdc from prev rnd, ch 2 (serves as first fpdc), fpdc around ea of next 29 sts, bpdc around next 5 sts, fpdc around ea of remaining sts to end of rnd, join with sl st in top of ch 2. (64)

RND 18: fpsc around first fpdc from prev rnd, ch 2 (serves as first fpdc), fpdc around ea of next 30 sts, bpdc around next 3 sts, fpdc around ea of remaining sts to end of rnd, join with sl st in top of ch 2. (64)

RND 19: fpsc around first fpdc from prev rnd, ch 2 (serves as first fpdc), fpdc around ea of next 31 sts, bpdc around next st, fpdc around ea of remaining sts to end of rnd, join with sl st in top of ch 2. (64)

RND 20: fpsc around first fpdc from prev rnd, ch 2 (serves as first fpdc), fpdc around ea st to end of rnd, join with sl st in top of ch 2. (64)

REPEAT RND 20 until the hat measures approximately 7" (18 cm) from crown to brim (center of the magic ring to the edge of the hat).

CONTINUE with Edging at end of pattern (page 163).

CHILD EMBOSSED HEART BEANIE

Use "J" (6 mm) hook, or match gauge checkpoint after Rnd 5.

NOTE: *The beginning ch 2 counts as the final dc in each round and is included in the stitch count. In this pattern, a dc following a fpdc will always be made in the top of the same post that was just used for the fpdc.*

RND 1: Magic ring, ch 2 (counts as dc), 15 dc in ring, join with sl st in top of ch 2. (16)

OR ch 2, 16 dc in 2nd ch from hook, join with sl st in first dc. (16)

RND 2: ch 2, *fpdc around ea of next 2 dc, dc in top of same post just used for fpdc*, repeat between *...* to end of rnd, last fpdc will be around ch 2 from prev rnd, beg ch 2 counts as last dc, join with sl st in top of ch 2. (24)

RND 3: ch 2, *fpdc around ea of next 2 fpdc, fpdc around next dc, dc in top of same post just used*, repeat between *...* to end of rnd, last fpdc will be around ch 2 from prev rnd, beg ch 2 counts as last dc, join with sl st in top of ch 2. (32)

RND 4: ch 2, *fpdc around ea of next 3 fpdc, fpdc around next dc, dc in top of same post just used*, repeat between *...* to end of rnd, last fpdc will be around ch 2 from prev rnd, beg ch 2 counts as last dc, join with sl st in top of ch 2. (40)

RND 5: ch 2, *fpdc around ea of next 4 fpdc, fpdc around next dc, dc in top of same post just used*, repeat between *...* to end of rnd, last fpdc will be around ch 2 from prev rnd, beg ch 2 counts as last dc, join with sl st in top of ch 2. (48)

GAUGE CHECKPOINT: *Diameter of the circle should measure approximately 4.5" (11 cm) here.*

RND 6: ch 2, *fpdc around ea of next 5 fpdc, fpdc around next dc, dc in top of same post just used*, repeat between *...* to end of rnd, last fpdc will be around ch 2 from prev rnd, beg ch 2 counts as last dc, join with sl st in top of ch 2. (56)

RND 7: ch 2, *fpdc around ea of next 6 fpdc, fpdc around next dc, dc in top of same post just used*, repeat between *...* to end of rnd, last fpdc will be around ch 2 from prev rnd, beg ch 2 counts as last dc, join with sl st in top of ch 2. (64)

RND 8: ch 2, *[fpdc around ea of next 7 fpdc, fpdc around next dc] twice, dc in top of same post just used*, repeat between *...* to end of rnd, last fpdc will be around ch 2 from prev rnd, beg ch 2 counts as last dc, join with sl st in top of ch 2. (68)

RND 9: fpsc around first fpdc from prev rnd, ch 2 (serves as first fpdc), fpdc around ea st to end of rnd, last fpdc will be around beg ch 2 from prev rnd, join with sl st in top of ch 2. (68)

RND 10: fpsc around first fpdc from prev rnd, ch 2 (serves as first fpdc), fpdc around ea of next 29 sts, bpdc around next 3 sts, fpdc around next 5 sts, bpdc around next 3 sts, fpdc around ea of remaining sts to end of rnd, join with sl st in top of ch 2. (68)

RND 11: fpsc around first fpdc from prev rnd, ch 2 (serves as first fpdc), fpdc around ea of next 28 sts, bpdc around next 5 sts, fpdc around next 3 sts, bpdc around next 5 sts, fpdc around ea of remaining sts to end of rnd, join with sl st in top of ch 2. (68)

RND 12: fpsc around first fpdc from prev rnd, ch 2 (serves as first fpdc), fpdc around ea of next 27 sts, bpdc around next 7 sts, fpdc around next st, bpdc around next 7 sts, fpdc around ea of remaining sts to end of rnd, join with sl st in top of ch 2. (68)

RND 13: fpsc around first fpdc from prev rnd, ch 2 (serves as first fpdc), fpdc around ea of next 26 sts, bpdc around next 17 sts, fpdc around ea of remaining sts to end of rnd, join with sl st in top of ch 2. (68)

RNDS 14–15: Repeat Rnd 13.

RND 16: fpsc around first fpdc from prev rnd, ch 2 (serves as first fpdc), fpdc around ea of next 27 sts, bpdc around next 15 sts, fpdc around ea of remaining sts to end of rnd, join with sl st in top of ch 2. (68)

RND 17: fpsc around first fpdc from prev rnd, ch 2 (serves as first fpdc), fpdc around ea of next 28 sts, bpdc around next 13 sts, fpdc around ea of remaining sts to end of rnd, join with sl st in top of ch 2. (68)

RND 18: fpsc around first fpdc from prev rnd, ch 2 (serves as first fpdc), fpdc around ea of next 29 sts, bpdc around next 11 sts, fpdc around ea of remaining sts to end of rnd, join with sl st in top of ch 2. (68)

RND 19: fpsc around first fpdc from prev rnd, ch 2 (serves as first fpdc), fpdc around ea of next 30 sts, bpdc around next 9 sts, fpdc around ea of remaining sts to end of rnd, join with sl st in top of ch 2. (68)

RND 20: fpsc around first fpdc from prev rnd, ch 2 (serves as first fpdc), fpdc around ea of next 31 sts, bpdc around next 7 sts, fpdc around ea of remaining sts to end of rnd, join with sl st in top of ch 2. (68)

RND 21: fpsc around first fpdc from prev rnd, ch 2 (serves as first fpdc), fpdc around ea of next 32 sts, bpdc around next 5 sts, fpdc around ea of remaining sts to end of rnd, join with sl st in top of ch 2. (68)

RND 22: fpsc around first fpdc from prev rnd, ch 2 (serves as first fpdc), fpdc around ea of next 33 sts, bpdc around next 3 sts, fpdc around ea of remaining sts to end of rnd, join with sl st in top of ch 2. (68)

RND 23: fpsc around first fpdc from prev rnd, ch 2 (serves as first fpdc), fpdc around ea of next 34 sts, bpdc around next st, fpdc around ea of remaining sts to end of rnd, join with sl st in top of ch 2. (68)

RND 24: fpsc around first fpdc from prev rnd, ch 2 (serves as first fpdc), fpdc around ea st to end of rnd, join with sl st in top of ch 2. (68)

REPEAT RND 24 until the hat measures approximately 7.5" (19 cm) from crown to brim (center of the magic ring to the edge of the hat).

CONTINUE with Edging at end of pattern (page 163).

TEEN/ADULT EMBOSSED HEART BEANIE

Use "J" (6 mm) hook, or match gauge checkpoint after Rnd 5.

NOTE: *The beginning ch 2 counts as the final dc in each round and is included in the stitch count. In this pattern, a dc following a fpdc will always be made in the top of the same post that was just used for the fpdc.*

RND 1: Magic ring, ch 2 (counts as dc), 15 dc in ring, join with sl st in top of ch 2. (16)

OR ch 2, 16 dc in 2nd ch from hook, join with sl st in first dc. (16)

RND 2: ch 2, *fpdc around ea of next 2 dc, dc in top of same post just used for fpdc*, repeat between *...* to end of rnd, last fpdc will be around ch 2 from prev rnd, beg ch 2 counts as last dc, join with sl st in top of ch 2. (24)

RND 3: ch 2, *fpdc around ea of next 2 fpdc, fpdc around next dc, dc in top of same post just used*, repeat between *...* to end of rnd, last fpdc will be around ch 2 from prev rnd, beg ch 2 counts as last dc, join with sl st in top of ch 2. (32)

RND 4: ch 2, *fpdc around ea of next 3 fpdc, fpdc around next dc, dc in top of same post just used*, repeat between *...* to end of rnd, last fpdc will be around ch 2 from prev rnd, beg ch 2 counts as last dc, join with sl st in top of ch 2. (40)

RND 5: ch 2, *fpdc around ea of next 4 fpdc, fpdc around next dc, dc in top of same post just used*, repeat between *...* to end of rnd, last fpdc will be around ch 2 from prev rnd, beg ch 2 counts as last dc, join with sl st in top of ch 2. (48)

GAUGE CHECKPOINT: *Diameter of the circle should measure approximately 4.5" (11 cm) here.*

RND 6: ch 2, *fpdc around ea of next 5 fpdc, fpdc around next dc, dc in top of same post just used*, repeat between *...* to end of rnd, last fpdc will be around ch 2 from prev rnd, beg ch 2 counts as last dc, join with sl st in top of ch 2. (56)

RND 7: ch 2, *fpdc around ea of next 6 fpdc, fpdc around next dc, dc in top of same post just used*, repeat between *...* to end of rnd, last fpdc will be around ch 2 from prev rnd, beg ch 2 counts as last dc, join with sl st in top of ch 2. (64)

RND 8: ch 2, *fpdc around ea of next 7 fpdc, fpdc around next dc, dc in top of same post just used*, repeat between *...* to end of rnd, last fpdc will be around ch 2 from prev rnd, beg ch 2 counts as last dc, join with sl st in top of ch 2. (72)

NOTE: *The "fpsc and ch 2" at the beginnings of the following rounds creates a stitch that looks like a fpdc. Be sure to crochet the fpsc tightly around the post so it doesn't bulge at the base of the ch 2. It is correct if it looks very similar to a fpdc. Starting the round in this fashion (instead of a standard ch 2) will result in a seam that is almost completely invisible. This fpsc + ch 2 combo counts as the first fpdc of every round from this point.*

RND 9: fpsc around first fpdc from prev rnd, ch 2 (serves as first fpdc), fpdc around ea st to end of rnd, last fpdc will be around beg ch 2 from prev rnd, join with sl st in top of ch 2. (72)

RND 10: fpsc around first fpdc from prev rnd, ch 2 (serves as first fpdc), fpdc around ea of next 31 sts, bpdc around next 3 sts, fpdc around next 5 sts, bpdc around next 3 sts, fpdc around ea of remaining sts to end of rnd, join with sl st in top of ch 2. (72)

RND 11: fpsc around first fpdc from prev rnd, ch 2 (serves as first fpdc), fpdc around ea of next 30 sts, bpdc around next 5 sts, fpdc around next 3 sts, bpdc around next 5 sts, fpdc around ea of remaining sts to end of rnd, join with sl st in top of ch 2. (72)

RND 12: fpsc around first fpdc from prev rnd, ch 2 (serves as first fpdc), fpdc around ea of next 29 sts, bpdc around next 7 sts, fpdc around next st, bpdc around next 7 sts, fpdc around ea of remaining sts to end of rnd, join with sl st in top of ch 2. (72)

RND 13: fpsc around first fpdc from prev rnd, ch 2 (serves as first fpdc), fpdc around ea of next 28 sts, bpdc around next 17 sts, fpdc around ea of remaining sts to end of rnd, join with sl st in top of ch 2. (72)

RNDS 14–16: Repeat Rnd 13.

RND 17: fpsc around first fpdc from prev rnd, ch 2 (serves as first fpdc), fpdc around ea of next 29 sts, bpdc around next 15 sts, fpdc around ea of remaining sts to end of rnd, join with sl st in top of ch 2. (72)

RND 18: fpsc around first fpdc from prev rnd, ch 2 (serves as first fpdc), fpdc around ea of next 30 sts, bpdc around next 13 sts, fpdc around ea of remaining sts to end of rnd, join with sl st in top of ch 2. (72)

RND 19: fpsc around first fpdc from prev rnd, ch 2 (serves as first fpdc), fpdc around ea of next 31 sts, bpdc around next 11 sts, fpdc around ea of remaining sts to end of rnd, join with sl st in top of ch 2. (72)

RND 20: fpsc around first fpdc from prev rnd, ch 2 (serves as first fpdc), fpdc around ea of next 32 sts, bpdc around next 9 sts, fpdc around ea of remaining sts to end of rnd, join with sl st in top of ch 2. (72)

RND 21: fpsc around first fpdc from prev rnd, ch 2 (serves as first fpdc), fpdc around ea of next 33 sts, bpdc around next 7 sts, fpdc around ea of remaining sts to end of rnd, join with sl st in top of ch 2. (72)

RND 22: fpsc around first fpdc from prev rnd, ch 2 (serves as first fpdc), fpdc around ea of next 34 sts, bpdc around next 5 sts, fpdc around ea of remaining sts to end of rnd, join with sl st in top of ch 2. (72)

RND 23: fpsc around first fpdc from prev rnd, ch 2 (serves as first fpdc), fpdc around ea of next 35 sts, bpdc around next 3 sts, fpdc around ea of remaining sts to end of rnd, join with sl st in top of ch 2. (72)

RND 24: fpsc around first fpdc from prev rnd, ch 2 (serves as first fpdc), fpdc around ea of next 36 sts, bpdc around next st, fpdc around ea of remaining sts to end of rnd, join with sl st in top of ch 2. (72)

RND 25: fpsc around first fpdc from prev rnd, ch 2 (serves as first fpdc), fpdc around ea st to end of rnd, join with sl st in top of ch 2. (72)

REPEAT RND 25 until the hat measures approximately 7.5 to 8″ (19 to 20 cm) from crown to brim (center of the magic ring to the edge of the hat).

CONTINUE with Edging at end of pattern (page 163).

LARGE ADULT EMBOSSED HEART BEANIE

Use "J" (6 mm) hook, or match gauge checkpoint after Rnd 5.

NOTE: *The beginning ch 2 counts as the final dc in each round and is included in the stitch count. In this pattern, a dc following a fpdc will always be made in the top of the same post that was just used for the fpdc.*

RND 1: Magic ring, ch 2 (counts as dc), 15 dc in ring, join with sl st in top of ch 2. (16)

OR ch 2, 16 dc in 2nd ch from hook, join with sl st in first dc. (16)

RND 2: ch 2, *fpdc around ea of next 2 dc, dc in top of same post just used for fpdc*, repeat between *...* to end of rnd, last fpdc will be around ch 2 from prev rnd, beg ch 2 counts as last dc, join with sl st in top of ch 2. (24)

RND 3: ch 2, *fpdc around ea of next 2 fpdc, fpdc around next dc, dc in top of same post just used*, repeat between *...* to end of rnd, last fpdc will be around ch 2 from prev rnd, beg ch 2 counts as last dc, join with sl st in top of ch 2. (32)

RND 4: ch 2, *fpdc around ea of next 3 fpdc, fpdc around next dc, dc in top of same post just used*, repeat between *...* to end of rnd, last fpdc will be around ch 2 from prev rnd, beg ch 2 counts as last dc, join with sl st in top of ch 2. (40)

RND 5: ch 2, *fpdc around ea of next 4 fpdc, fpdc around next dc, dc in top of same post just used*, repeat between *...* to end of rnd, last fpdc will be around ch 2 from prev rnd, beg ch 2 counts as last dc, join with sl st in top of ch 2. (48)

GAUGE CHECKPOINT: *Diameter of the circle should measure approximately 4.5" (11 cm) here.*

RND 6: ch 2, *fpdc around ea of next 5 fpdc, fpdc around next dc, dc in top of same post just used*, repeat between *...* to end of rnd, last fpdc will be around ch 2 from prev rnd, beg ch 2 counts as last dc, join with sl st in top of ch 2. (56)

RND 7: ch 2, *fpdc around ea of next 6 fpdc, fpdc around next dc, dc in top of same post just used*, repeat between *...* to end of rnd, last fpdc will be around ch 2 from prev rnd, beg ch 2 counts as last dc, join with sl st in top of ch 2. (64)

RND 8: ch 2, *fpdc around ea of next 7 fpdc, fpdc around next dc, dc in top of same post just used*, repeat between *...* to end of rnd, last fpdc will be around ch 2 from prev rnd, beg ch 2 counts as last dc, join with sl st in top of ch 2. (72)

RND 9: ch 2, *fpdc around ea of next 8 fpdc, fpdc around next dc, dc in top of same post just used*, repeat between *...* to end of rnd, last fpdc will be around ch 2 from prev rnd, beg ch 2 counts as last dc, join with sl st in top of ch 2. (80)

NOTE: *The "fpsc and ch 2" at the beginnings of the following rounds creates a stitch that looks like a fpdc. Be sure to crochet the fpsc tightly around the post so it doesn't bulge at the base of the ch 2. It is correct if it looks very similar to a fpdc. Starting the round in this fashion (instead of a standard ch 2) will result in a seam that is almost completely invisible. This fpsc + ch 2 combo counts as the first fpdc of every round from this point.*

RND 10: fpsc around first fpdc from prev rnd, ch 2 (serves as first fpdc), fpdc around ea st to end of rnd, last fpdc will be around beg ch 2 from prev rnd, join with sl st in top of ch 2. (80)

RND 11: fpsc around first fpdc from prev rnd, ch 2 (serves as first fpdc), fpdc around ea of next 34 sts, bpdc around next 4 sts, fpdc around next 5 sts, bpdc around next 4 sts, fpdc around ea of remaining sts to end of rnd, join with sl st in top of ch 2. (80)

RND 12: fpsc around first fpdc from prev rnd, ch 2 (serves as first fpdc), fpdc around ea of next 33 sts, bpdc around next 6 sts, fpdc around next 3 sts, bpdc around next 6 sts, fpdc around ea of remaining sts to end of rnd, join with sl st in top of ch 2. (80)

RND 13: fpsc around first fpdc from prev rnd, ch 2 (serves as first fpdc), fpdc around ea of next 32 sts, bpdc around next 8 sts, fpdc around next st, bpdc around next 8 sts, fpdc around ea of remaining sts to end of rnd, join with sl st in top of ch 2. (80)

RND 14: fpsc around first fpdc from prev rnd, ch 2 (serves as first fpdc), fpdc around ea of next 31 sts, bpdc around next 19 sts, fpdc around ea of remaining sts to end of rnd, join with sl st in top of ch 2. (80)

RNDS 15–17: Repeat Rnd 14.

RND 18: fpsc around first fpdc from prev rnd, ch 2 (serves as first fpdc), fpdc around ea of next 32 sts, bpdc around next 17 sts, fpdc around ea of remaining sts to end of rnd, join with sl st in top of ch 2. (80)

RND 19: fpsc around first fpdc from prev rnd, ch 2 (serves as first fpdc), fpdc around ea of next 33 sts, bpdc around next 15 sts, fpdc around ea of remaining sts to end of rnd, join with sl st in top of ch 2. (80)

RND 20: fpsc around first fpdc from prev rnd, ch 2 (serves as first fpdc), fpdc around ea of next 34 sts, bpdc around next 13 sts, fpdc around ea of remaining sts to end of rnd, join with sl st in top of ch 2. (80)

RND 21: fpsc around first fpdc from prev rnd, ch 2 (serves as first fpdc), fpdc around ea of next 35 sts, bpdc around next 11 sts, fpdc around ea of remaining sts to end of rnd, join with sl st in top of ch 2. (80)

RND 22: fpsc around first fpdc from prev rnd, ch 2 (serves as first fpdc), fpdc around ea of next 36 sts, bpdc around next 9 sts, fpdc around ea of remaining sts to end of rnd, join with sl st in top of ch 2. (80)

RND 23: fpsc around first fpdc from prev rnd, ch 2 (serves as first fpdc), fpdc around ea of next 37 sts, bpdc around next 7 sts, fpdc around ea of remaining sts to end of rnd, join with sl st in top of ch 2. (80)

RND 24: fpsc around first fpdc from prev rnd, ch 2 (serves as first fpdc), fpdc around ea of next 38 sts, bpdc around next 5 sts, fpdc around ea of remaining sts to end of rnd, join with sl st in top of ch 2. (80)

RND 25: fpsc around first fpdc from prev rnd, ch 2 (serves as first fpdc), fpdc around ea of next 39 sts, bpdc around next 3 sts, fpdc around ea of remaining sts to end of rnd, join with sl st in top of ch 2. (80)

RND 26: fpsc around first fpdc from prev rnd, ch 2 (serves as first fpdc), fpdc around ea of next 40 sts, bpdc around next st, fpdc around ea of remaining sts to end of rnd, join with sl st in top of ch 2. (80)

RND 27: fpsc around first fpdc from prev rnd, ch 2 (serves as first fpdc), fpdc around ea st to end of rnd, join with sl st in top of ch 2. (80)

REPEAT RND 27 until the hat measures approximately 8.5″ (22 cm) from crown to brim (center of the magic ring to the edge of the hat).

EDGING (ALL SIZES)

Ch 1, sc in same st and ea st to end of rnd, fasten off with invisible join (or sl st) in first sc. (40, 48, 56, 64, 68, 72, 80) Weave in ends.

NOTE: *Measure after completing the Edging. If the circumference does not fall within the large end of the size range on page 150, redo with a smaller hook.*

MAKING WAVES BEANIE

One of my favorite textured beanie patterns of all time, this hat is one that I just love to make over and over. Fabulously squishy, the unique texture will keep you entertained as you are crocheting this one. The unisex design also looks great on every member of the family. Pair it up with the matching Making Waves Baby Cocoon (page 89) for the little ones.

SKILL LEVEL: ◖■▮▯◗ **INTERMEDIATE**

MATERIALS

TOOLS	Stitch marker, measuring tape, yarn needle
YARN	5 oz (142 g) or less of #4 worsted weight yarn
GAUGE	Gauge checkpoint given in pattern for each size after Rnd 4
HOOK SIZE	"J" (6 mm) crochet hook or to match gauge checkpoint

BEANIE SIZE CHART

0-3 MONTHS	12-14" (30-36 cm) circumference, approximately 5.5" (14 cm) from crown to brim
3-6 MONTHS	14-16" (36-41 cm) circumference, approximately 5.5-6" (14-15 cm) from crown to brim
6-12 MONTHS	16-18" (41-46 cm) circumference, approximately 6.5-7" (17-18 cm) from crown to brim
TODDLER/CHILD	18-20" (46-51 cm) circumference, approximately 7.5-8" (19-20 cm) from crown to brim
TEEN/ADULT	20-22" (51-56 cm) circumference, approximately 8-8.5" (20-22 cm) from crown to brim
LARGE ADULT	22-24" (56-61 cm) circumference, approximately 8.5-9" (22-23 cm) from crown to brim

ABBREVIATIONS USED

ST(S)	stitch(es)
CH	chain stitch
SC	single crochet
HDC	half double crochet
DC	double crochet
FPSC	front post single crochet
FPDC	front post double crochet
HDC2TOG	half double crochet 2 stitches together
SL ST	slip stitch
RND(S)	round(s)
SK	skip
SP	space
EA	each
BEG	beginning
PREV	previous
YO	Yarn Over

SPECIAL STITCHES DEFINITIONS

FRONT POST SINGLE CROCHET (FPSC): Insert hook from the front side of the work (right to left) under the post of the indicated stitch, YO and pull up a loop, YO and draw through 2 loops.

FRONT POST DOUBLE CROCHET (FPDC): Working from the front side of the work, YO and insert the hook from right to left under the post of the double crochet indicated from the previous round, YO and pull up a loop, [YO and draw through 2 loops] twice.

HALF DOUBLE CROCHET IN 3RD LOOP: There are 2 main loops in a stitch—the "V" on the top—referred to as the front and back loops. With a hdc, the YO (before the hook is inserted into the next stitch) creates a 3rd loop on the back side of the stitch. In this pattern, all hdc in the 3rd loop will be worked in the BACK 3rd loop. The only difference is where the stitch is placed, not how it is worked. (See hdc2tog definition.)

HALF DOUBLE CROCHET 2 STITCHES TOGETHER (HDC2TOG): [YO, insert hook in next stitch, YO and pull up a loop] twice, YO and draw through all 5 loops on hook. (In this pattern, this stitch is always worked in the 3rd loop.)

FRONT POST DOUBLE CROCHET DECREASE (FPDC DECREASE): Work 1 fpdc around both posts of indicated stitches from previous round at the same time.

SPECIAL TECHNIQUES

USING THE BEG "CH 2" AS THE FINAL DC IN THE ROUND: If there is a "ch 2" at the beg of a round, it will stand in as the last dc in the round. This avoids having a noticeable seam. If the repeat ends on a dc at the end of the round, don't make that last dc because the "ch 2" is there and will look like a dc when you join to the top of it. If the repeat ends with 2 dc worked in one stitch, make the first dc in the same stitch as the "ch 2." This will look almost exactly the same as working 2 dc in one stitch.

JOINING IN THE "TOP" OF THE CH 2: If there is any confusion on where to join at the end of each round, use the following method: Complete the first ch 2 of the round, then add a stitch marker around the loop that is on the hook. At the end of the round, this is the stitch that will be used for joining.

0–3 MONTHS MAKING WAVES BEANIE

Use "J" (6 mm) hook, or match gauge checkpoint after Rnd 4.

NOTE: *The beginning ch 2 counts as the final dc or hdc in each round and is included in the stitch count for the first 2 rounds.*

RND 1: Magic ring, ch 2 (counts as dc), 9 dc in ring, join with sl st in top of ch 2. (10)

OR ch 2, 10 dc in 2nd ch from hook, join with sl st in first dc. (10)

RND 2: ch 2, *fpdc around ea of next 2 dc, dc in top of same post just used for fpdc*, repeat between *...* to end of rnd, last fpdc will be around ch 2 from prev rnd, beg ch 2 counts as last dc, join with sl st in top of ch 2. (15)

NOTE: *From this point on, the first fpdc of EVERY round is worked as follows: fpsc around post of first fpdc from prev rnd, ch 2. The "fpsc + ch 2" creates a stitch that looks like a fpdc. Crochet the fpsc tightly around the post so it doesn't bulge at the base of the ch 2. It is correct if it looks very similar to a fpdc. Starting the round in this fashion (instead of a standard ch 2) will result in a seam that is almost completely invisible. This fpsc + ch 2 combo counts as the first fpdc of every round from this point. All hdc in "3rd loop" are worked in the back 3rd loop (see Special Stitches Definitions, page 166).*

RND 3: *fpdc around ea of next 2 fpdc, fpdc around next dc, hdc in top of same post just used*, repeat between *...* to end of rnd, join with sl st in top of ch 2. (20)

RND 4: *fpdc around ea of next 3 fpdc, 2 hdc in 3rd loop of next hdc*, repeat between *...* to end of rnd, join with sl st in top of ch 2. (25)

GAUGE CHECKPOINT: *Diameter of the circle should measure approximately 3" (8 cm) here.*

RND 5: *fpdc around next fpdc, 2 fpdc around next fpdc, fpdc around next fpdc, hdc in 3rd loop of next hdc, 2 hdc in 3rd loop of next hdc*, repeat between *...* to end of rnd, join with sl st in top of ch 2. (35)

RND 6: *fpdc around next 2 fpdc, 2 dc in top of same post just used (between 2nd and 3rd fpdc of prev round), fpdc around next 2 fpdc, hdc in 3rd loop of next hdc, hdc2tog (3rd loop) over next 2 hdc*, repeat between *...* to end of rnd, join with sl st in top of ch 2. (40)

RND 7: *fpdc around next 2 fpdc, fpdc around next dc, hdc in top of same post just used (between 2 dc of prev round), fpdc around next dc, fpdc around next 2 fpdc, hdc2tog (3rd loop) over next 2 hdc*, repeat between *...* to end of rnd, join with sl st in top of ch 2. (40)

RND 8: *fpdc around next 3 fpdc, 2 hdc (3rd loop) in next hdc, fpdc around next 3 fpdc, sk next hdc*, repeat between *...* to end of rnd, join with sl st in top of ch 2. (40)

NOTE: *A fpdc decrease is worked as follows: Work* **one** *fpdc around* **both** *middle stitches of the 6 fpdc from prev round at the same time. This method will leave less of a hole than a regular fpdc2tog. (The first time Rnd 9 is worked, the fpdc [fpsc + ch 2] decrease of the next round is worked around both the LAST fpdc [prev rnd] and the FIRST fpdc [prev rnd] at the same time. When repeated, just use the middle 2 fpdc.)*

RND 9: *fpdc decrease, fpdc around next 2 fpdc, hdc (3rd loop) in next hdc, 2 hdc (3rd loop) in next hdc, fpdc around next 2 fpdc*, repeat between *...* to end of rnd, join with sl st in top of ch 2. (40)

RND 10: *2 fpdc around next fpdc, fpdc around next 2 fpdc, hdc (3rd loop) next hdc, hdc2tog (3rd loop) over next 2 hdc, fpdc around next 2 fpdc*, repeat to end of rnd, join with sl st in top of ch 2. (40)

RND 11: *fpdc around next fpdc, hdc in top of post just used, fpdc around next 3 fpdc, hdc2tog (3rd loop) over next 2 hdc, fpdc around next 2 fpdc*, repeat to end of rnd, join with sl st in top of ch 2. (40)

RND 12: *fpdc around next fpdc, 2 hdc (3rd loop) in next hdc, fpdc around next 3 fpdc, sk next hdc, fpdc around next 2 fpdc*, repeat to end of rnd, join with sl st in top of ch 2. (40)

RND 13: *fpdc around next fpdc, hdc (3rd loop) in next hdc, 2 hdc (3rd loop) in next hdc, fpdc around next 2 fpdc, fpdc decrease, fpdc around next fpdc*, repeat to end of rnd, join with sl st in top of ch 2. (40)

RND 14: *fpdc around next fpdc, hdc (3rd loop) in next hdc, hdc2tog (3rd loop) over next 2 hdc, fpdc around next 2 fpdc, 2 fpdc around next fpdc, fpdc around next fpdc*, repeat to end of rnd, join with sl st in top of ch 2. (40)

RND 15: *fpdc around next fpdc, hdc2tog (3rd loop) over next 2 hdc, fpdc around next 3 fpdc, hdc in top of same post just used, fpdc around next 2 fpdc*, repeat to end of rnd, join with sl st in top of ch 2. (40)

RND 16: *fpdc around next fpdc, sk next hdc, fpdc around next 3 fpdc, 2 hdc (3rd loop) in next hdc, fpdc around next 2 fpdc*, repeat to end of rnd, join with sl st in top of ch 2. (40)

REPEAT RNDS 9–16 (Read Note before Rnd 9) until the beanie reaches approximately 5.5" (14 cm) from top to bottom. Stop at any point when the beanie has reached this measurement.

> **NOTE:** *Measure the circumference after completing the Edging (before fastening off). If it's not within the size range listed in the size chart (page 165), adjust the hook size and redo last rnd.*

EDGING: ch 1, sc in same st as ch 1 and ea st to end of rnd, fasten off with invisible join (or sl st) in first st. (40) Weave in ends.

3-6 MONTHS MAKING WAVES BEANIE

Use "J" (6 mm) hook, or match gauge checkpoint after Rnd 4.

> **NOTE:** *The beginning ch 2 counts as the final dc or hdc in each round and is included in the stitch count for the first 2 rounds.*

RND 1: Magic ring, ch 2 (counts as dc), 11 dc in ring, join with sl st in top of ch 2. (12)

OR ch 2, 12 dc in 2nd ch from hook, join with sl st in first dc. (12)

RND 2: ch 2, *fpdc around ea of next 2 dc, dc in top of same post just used for fpdc*, repeat between *...* to end of rnd, last fpdc will be around ch 2 from prev rnd, beg ch 2 counts as last dc, join with sl st in top of ch 2. (18)

> **NOTE:** *From this point on, the first fpdc of EVERY round is worked as follows: fpsc around post of first fpdc from prev rnd, ch 2. The "fpsc + ch 2" creates a stitch that looks like a fpdc. Crochet the fpsc tightly around the post so it doesn't bulge at the base of the ch 2. It is correct if it looks very similar to a fpdc. Starting the round in this fashion (instead of a standard ch 2) will result in a seam that is almost completely invisible. This fpsc + ch 2 combo counts as the first fpdc of every round from this point. All hdc in "3rd loop" are worked in the back 3rd loop (see Special Stitches Definitions, page 166).*

RND 3: *fpdc around ea of next 2 fpdc, fpdc around next dc, hdc in top of same post just used*, repeat between *...* to end of rnd, join with sl st in top of ch 2. (24)

RND 4: *fpdc around ea of next 3 fpdc, 2 hdc in 3rd loop of next hdc*, repeat between *...* to end of rnd, join with sl st in top of ch 2. (30)

> **GAUGE CHECKPOINT:** *Diameter of the circle should measure approximately 3.5" (9 cm) here.*

RND 5: *fpdc around next fpdc, 2 fpdc around next fpdc, fpdc around next fpdc, hdc in 3rd loop of next hdc, 2 hdc in 3rd loop of next hdc*, repeat between *...* to end of rnd, join with sl st in top of ch 2. (42)

RND 6: *fpdc around next 2 fpdc, 2 dc in top of same post just used (between 2nd and 3rd fpdc of prev round), fpdc around next 2 fpdc, hdc in 3rd loop of next hdc, hdc2tog (3rd loop) over next 2 hdc*, repeat between *...* to end of rnd, join with sl st in top of ch 2. (48)

RND 7: *fpdc around next 2 fpdc, fpdc around next dc, hdc in top of same post just used (between 2 dc of prev round), fpdc around next dc, fpdc around next 2 fpdc, hdc2tog (3rd loop) over next 2 hdc*, repeat between *...* to end of rnd, join with sl st in top of ch 2. (48)

RND 8: *fpdc around next 3 fpdc, 2 hdc (3rd loop) in next hdc, fpdc around next 3 fpdc, sk next hdc*, repeat between *...* to end of rnd, join with sl st in top of ch 2. (48)

> **NOTE:** A fpdc decrease is worked as follows: Work **one** fpdc around **both** middle stitches of the 6 fpdc from prev round at the same time. This method will leave less of a hole than a regular fpdc2tog. (The first time Rnd 9 is worked, the fpdc [fpsc + ch 2] decrease of the next round is worked around both the LAST fpdc [prev rnd] and the FIRST fpdc [prev rnd] at the same time. When repeated, just use the middle 2 fpdc.)

RND 9: *fpdc decrease, fpdc around next 2 fpdc, hdc (3rd loop) in next hdc, 2 hdc (3rd loop) in next hdc, fpdc around next 2 fpdc*, repeat between *...* to end of rnd, join with sl st in top of ch 2. (48)

RND 10: *2 fpdc around next fpdc, fpdc around next 2 fpdc, hdc (3rd loop) next hdc, hdc2tog (3rd loop) over next 2 hdc, fpdc around next 2 fpdc*, repeat to end of rnd, join with sl st in top of ch 2. (48)

RND 11: *fpdc around next fpdc, hdc in top of post just used, fpdc around next 3 fpdc, hdc2tog (3rd loop) over next 2 hdc, fpdc around next 2 fpdc*, repeat to end of rnd, join with sl st in top of ch 2. (48)

RND 12: *fpdc around next fpdc, 2 hdc (3rd loop) in next hdc, fpdc around next 3 fpdc, sk next hdc, fpdc around next 2 fpdc*, repeat to end of rnd, join with sl st in top of ch 2. (48)

RND 13: *fpdc around next fpdc, hdc (3rd loop) in next hdc, 2 hdc (3rd loop) in next hdc, fpdc around next 2 fpdc, fpdc decrease, fpdc around next fpdc*, repeat to end of rnd, join with sl st in top of ch 2. (48)

RND 14: *fpdc around next fpdc, hdc (3rd loop) in next hdc, hdc2tog (3rd loop) over next 2 hdc, fpdc around next 2 fpdc, 2 fpdc around next fpdc, fpdc around next fpdc*, repeat to end of rnd, join with sl st in top of ch 2. (48)

RND 15: *fpdc around next fpdc, hdc2tog (3rd loop) over next 2 hdc, fpdc around next 3 fpdc, hdc in top of same post just used, fpdc around next 2 fpdc*, repeat to end of rnd, join with sl st in top of ch 2. (48)

RND 16: *fpdc around next fpdc, sk next hdc, fpdc around next 3 fpdc, 2 hdc (3rd loop) in next hdc, fpdc around next 2 fpdc*, repeat to end of rnd, join with sl st in top of ch 2. (48)

REPEAT RNDS 9–16 (Read Note before Rnd 9) until the beanie reaches approximately 5.5 to 6″ (14 to 15 cm) from top to bottom. Stop at any point when the beanie has reached this measurement.

> **NOTE:** Measure the circumference after completing the Edging (before fastening off). If it's not within size range listed in the size chart (page 165), adjust the hook size and redo last rnd.

EDGING: ch 1, sc in same st as ch 1 and ea st to end of rnd, fasten off with invisible join (or sl st) in first st. (48) Weave in ends.

6-12 MONTHS MAKING WAVES BEANIE

Use "J" (6 mm) hook, or match gauge checkpoint after Rnd 4.

> **NOTE:** The beginning ch 2 counts as the final dc or hdc in each round and is included in the stitch count for the first 2 rounds.

RND 1: Magic ring, ch 2 (counts as dc), 13 dc in ring, join with sl st in top of ch 2. (14)

OR ch 2, 14 dc in 2nd ch from hook, join with sl st in first dc. (14)

RND 2: ch 2, *fpdc around ea of next 2 dc, dc in top of same post just used for fpdc*, repeat between *...* to end of rnd, last fpdc will be around ch 2 from prev rnd, beg ch 2 counts as last dc, join with sl st in top of ch 2. (21)

> **NOTE:** *From this point on, the first fpdc of EVERY round is worked as follows: fpsc around post of first fpdc from prev rnd, ch 2. The "fpsc + ch 2" creates a stitch that looks like a fpdc. Crochet the fpsc tightly around the post so it doesn't bulge at the base of the ch 2. It is correct if it looks very similar to a fpdc. Starting the round in this fashion (instead of a standard ch 2) will result in a seam that is almost completely invisible. This fpsc + ch 2 combo counts as the first fpdc of every round from this point. All hdc in "3rd loop" are worked in the back 3rd loop (see Special Stitches Definitions, page 166).*

RND 3: *fpdc around ea of next 2 fpdc, fpdc around next dc, hdc in top of same post just used*, repeat between *...* to end of rnd, join with sl st in top of ch 2. (28)

RND 4: *fpdc around ea of next 3 fpdc, 2 hdc in 3rd loop of next hdc*, repeat between *...* to end of rnd, join with sl st in top of ch 2. (35)

> **GAUGE CHECKPOINT:** *Diameter of the circle should measure approximately 3.75 to 4" (9 to 10 cm) here.*

RND 5: *fpdc around next fpdc, 2 fpdc around next fpdc, fpdc around next fpdc, hdc in 3rd loop of next hdc, 2 hdc in 3rd loop of next hdc*, repeat between *...* to end of rnd, join with sl st in top of ch 2. (49)

RND 6: *fpdc around next 2 fpdc, 2 dc in top of same post just used (between 2nd and 3rd fpdc of prev round), fpdc around next 2 fpdc, hdc in 3rd loop of next hdc, hdc2tog (3rd loop) over next 2 hdc*, repeat between *...* to end of rnd, join with sl st in top of ch 2. (56)

RND 7: *fpdc around next 2 fpdc, fpdc around next dc, hdc in top of same post just used (between 2 dc of prev round), fpdc around next dc, fpdc around next 2 fpdc, hdc2tog (3rd loop) over next 2 hdc*, repeat between *...* to end of rnd, join with sl st in top of ch 2. (56)

RND 8: *fpdc around next 3 fpdc, 2 hdc (3rd loop) in next hdc, fpdc around next 3 fpdc, sk next hdc*, repeat between *...* to end of rnd, join with sl st in top of ch 2. (56)

> **NOTE:** *A fpdc decrease is worked as follows: Work **one** fpdc around **both** middle stitches of the 6 fpdc from prev round at the same time. This method will leave less of a hole than a regular fpdc2tog. (The first time Rnd 9 is worked, the fpdc [fpsc + ch 2] decrease of the next round is worked around both the LAST fpdc [prev rnd] and the FIRST fpdc [prev rnd] at the same time. When repeated, just use the middle 2 fpdc.)*

RND 9: *fpdc decrease, fpdc around next 2 fpdc, hdc (3rd loop) in next hdc, 2 hdc (3rd loop) in next hdc, fpdc around next 2 fpdc*, repeat between *...* to end of rnd, join with sl st in top of ch 2. (56)

RND 10: *2 fpdc around next fpdc, fpdc around next 2 fpdc, hdc (3rd loop) next hdc, hdc2tog (3rd loop) over next 2 hdc, fpdc around next 2 fpdc*, repeat to end of rnd, join with sl st in top of ch 2. (56)

RND 11: *fpdc around next fpdc, hdc in top of post just used, fpdc around next 3 fpdc, hdc2tog (3rd loop) over next 2 hdc, fpdc around next 2 fpdc*, repeat to end of rnd, join with sl st in top of ch 2. (56)

RND 12: *fpdc around next fpdc, 2 hdc (3rd loop) in next hdc, fpdc around next 3 fpdc, sk next hdc, fpdc around next 2 fpdc*, repeat to end of rnd, join with sl st in top of ch 2. (56)

RND 13: *fpdc around next fpdc, hdc (3rd loop) in next hdc, 2 hdc (3rd loop) in next hdc, fpdc around next 2 fpdc, fpdc decrease, fpdc around next fpdc*, repeat to end of rnd, join with sl st in top of ch 2. (56)

RND 14: *fpdc around next fpdc, hdc (3rd loop) in next hdc, hdc2tog (3rd loop) over next 2 hdc, fpdc around next 2 fpdc, 2 fpdc around next fpdc, fpdc around next fpdc*, repeat to end of rnd, join with sl st in top of ch 2. (56)

RND 15: *fpdc around next fpdc, hdc2tog (3rd loop) over next 2 hdc, fpdc around next 3 fpdc, hdc in top of same post just used, fpdc around next 2 fpdc*, repeat to end of rnd, join with sl st in top of ch 2. (56)

RND 16: *fpdc around next fpdc, sk next hdc, fpdc around next 3 fpdc, 2 hdc (3rd loop) in next hdc, fpdc around next 2 fpdc*, repeat to end of rnd, join with sl st in top of ch 2. (56)

REPEAT RNDS 9–16 (Read Note before Rnd 9) until the beanie reaches approximately 6.5 to 7" (17 to 18 cm) from top to bottom. Stop at any point when beanie has reached this measurement.

> **NOTE:** *Measure the circumference after completing the Edging (before fastening off). If it's not within the size range listed in the size chart (page 165), adjust the hook size and redo last rnd.*

EDGING: ch 1, sc in same st as ch 1 and ea st to end of rnd, fasten off with invisible join (or sl st) in first st. (56) Weave in ends.

TODDLER/CHILD MAKING WAVES BEANIE

Use "J" (6 mm) hook, or match gauge checkpoint after Rnd 4.

> **NOTE:** *The beginning ch 2 counts as the final dc or hdc in each round and is included in the stitch count for the first 3 rounds.*

RND 1: Magic ring, ch 2 (counts as dc), 7 dc in ring, join with sl st in top of ch 2. (8)

OR ch 2, 8 dc in 2nd ch from hook, join with sl st in first dc. (8)

RND 2: ch 2, *fpdc around next dc, dc in top of same post just used for fpdc*, repeat between *...* to end of rnd, last fpdc will be around ch 2 from prev rnd, beg ch 2 counts as last dc, join with sl st in top of ch 2. (16)

RND 3: ch 2, *fpdc around next fpdc, fpdc around next dc, dc in top of same post just used*, repeat between *...* to end of rnd, last fpdc will be around ch 2 from prev rnd, beg ch 2 counts as last dc, join with sl st in top of ch 2. (24)

> **NOTE:** *From this point on, the first fpdc of EVERY round is worked as follows: fpsc around post of first fpdc from prev rnd, ch 2. The "fpsc + ch 2" creates a stitch that looks like a fpdc. Crochet the fpsc tightly around the post so it doesn't bulge at the base of the ch 2. It is correct if it looks very similar to a fpdc. Starting the round in this fashion (instead of a standard ch 2) will result in a seam that is almost completely invisible. This fpsc + ch 2 combo counts as the first fpdc of every round from this point. All hdc in "3rd loop" are worked in the back 3rd loop (see Special Stitches Definitions, page 166).*

RND 4: *fpdc around ea of next 2 fpdc, fpdc around next dc, hdc in top of same post just used*, repeat between *...* to end of rnd, join with sl st in top of ch 2. (32)

> **GAUGE CHECKPOINT:** *Diameter of circle should measure approximately 3.25" (8 cm) here.*

RND 5: *fpdc around ea of next 3 fpdc, 2 hdc in 3rd loop of next hdc*, repeat between *...* to end of rnd, join with sl st in top of ch 2. (40)

RND 6: *fpdc around next fpdc, 2 fpdc around next fpdc, fpdc around next fpdc, hdc in 3rd loop of next hdc, 2 hdc in 3rd loop of next hdc*, repeat between *...* to end of rnd, join with sl st in top of ch 2. (56)

RND 7: *fpdc around next 2 fpdc, 2 dc in top of same post just used (between 2nd and 3rd fpdc of prev round), fpdc around next 2 fpdc, hdc in 3rd loop of next hdc, hdc2tog (3rd loop) over next 2 hdc*, repeat between *...* to end of rnd, join with sl st in top of ch 2. (64)

RND 8: *fpdc around next 2 fpdc, fpdc around next dc, hdc in top of same post just used (between 2 dc of prev round), fpdc around next dc, fpdc around next 2 fpdc, hdc2tog (3rd loop) over next 2 hdc*, repeat between *...* to end of rnd, join with sl st in top of ch 2. (64)

RND 9: *fpdc around next 3 fpdc, 2 hdc (3rd loop) in next hdc, fpdc around next 3 fpdc, sk next hdc*, repeat between *...* to end of rnd, join with sl st in top of ch 2. (64)

> **NOTE:** *A fpdc decrease is worked as follows: Work **one** fpdc around **both** middle stitches of the 6 fpdc from prev round at the same time. This method will leave less of a hole than a regular fpdc2tog. (The first time Rnd 10 is worked, the fpdc [fpsc + ch 2] decrease of the next round is worked around both the LAST fpdc [prev rnd] and the FIRST fpdc [prev rnd] at the same time. When repeated, just use the middle 2 fpdc.)*

RND 10: *fpdc decrease, fpdc around next 2 fpdc, hdc (3rd loop) in next hdc, 2 hdc (3rd loop) in next hdc, fpdc around next 2 fpdc*, repeat between *...* to end of rnd, join with sl st in top of ch 2. (64)

RND 11: *2 fpdc around next fpdc, fpdc around next 2 fpdc, hdc (3rd loop) next hdc, hdc2tog over next 2 hdc, fpdc around next 2 fpdc*, repeat to end of rnd, join with sl st in top of ch 2. (64)

RND 12: *fpdc around next fpdc, hdc in top of post just used, fpdc around next 3 fpdc, hdc2tog (3rd loop) over next 2 hdc, fpdc around next 2 fpdc*, repeat to end of rnd, join with sl st in top of ch 2. (64)

RND 13: *fpdc around next fpdc, 2 hdc (3rd loop) in next hdc, fpdc around next 3 fpdc, sk next hdc, fpdc around next 2 fpdc*, repeat to end of rnd, join with sl st in top of ch 2. (64)

RND 14: *fpdc around next fpdc, hdc (3rd loop) in next hdc, 2 hdc (3rd loop) in next hdc, fpdc around next 2 fpdc, fpdc decrease, fpdc around next fpdc*, repeat to end of rnd, join with sl st in top of ch 2. (64)

RND 15: *fpdc around next fpdc, hdc (3rd loop) in next hdc, hdc2tog (3rd loop) over next 2 hdc, fpdc around next 2 fpdc, 2 fpdc around next fpdc, fpdc around next fpdc*, repeat to end of rnd, join with sl st in top of ch 2. (64)

RND 16: *fpdc around next fpdc, hdc2tog (3rd loop) over next 2 hdc, fpdc around next 3 fpdc, hdc in top of same post just used, fpdc around next 2 fpdc*, repeat to end of rnd, join with sl st in top of ch 2. (64)

RND 17: *fpdc around next fpdc, sk next hdc, fpdc around next 3 fpdc, 2 hdc (3rd loop) in next hdc, fpdc around next 2 fpdc*, repeat to end of rnd, join with sl st in top of ch 2. (64)

REPEAT RNDS 10–17 (Read Note before Rnd 10) until the beanie reaches approximately 7.5 to 8" (19 to 20 cm) from top to bottom. Stop at any point when beanie has reached this measurement.

> **NOTE:** *Measure the circumference after completing the Edging (before fastening off). If it's not within the size range listed in the size chart (page 165), adjust the hook size and redo.*

EDGING: CH 1, sc in same st as ch 1 and ea st to end of rnd, fasten off with invisible join (or sl st) in first st. (64) Weave in ends.

TEEN/ADULT MAKING WAVES BEANIE

Use "J" (6 mm) hook, or match gauge checkpoint after Rnd 4.

> **NOTE:** *The beginning ch 2 counts as the final dc or hdc in each round and is included in the stitch count for the first 3 rounds.*

RND 1: Magic ring, ch 2 (counts as dc), 8 dc in ring, join with sl st in top of ch 2. (9)

OR ch 2, 9 dc in 2nd ch from hook, join with sl st in first dc. (9)

RND 2: ch 2, *fpdc around next dc, dc in top of same post just used for fpdc*, repeat between *...* to end of rnd, last fpdc will be around ch 2 from prev rnd, beg ch 2 counts as last dc, join with sl st in top of ch 2. (18)

RND 3: ch 2, *fpdc around next fpdc, fpdc around next dc, dc in top of same post just used*, repeat between *...* to end of rnd, last fpdc will be around ch 2 from prev rnd, beg ch 2 counts as last dc, join with sl st in top of ch 2. (27)

> **NOTE:** *From this point on, the first fpdc of EVERY round is worked as follows: fpsc around post of first fpdc from prev rnd, ch 2. The "fpsc + ch 2" creates a stitch that looks like a fpdc. Crochet the fpsc tightly around the post so it doesn't bulge at the base of the ch 2. It is correct if it looks very similar to a fpdc. Starting the round in this fashion (instead of a standard ch 2) will result in a seam that is almost completely invisible. This fpsc + ch 2 combo counts as the first fpdc of every round from this point. All hdc in "3rd loop" are worked in the back 3rd loop (see Special Stitches Definitions, page 166).*

RND 4: *fpdc around ea of next 2 fpdc, fpdc around next dc, hdc in top of same post just used*, repeat between *...* to end of rnd, join with sl st in top of ch 2. (36)

> **GAUGE CHECKPOINT:** *Diameter of the circle should measure approximately 3.25" (8 cm) here.*

RND 5: *fpdc around ea of next 3 fpdc, 2 hdc in 3rd loop of next hdc*, repeat between *...* to end of rnd, join with sl st in top of ch 2. (45)

RND 6: *fpdc around next fpdc, 2 fpdc around next fpdc, fpdc around next fpdc, hdc in 3rd loop of next hdc, 2 hdc in 3rd loop of next hdc*, repeat between *...* to end of rnd, join with sl st in top of ch 2. (63)

RND 7: *fpdc around next 2 fpdc, 2 dc in top of same post just used (between 2nd and 3rd fpdc of prev round), fpdc around next 2 fpdc, hdc in 3rd loop of next hdc, hdc2tog (3rd loop) over next 2 hdc*, repeat between *...* to end of rnd, join with sl st in top of ch 2. (72)

RND 8: *fpdc around next 2 fpdc, fpdc around next dc, hdc in top of same post just used (between 2 dc of prev round), fpdc around next dc, fpdc around next 2 fpdc, hdc2tog (3rd loop) over next 2 hdc*, repeat between *...* to end of rnd, join with sl st in top of ch 2. (72)

RND 9: *fpdc around next 3 fpdc, 2 hdc (3rd loop) in next hdc, fpdc around next 3 fpdc, sk next hdc*, repeat between *...* to end of rnd, join with sl st in top of ch 2. (72)

> **NOTE:** *A fpdc decrease is worked as follows: Work **one** fpdc around **both** middle stitches of the 6 fpdc from prev round at the same time. This method will leave less of a hole than a regular fpdc2tog. (The first time Rnd 10 is worked, the fpdc [fpsc + ch 2] decrease of the next round is worked around both the LAST fpdc [prev rnd] and the FIRST fpdc [prev rnd] at the same time. When repeated, just use the middle 2 fpdc.)*

RND 10: *fpdc decrease, fpdc around next 2 fpdc, hdc (3rd loop) in next hdc, 2 hdc (3rd loop) in next hdc, fpdc around next 2 fpdc*, repeat between *...* to end of rnd, join with sl st in top of ch 2. (72)

RND 11: *2 fpdc around next fpdc, fpdc around next 2 fpdc, hdc (3rd loop) next hdc, hdc2tog (3rd loop) over next 2 hdc, fpdc around next 2 fpdc*, repeat to end of rnd, join with sl st in top of ch 2. (72)

RND 12: *fpdc around next fpdc, hdc in top of post just used, fpdc around next 3 fpdc, hdc2tog (3rd loop) over next 2 hdc, fpdc around next 2 fpdc*, repeat to end of rnd, join with sl st in top of ch 2. (72)

RND 13: *fpdc around next fpdc, 2 hdc (3rd loop) in next hdc, fpdc around next 3 fpdc, sk next hdc, fpdc around next 2 fpdc*, repeat to end of rnd, join with sl st in top of ch 2. (72)

RND 14: *fpdc around next fpdc, hdc (3rd loop) in next hdc, 2 hdc (3rd loop) in next hdc, fpdc around next 2 fpdc, fpdc decrease, fpdc around next fpdc*, repeat to end of rnd, join with sl st in top of ch 2. (72)

RND 15: *fpdc around next fpdc, hdc (3rd loop) in next hdc, hdc2tog (3rd loop) over next 2 hdc, fpdc around next 2 fpdc, 2 fpdc around next fpdc, fpdc around next fpdc*, repeat to end of rnd, join with sl st in top of ch 2. (72)

RND 16: *fpdc around next fpdc, hdc2tog (3rd loop) over next 2 hdc, fpdc around next 3 fpdc, hdc in top of same post just used, fpdc around next 2 fpdc*, repeat to end of rnd, join with sl st in top of ch 2. (72)

RND 17: *fpdc around next fpdc, sk next hdc, fpdc around next 3 fpdc, 2 hdc (3rd loop) in next hdc, fpdc around next 2 fpdc*, repeat to end of rnd, join with sl st in top of ch 2. (72)

REPEAT RNDS 10–17 (Read Note before Rnd 10) until the beanie reaches approximately 8 to 8.5" (20 to 22 cm) from top to bottom. Stop at any point when beanie has reached this measurement.

> **NOTE:** *Measure the circumference after completing the Edging (before fastening off). If it's not within size range listed in the size chart (page 165), adjust the hook size and redo last rnd.*

EDGING: ch 1, sc in same st as ch 1 and ea st to end of rnd, fasten off with invisible join (or sl st) in first st. (72) Weave in ends.

LARGE ADULT MAKING WAVES BEANIE

Use "J" (6 mm) hook, or match gauge checkpoint after Rnd 4.

> **NOTE:** *The beginning ch 2 counts as the final dc or hdc in each round and is included in the stitch count for the first 3 rounds.*

RND 1: Magic ring, ch 2 (counts as dc), 9 dc in ring, join with sl st in top of ch 2. (10)

OR ch 2, 10 dc in 2nd ch from hook, join with sl st in first dc. (10)

RND 2: ch 2, *fpdc around next dc, dc in top of same post just used for fpdc*, repeat between *...* to end of rnd, last fpdc will be around ch 2 from prev rnd, beg ch 2 counts as last dc, join with sl st in top of ch 2. (20)

RND 3: ch 2, *fpdc around next fpdc, fpdc around next dc, dc in top of same post just used*, repeat between *...* to end of rnd, last fpdc will be around ch 2 from prev rnd, beg ch 2 counts as last dc, join with sl st in top of ch 2. (30)

> **NOTE:** *From this point on, the first fpdc of EVERY round is worked as follows: fpsc around post of first fpdc from prev rnd, ch 2. The "fpsc + ch 2" creates a stitch that looks like a fpdc. Crochet the fpsc tightly around the post so it doesn't bulge at the base of the ch 2. It is correct if it looks very similar to a fpdc. Starting the round in this fashion (instead of a standard ch 2) will result in a seam that is almost completely invisible. This fpsc + ch 2 combo counts as the first fpdc of every round from this point. All hdc in "3rd loop" are worked in the back 3rd loop (see Special Stitches Definitions, page 165).*

RND 4: *fpdc around ea of next 2 fpdc, fpdc around next dc, hdc in top of same post just used*, repeat between *...* to end of rnd, join with sl st in top of ch 2. (40)

> **GAUGE CHECKPOINT:** *Diameter of circle should measure approximately 3.5" (9 cm) here.*

RND 5: *fpdc around ea of next 3 fpdc, 2 hdc in 3rd loop of next hdc*, repeat between *...* to end of rnd, join with sl st in top of ch 2. (50)

RND 6: *fpdc around next fpdc, 2 fpdc around next fpdc, fpdc around next fpdc, hdc in 3rd loop of next hdc, 2 hdc in 3rd loop of next hdc*, repeat between *...* to end of rnd, join with sl st in top of ch 2. (70)

RND 7: *fpdc around next 2 fpdc, 2 dc in top of same post just used (between 2nd and 3rd fpdc of prev round), fpdc around next 2 fpdc, hdc in 3rd loop of next hdc, hdc2tog (3rd loop) over next 2 hdc*, repeat between *...* to end of rnd, join with sl st in top of ch 2. (80)

RND 8: *fpdc around next 2 fpdc, fpdc around next dc, hdc in top of same post just used (between 2 dc of prev round), fpdc around next dc, fpdc around next 2 fpdc, hdc2tog (3rd loop) over next 2 hdc*, repeat between *...* to end of rnd, join with sl st in top of ch 2. (80)

RND 9: *fpdc around next 3 fpdc, 2 hdc (3rd loop) in next hdc, fpdc around next 3 fpdc, sk next hdc*, repeat between *...* to end of rnd, join with sl st in top of ch 2. (80)

> **NOTE:** *A fpdc decrease is worked as follows: Work **one** fpdc around **both** middle stitches of the 6 fpdc from prev round at the same time. This method will leave less of a hole than a regular fpdc2tog. (The first time Rnd 10 is worked, the fpdc [fpsc + ch 2] decrease of the next round is worked around both the LAST fpdc [prev rnd] and the FIRST fpdc [prev rnd] at the same time. When repeated, just use the middle 2 fpdc.)*

RND 10: *fpdc decrease, fpdc around next 2 fpdc, hdc (3rd loop) in next hdc, 2 hdc (3rd loop) in next hdc, fpdc around next 2 fpdc*, repeat between *...* to end of rnd, join with sl st in top of ch 2. (80)

RND 11: *2 fpdc around next fpdc, fpdc around next 2 fpdc, hdc (3rd loop) next hdc, hdc2tog (3rd loop) over next 2 hdc, fpdc around next 2 fpdc*, repeat to end of rnd, join with sl st in top of ch 2. (80)

RND 12: *fpdc around next fpdc, hdc in top of post just used, fpdc around next 3 fpdc, hdc2tog (3rd loop) over next 2 hdc, fpdc around next 2 fpdc*, repeat to end of rnd, join with sl st in top of ch 2. (80)

RND 13: *fpdc around next fpdc, 2 hdc (3rd loop) in next hdc, fpdc around next 3 fpdc, sk next hdc, fpdc around next 2 fpdc*, repeat to end of rnd, join with sl st in top of ch 2. (80)

RND 14: *fpdc around next fpdc, hdc (3rd loop) in next hdc, 2 hdc (3rd loop) in next hdc, fpdc around next 2 fpdc, fpdc decrease, fpdc around next fpdc*, repeat to end of rnd, join with sl st in top of ch 2. (80)

RND 15: *fpdc around next fpdc, hdc (3rd loop) in next hdc, hdc2tog (3rd loop) over next 2 hdc, fpdc around next 2 fpdc, 2 fpdc around next fpdc, fpdc around next fpdc*, repeat to end of rnd, join with sl st in top of ch 2. (80)

RND 16: *fpdc around next fpdc, hdc2tog (3rd loop) over next 2 hdc, fpdc around next 3 fpdc, hdc in top of same post just used, fpdc around next 2 fpdc*, repeat to end of rnd, join with sl st in top of ch 2. (80)

RND 17: *fpdc around next fpdc, sk next hdc, fpdc around next 3 fpdc, 2 hdc (3rd loop) in next hdc, fpdc around next 2 fpdc*, repeat to end of rnd, join with sl st in top of ch 2. (80)

REPEAT RNDS 10–17 (Read Note before Rnd 10) until the beanie reaches approximately 8.5 to 9" (22 to 23 cm) from top to bottom. Stop at any point when beanie has reached this measurement.

> **NOTE:** *Measure the circumference after completing the Edging (before fastening off). If it's not within the size range listed in the size chart (page 165), adjust the hook size and redo.*

EDGING: ch 1, sc in same st as ch 1 and ea st to end of rnd, fasten off with invisible join (or sl st) in first st. (80) Weave in ends.

CHINOOK BRAIDED CABLE BEANIE

The Chinook Braided Cable Beanie has options for both a regular closed-top beanie and the trendy ponytail or "messy bun" opening. With multiple options, this hat covers the whole family! Whether it's a warm "chinook wind" type of day or you're dealing with frigid temperatures, this hat will keep you cozy.

SKILL LEVEL: **INTERMEDIATE**

MATERIALS

TOOLS	Stitch marker, measuring tape, yarn needle, elastic hair tie (optional)
YARN	5 oz (142 g) or less of #4 worsted weight yarn
GAUGE	15 stitches and 7 rows in dc = 4" x 4" (10 x 10 cm) with 6 mm hook, or see Gauge Checkpoint on page 179 (Closed Top Beginning, either size)
HOOK SIZE	"J" (6 mm) for main portion of hat, "H" (5 mm) for edging

BEANIE SIZE CHART

BABY	16-18" (41-46 cm) circumference, approximately 6-7" (15-18 cm) from crown to brim
TODDLER/CHILD	18-20" (46-51 cm) circumference, approximately 6.5-7.5" (17-19 cm) from crown to brim
TEEN/ADULT	20-22" (51-56 cm) circumference, approximately 7.5-8.5" (17-22 cm) from crown to brim
LARGE ADULT	22-24" (56-61 cm) circumference, approximately 8-9" (20-23 cm) from crown to brim

ABBREVIATIONS USED

ST(S)	stitch(es)
CH	chain stitch
SC	single crochet
DC	double crochet
FPSC	front post single crochet
FPDC	front post double crochet
BPDC	back post double crochet
FPTR	front post treble crochet
SL ST	slip stitch
RND(S)	round(s)
SK	skip
EA	each
BEG	beginning
PREV	previous
YO	Yarn Over

SPECIAL STITCHES DEFINITIONS

FRONT POST SINGLE CROCHET (FPSC): Insert hook from the front side of the work (right to left) under the post of the indicated stitch, YO and pull up a loop, YO and draw through 2 loops.

FRONT POST DOUBLE CROCHET (FPDC): Working from the front side of the work, YO and insert the hook from right to left under the post of the double crochet indicated from the previous round, YO and pull up a loop, [YO and draw through 2 loops] twice.

BACK POST DOUBLE CROCHET (BPDC): Working from the back side of the work, YO and insert the hook from right to left over the post of the double crochet indicated from the previous round, YO and pull up a loop, [YO and draw through 2 loops] twice.

FRONT POST TREBLE CROCHET (FPTR): YO hook twice, insert hook from right to left under the post of the stitch indicated, YO and pull up loop, [YO and draw through 2 loops] 3 times.

FRONT TWIST: Skip next 2 stitches, fptr around each of next 2 stitches, working over (in front of) first 2 stitches just made, fptr around first skipped stitch, fptr around second skipped stitch, now moving forward again, fptr around each of next 2 stitches.

BACK TWIST: Fptr around each of next 2 stitches, skip next 2 stitches, fptr around each of next 2 stitches, working under (behind) first 2 stitches just made, fptr around first skipped stitch, fptr around second skipped stitch.

SPECIAL TECHNIQUES

USING THE BEG "CH 2" AS THE FINAL DC IN THE ROUND: If there is a "ch 2" at the beg of a round, it will stand in as the last dc in the round. This avoids having a noticeable seam. If the repeat ends on a dc at the end of the round, don't make that last dc because the "ch 2" is there and will look like a dc when you join to the top of it. If the repeat ends with 2 dc worked in one stitch, make the first dc in the same stitch as the "ch 2." This will look almost exactly the same as working 2 dc in one stitch.

JOINING IN THE "TOP" OF THE CH 2 OR CH 3: If there is any confusion on where to join at the end of each round, use the following method: Complete the first ch 2 or ch 3 of the round, then add a stitch marker around the loop that is on the hook. At the end of the round, this is the stitch that will be used for joining.

ALTERNATIVE CLOSED TOP BEGINNING (BABY SIZE ONLY)

Use "J" (6 mm) hook, or match gauge checkpoint after Rnd 3.

RND 1: Magic ring, ch 2 (counts as dc), 14 dc in ring, join with sl st in top of ch 2. (15)

OR ch 2, 15 dc in 2nd ch from hook, join with sl st in first dc. (15)

RND 2: ch 2, *fpdc around next dc, dc in top of same post just used for fpdc*, repeat between *...* to end of rnd, last fpdc will be around ch 2 from prev rnd, beg ch 2 counts as last dc, join with sl st in top of ch 2. (30)

RND 3: ch 2, *fpdc around ea of next 6 sts, dc in top of same post just used for last fpdc*, repeat between *...* to end of rnd, last fpdc will be around ch 2 from prev rnd, beg ch 2 counts as last dc, join with sl st in top of ch 2. (35)

> **GAUGE CHECKPOINT:** *Diameter of the circle should measure approximately 3" (8 cm) here.*

CONTINUE with Rnd 3 in main pattern of Baby Size (page 180).

ALTERNATIVE CLOSED TOP BEGINNING (TODDLER/CHILD, TEEN/ADULT AND LARGE ADULT)

Use "J" (6 mm) hook, or match gauge checkpoint after Rnd 5.

RND 1: Magic ring, ch 2 (counts as dc), 11 dc in ring, join with sl st in top of ch 2. (12)

OR ch 2, 12 dc in 2nd ch from hook, join with sl st in first dc. (12)

RND 2: ch 2, *fpdc around next dc, dc in top of same post just used for fpdc*, repeat between *...* to end of rnd, last fpdc will be around ch 2 from prev rnd, beg ch 2 counts as last dc, join with sl st in top of ch 2. (24)

RND 3: ch 2, *[fpdc around next fpdc, fpdc around next dc] twice, dc in top of same post just used*, repeat between *...* to end of rnd, last fpdc will be around ch 2 from prev rnd, beg ch 2 counts as last dc, join with sl st in top of ch 2. (30)

RND 4: ch 2, *fpdc around ea of next 4 fpdc, fpdc around next dc, dc in top of same post just used*, repeat between *...* to end of rnd, last fpdc will be around ch 2 from prev rnd, beg ch 2 counts as last dc, join with sl st in top of ch 2. (36)

RND 5: ch 2, *fpdc around ea of next 5 fpdc, fpdc around next dc, dc in top of same post just used*, repeat between *...* to end of rnd, last fpdc will be around ch 2 from prev rnd, beg ch 2 counts as last dc, join with sl st in top of ch 2. (42)

> **GAUGE CHECKPOINT:** *Diameter of the circle should measure approximately 4 to 4.25" (10 to 11 cm) here.*

CONTINUE with Rnd 3 in main pattern of desired size (page 181, page 182, page 183).

BABY CHINOOK BRAIDED CABLE (PONYTAIL) BEANIE

Use "J" (6 mm) hook, or match gauge. See page 179 for closed top beginning.

> **NOTE:** *The beg ch 2 counts as final dc in each round and is included in the stitch count.*

RND 1: Make slipknot, work sc (tightly) around hair tie, ch 2 (counts as first dc), work 29 dc around elastic hair tie, join with sl st in top of ch 2 (see Joining Tip under Special Techniques [page 178]). (30)

RND 2: ch 2, *fpdc around next 6 dc, dc in top of same post just used*, repeat between *...* to end of rnd, last fpdc will be around ch 2 from prev rnd, beg ch 2 counts as last dc, join with sl st in top of ch 2. (35)

NOTE: *The "fpsc and ch 3" at the beginning of the following rounds creates a stitch that looks like a fptr. Be sure to crochet the fpsc tightly around the post so it doesn't bulge at the base of the ch 3. It is correct if it looks very similar to a fptr. Starting the round in this fashion (instead of a standard ch 3) will result in a seam that is almost completely invisible. When using skipped stitches, work them in order from "right to left" for right-handed people, "left to right" for lefties.*

RND 3 (SEE NOTE ABOVE): sl st in ea of next 2 sts, fpsc around post of third fpdc from prev rnd, ch 3 (serves as first fptr), fptr around next fpdc, working **over (in front of)** 2 sts just made, fptr around first skipped fpdc of rnd, fptr around second skipped fpdc, now moving forward again, fptr around ea of next 2 fpdc, work 2 bpdc around next dc, ***front twist** (see Special Stitches Definitions [page 178]), 2 bpdc around next dc*, repeat between *...* to end of rnd, join with sl st in top of ch 3. (40)

RND 4: fpsc around post of first fptr from prev rnd directly below, ch 3 (serves as first fptr), fptr around next fptr, sk next 2 fptr, fptr around ea of next 2 fptr, working **under (behind)** 2 sts just made, fptr around ea skipped fptr, bpdc around next bpdc, 2 bpdc around next bpdc, ***back twist** (see Special Stitches Definitions [page 178]), bpdc around next bpdc, 2 bpdc around next bpdc*, repeat between *...* to end of rnd, join with sl st in top of ch 3. (45)

RND 5: sl st in next st, fpsc around post of third fptr from prev rnd, ch 3 (serves as first fptr), fptr around next fptr, working **over (in front of)** 2 sts just made, fptr around first skipped fptr of rnd, fptr around second skipped fptr, now moving forward again, fptr around ea of next 2 fptr, bpdc around ea of next 2 bpdc, 2 bpdc around next bpdc, ***front twist**, bpdc around ea of next 2 bpdc, 2 bpdc around next bpdc*, repeat between *...* to end of rnd, join with sl st in top of ch 3. (50)

RND 6: fpsc around post of first fptr from prev rnd directly below, ch 3 (serves as first fptr), fptr around next fptr, sk next 2 fptr, fptr around ea of next 2 fptr, working **under (behind)** 2 sts just made, fptr around ea skipped fptr, bpdc around ea of next 3 bpdc, 2 bpdc around next bpdc, ***back twist**, bpdc around ea of next 3 bpdc, 2 bpdc around next bpdc*, repeat between *...* to end of rnd, join with sl st in top of ch 3. (55)

RND 7: sl st in next st, fpsc around post of third fptr from prev rnd, ch 3 (serves as first fptr), fptr around next fptr, working **over (in front of)** 2 sts just made, fptr around first skipped fptr of rnd, fptr around second skipped fptr, now moving forward again, fptr around ea of next 2 fptr, bpdc around ea of next 4 bpdc, 2 bpdc around next bpdc, ***front twist**, bpdc around ea of next 4 bpdc, 2 bpdc around next bpdc*, repeat between *...* to end of rnd, join with sl st in top of ch 3. (60)

RND 8: fpsc around post of first fptr from prev rnd directly below, ch 3 (serves as first fptr), fptr around next fptr, sk next 2 fptr, fptr around ea of next 2 fptr, working **under (behind)** 2 sts just made, fptr around ea skipped fptr, 6 bpdc, ***back twist**, 6 bpdc*, repeat between *...* to end of rnd, join with sl st in top of ch 3. (60)

RND 9: sl st in next st, fpsc around post of third fptr from prev rnd, ch 3 (serves as first fptr), fptr around next fptr, working **over (in front of)** 2 sts just made, fptr around first skipped fptr of rnd, fptr around second skipped fptr, now moving forward again, fptr around ea of next 2 fptr, 6 bpdc, ***front twist**, 6 bpdc*, repeat between *...* to end of rnd, join with sl st in top of ch 3. (60)

REPEAT RNDS 8 AND 9 until the hat measures 5″ (13 cm) from top to bottom for the ponytail version (or 5.5″ [14 cm] for the closed-top beanie).

CONTINUE with the Edging on page 184.

TODDLER/CHILD CHINOOK BRAIDED CABLE (PONYTAIL) BEANIE

Use "J" (6 mm) hook, or match gauge. See page 179 for closed top beginning.

RND 1: Make slipknot, work sc (tightly) around hair tie, ch 2 (counts as first dc), work 35 dc around elastic hair tie, join with sl st in top of ch 2 (see Joining Tip under Special Techniques [page 178]). (36)

RND 2: ch 2, *fpdc around next 6 dc, dc in top of same post just used*, repeat between *...* to end of rnd, last fpdc will be around ch 2 from prev rnd, beg ch 2 counts as last dc, join with sl st in top of ch 2. (42)

RND 3 (SEE NOTE ABOVE): sl st in ea of next 2 sts, fpsc around post of third fpdc from prev rnd, ch 3 (serves as first fptr), fptr around next fpdc, working **over (in front of)** 2 sts just made, fptr around first skipped fpdc of rnd, fptr around second skipped fpdc, now moving forward again, fptr around ea of next 2 fpdc, work 2 bpdc around next dc, ***front twist** (see Special Stitches Definitions [page 178]), 2 bpdc around next dc*, repeat between *...* to end of rnd, join with sl st in top of ch 3. (48)

RND 4: fpsc around post of first fptr from prev rnd directly below, ch 3 (serves as first fptr), fptr around next fptr, sk next 2 fptr, fptr around ea of next 2 fptr, working **under (behind)** 2 sts just made, fptr around ea skipped fptr, bpdc around next bpdc, 2 bpdc around next bpdc, ***back twist** (see Special Stitches Definitions [page 178]), bpdc around next bpdc, 2 bpdc around next bpdc*, repeat between *...* to end of rnd, join with sl st in top of ch 3. (54)

RND 5: sl st in next st, fpsc around post of third fptr from prev rnd, ch 3 (serves as first fptr), fptr around next fptr, working **over (in front of)** 2 sts just made, fptr around first skipped fptr of rnd, fptr around second skipped fptr, now moving forward again, fptr around ea of next 2 fptr, bpdc around ea of next 2 bpdc, 2 bpdc around next bpdc, ***front twist**, bpdc around ea of next 2 bpdc, 2 bpdc around next bpdc*, repeat between *...* to end of rnd, join with sl st in top of ch 3. (60)

RND 6: fpsc around post of first fptr from prev rnd directly below, ch 3 (serves as first fptr), fptr around next fptr, sk next 2 fptr, fptr around ea of next 2 fptr, working **under (behind)** 2 sts just made, fptr around ea skipped fptr, bpdc around ea of next 3 bpdc, 2 bpdc around next bpdc, ***back twist**, bpdc around ea of next 3 bpdc, 2 bpdc around next bpdc*, repeat between *...* to end of rnd, join with sl st in top of ch 3. (66)

RND 7: sl st in next st, fpsc around post of third fptr from prev rnd, ch 3 (serves as first fptr), fptr around next fptr, working **over (in front of)** 2 sts just made, fptr around first skipped fptr of rnd, fptr around second skipped fptr, now moving forward again, fptr around ea of next 2 fptr, 5 bpdc, ***front twist**, 5 bpdc*, repeat between *...* to end of rnd, join with sl st in top of ch 3. (66)

RND 8: fpsc around post of first fptr from prev rnd directly below, ch 3 (serves as first fptr), fptr around next fptr, sk next 2 fptr, fptr around ea of next 2 fptr, working **under (behind)** 2 sts just made, fptr around ea skipped fptr, 5 bpdc, ***back twist**, 5 bpdc*, repeat between *...* to end of rnd, join with sl st in top of ch 3. (66)

REPEAT RNDS 7 AND 8 until the hat reaches the following measurement:

TODDLER BEANIE	6" (15 cm)
TODDLER SLOUCH	6.5" (17 cm)
CHILD BEANIE	6.5" (17 cm)
CHILD SLOUCH	7" (18 cm)

CONTINUE with the Edging on page 184.

TEEN/ADULT CHINOOK BRAIDED CABLE (PONYTAIL) BEANIE

Use "J" (6 mm) hook, or match gauge. See page 179 for closed top beginning.

NOTE: *The beg ch 2 counts as final dc in each round and is included in the stitch count.*

RND 1: Make slipknot, work sc (tightly) around hair tie, ch 2 (counts as first dc), work 35 dc around elastic hair tie, join with sl st in top of ch 2 (see Joining Tip under Special Techniques [page 178]). (36)

RND 2: ch 2, *fpdc around next 6 dc, dc in top of same post just used*, repeat between *...* to end of rnd, last fpdc will be around ch 2 from prev rnd, beg ch 2 counts as last dc, join with sl st in top of ch 2. (42)

NOTE: *The "fpsc and ch 3" at the beginning of the following rounds creates a stitch that looks like a fptr. Be sure to crochet the fpsc tightly around the post so it doesn't bulge at the base of the ch 3. It is correct if it looks very similar to a fptr. Starting the round in this fashion (instead of a standard ch 3) will result in a seam that is almost completely invisible. When using skipped stitches, work them in order from "right to left" for right-handed people, "left to right" for lefties.*

RND 3 (SEE NOTE ABOVE): sl st in ea of next 2 sts, fpsc around post of third fpdc from prev rnd, ch 3 (serves as first fptr), fptr around next fpdc, working **over (in front of)** 2 sts just made, fptr around first skipped fpdc of rnd, fptr around second skipped fpdc, now moving forward again, fptr around ea of next 2 fpdc, work 2 bpdc around next dc, ***front twist** (see Special Stitches Definitions [page 178]), 2 bpdc around next dc*, repeat between *...* to end of rnd, join with sl st in top of ch 3. (48)

RND 4: fpsc around post of first fptr from prev rnd directly below, ch 3 (serves as first fptr), fptr around next fptr, sk next 2 fptr, fptr around ea of next 2 fptr, working **under (behind)** 2 sts just made, fptr around ea skipped fptr, bpdc around next bpdc, 2 bpdc around next bpdc, ***back twist** (see Special Stitches Definitions), bpdc around next bpdc, 2 bpdc around next bpdc*, repeat between *...* to end of rnd, join with sl st in top of ch 3. (54)

RND 5: sl st in next st, fpsc around post of third fptr from prev rnd, ch 3 (serves as first fptr), fptr around next fptr, working **over (in front of)** 2 sts just made, fptr around first skipped fptr of rnd, fptr around second skipped fptr, now moving forward again, fptr around ea of next 2 fptr, bpdc around ea of next 2 bpdc, 2 bpdc around next bpdc, ***front twist**, bpdc around ea of next 2 bpdc, 2 bpdc around next bpdc*, repeat between *...* to end of rnd, join with sl st in top of ch 3. (60)

RND 6: fpsc around post of first fptr from prev rnd directly below, ch 3 (serves as first fptr), fptr around next fptr, sk next 2 fptr, fptr around ea of next 2 fptr, working **under (behind)** 2 sts just made, fptr around ea skipped fptr, bpdc around ea of next 3 bpdc, 2 bpdc around next bpdc, ***back twist**, bpdc around ea of next 3 bpdc, 2 bpdc around next bpdc*, repeat between *...* to end of rnd, join with sl st in top of ch 3. (66)

RND 7: sl st in next st, fpsc around post of third fptr from prev rnd, ch 3 (serves as first fptr), fptr around next fptr, working **over (in front of)** 2 sts just made, fptr around first skipped fptr of rnd, fptr around second skipped fptr, now moving forward again, fptr around ea of next 2 fptr, bpdc around ea of next 4 bpdc, 2 bpdc around next bpdc, ***front twist**, bpdc around ea of next 4 bpdc, 2 bpdc around next bpdc*, repeat between *...* to end of rnd, join with sl st in top of ch 3. (72)

RND 8: fpsc around post of first fptr from prev rnd directly below, ch 3 (serves as first fptr), fptr around next fptr, sk next 2 fptr, fptr around ea of next 2 fptr, working **under (behind)** 2 sts just made, fptr around ea skipped fptr, 6 bpdc, ***back twist**, 6 bpdc*, repeat between *...* to end of rnd, join with sl st in top of ch 3. (72)

RND 9: sl st in next st, fpsc around post of third fptr from prev rnd, ch 3 (serves as first fptr), fptr around next fptr, working **over (in front of)** 2 sts just made, fptr around first skipped fptr of rnd, fptr around second skipped fptr, now moving forward again, fptr around ea of next 2 fptr, 6 bpdc, ***front twist**, 6 bpdc*, repeat between *...* to end of rnd, join with sl st in top of ch 3. (72)

REPEAT RNDS 8 AND 9 until the hat measures 7" (18 cm) from top to bottom for the ponytail version, or 7.5" (19 cm) for closed-top beanie.

CONTINUE with the Edging on page 184.

LARGE ADULT CHINOOK BRAIDED CABLE (PONYTAIL) BEANIE

Use "J" (6 mm) hook, or to match gauge. See page 179 for closed top beginning.

NOTE: *The beg ch 2 counts as final dc in each round and is included in the stitch count.*

RND 1: Make slipknot, work sc (tightly) around hair tie, ch 2 (counts as first dc), work 35 dc around elastic hair tie, join with sl st in top of ch 2 (see Joining Tip under Special Techniques [page 178]). (36)

RND 2: ch 2, *fpdc around next 6 dc, dc in top of same post just used*, repeat between *...* to end of rnd, last fpdc will be around ch 2 from prev rnd, beg ch 2 counts as last dc, join with sl st in top of ch 2. (42)

NOTE: *The "fpsc and ch 3" at the beginning of the following rounds creates a stitch that looks like a fptr. Be sure to crochet the fpsc tightly around the post so it doesn't bulge at the base of the ch 3. It is correct if it looks very similar to a fptr. Starting the round in this fashion (instead of a standard ch 3) will result in a seam that is almost completely invisible. When using skipped stitches, work them in order from "right to left" for right-handed people, "left to right" for lefties.*

RND 3: (See Note bottom left) sl st in ea of next 2 sts, fpsc around post of third fpdc from prev rnd, ch 3 (serves as first fptr), fptr around next fpdc, working **over (in front of)** 2 sts just made, fptr around first skipped fpdc of rnd, fptr around second skipped fpdc, now moving forward again, fptr around ea of next 2 fpdc, work 2 bpdc around next dc, ***front twist** (see Special Stitches Definitions [page 178]), 2 bpdc around next dc*, repeat between *...* to end of rnd, join with sl st in top of ch 3. (48)

RND 4: fpsc around post of first fptr from prev rnd directly below, ch 3 (serves as first fptr), fptr around next fptr, sk next 2 fptr, fptr around ea of next 2 fptr, working **under (behind)** 2 sts just made, fptr around ea skipped fptr, bpdc around next bpdc, 2 bpdc around next bpdc, ***back twist** (see Special Stitches Definitions [page 178]), bpdc around next bpdc, 2 bpdc around next bpdc*, repeat between *...* to end of rnd, join with sl st in top of ch 3. (54)

RND 5: sl st in next st, fpsc around post of third fptr from prev rnd, ch 3 (serves as first fptr), fptr around next fptr, working **over (in front of)** 2 sts just made, fptr around first skipped fptr of rnd, fptr around second skipped fptr, now moving forward again, fptr around ea of next 2 fptr, bpdc around ea of next 2 bpdc, 2 bpdc around next bpdc, ***front twist**, bpdc around ea of next 2 bpdc, 2 bpdc around next bpdc*, repeat between *...* to end of rnd, join with sl st in top of ch 3. (60)

RND 6: fpsc around post of first fptr from prev rnd directly below, ch 3 (serves as first fptr), fptr around next fptr, sk next 2 fptr, fptr around ea of next 2 fptr, working **under (behind)** 2 sts just made, fptr around ea skipped fptr, bpdc around ea of next 3 bpdc, 2 bpdc around next bpdc, ***back twist**, bpdc around ea of next 3 bpdc, 2 bpdc around next bpdc*, repeat between *...* to end of rnd, join with sl st in top of ch 3. (66)

RND 7: sl st in next st, fpsc around post of third fptr from prev rnd, ch 3 (serves as first fptr), fptr around next fptr, working **over (in front of)** 2 sts just made, fptr around first skipped fptr of rnd, fptr around second skipped fptr, now moving forward again, fptr around ea of next 2 fptr, bpdc around ea of next 4 bpdc, 2 bpdc around next bpdc, ***front twist**, bpdc around ea of next 4 bpdc, 2 bpdc around next bpdc*, repeat between *...* to end of rnd, join with sl st in top of ch 3. (72)

RND 8: fpsc around post of first fptr from prev rnd directly below, ch 3 (serves as first fptr), fptr around next fptr, sk next 2 fptr, fptr around ea of next 2 fptr, working **under (behind)** 2 sts just made, fptr around ea skipped fptr, bpdc around ea of next 5 bpdc, 2 bpdc around next bpdc, *__back twist__, bpdc around ea of next 5 bpdc, 2 bpdc around next bpdc*, repeat between *...* to end of rnd, join with sl st in top of ch 3. (78)

RND 9: sl st in next st, fpsc around post of third fptr from prev rnd, ch 3 (serves as first fptr), fptr around next fptr, working **over (in front of)** 2 sts just made, fptr around first skipped fptr of rnd, fptr around second skipped fptr, now moving forward again, fptr around ea of next 2 fptr, 7 bpdc, *__front twist__, 7 bpdc*, repeat between *...* to end of rnd, join with sl st in top of ch 3. (78)

RND 10: fpsc around post of first fptr from prev rnd directly below, ch 3 (serves as first fptr), fptr around next fptr, sk next 2 fptr, fptr around ea of next 2 fptr, working **under (behind)** 2 sts just made, fptr around ea skipped fptr, 7 bpdc, *__back twist__, 7 bpdc*, repeat between *...* to end of rnd, join with sl st in top of ch 3. (78)

REPEAT RNDS 9 AND 10 until the hat measures 7.5" (19 cm) from top to bottom for the ponytail version, or 8" (20 cm) for the closed-top beanie.

CONTINUE with Edging.

EDGING (ALL SIZES)

NOTE: *Switch to "H" (5 mm) hook (or 2 hook sizes smaller than the beanie gauge). Measure after completing the first round. If the circumference doesn't fall within the large end of the size range on page 176, go down as many hook sizes as necessary to the match gauge.*

RND 1: ch 2 (counts as dc), dc in ea st to end of rnd, join with sl st in top of ch 2. (60, 66, 72, 78)

RND 2: ch 2, *fpdc around next dc, bpdc around next dc*, repeat between *...* to end of rnd, join with sl st in top of ch 2. (60, 66, 72, 78)

RND 3: ch 2, *fpdc around next fpdc, bpdc around next bpdc*, repeat between *...* to end of rnd, fasten off with invisible join (or sl st) in top of ch 2. (60, 66, 72, 78)

WEAVE in all ends.

WINTER FROST CHUNKY BEANIE

Using a chunky yarn, this textured beanie works up fast and the unisex cable design looks great on both boys and girls. Top it off with your favorite pom-pom or leave it plain. Make a matching set with the Winter Frost Chunky Cowl (page 193).

SKILL LEVEL: ◼◻◻ **INTERMEDIATE**

MATERIALS

TOOLS	Stitch markers, measuring tape, yarn needle, pom-pom (optional)
YARN	7 oz (198 g) or less of #5 chunky yarn
GAUGE	Gauge checkpoint given in pattern after Rnd 4
HOOK SIZE	"K" (6.5 mm) or 7 mm hook (see individual size in pattern)

BEANIE SIZE CHART

BABY	16–18" (41–46 cm) circumference, approximately 6–6.5" (15–17 cm) from crown to brim
TODDLER	17–19" (43–48 cm) circumference, approximately 7–7.5" (18–19 cm) from crown to brim
CHILD	18–20" (46–51 cm) circumference, approximately 7.5–8" (19–20 cm) from crown to brim
TEEN/ADULT	20–22" (51–56 cm) circumference, approximately 8–8.5" (20–22 cm) from crown to brim
LARGE ADULT	22–24" (56–61 cm) circumference, approximately 8.5–9" (22–23 cm) from crown to brim

ABBREVIATIONS USED

ST(S)	stitch(es)
CH	chain stitch
RND(S)	round(s)
SC	single crochet
HDC	half double crochet
DC	double crochet
FPSC	front post single crochet
FPDC	front post double crochet
FPTR	front post treble crochet
HDC2TOG	half double crochet 2 stitches together
SL ST	slip stitch
SK	skip
SP	space
EA	each
BEG	beginning
PREV	previous
YO	Yarn Over

SPECIAL STITCHES DEFINITIONS

FRONT POST SINGLE CROCHET (FPSC): Insert hook from the front side of the work (right to left) under the post of the indicated stitch, YO and pull up a loop, YO and draw through 2 loops.

FRONT POST DOUBLE CROCHET (FPDC): Working from the front side of the work, YO and insert the hook from right to left under the post of the double crochet indicated from the previous round, YO and pull up a loop, [YO and draw through 2 loops] twice.

FRONT POST TREBLE CROCHET (FPTR): YO hook twice, insert hook from right to left under the post of the stitch indicated, YO and pull up loop, [YO and draw through 2 loops] 3 times.

HALF DOUBLE CROCHET IN 3RD LOOP: There are 2 main loops in a stitch—the "V" on the top—referred to as the front and back loops. With a hdc, the YO (before the hook is inserted into the next stitch) creates a 3rd loop on the back side of the stitch. In this pattern, all hdc in the 3rd loop will be worked in the BACK 3rd loop. The only difference is where the stitch is placed, not how it is worked. (See hdc2tog definition.)

HALF DOUBLE CROCHET 2 STITCHES TOGETHER (HDC2TOG): [YO, insert hook in next stitch, YO and pull up a loop] twice, YO and draw through all 5 loops on hook.

SPECIAL TECHNIQUES

USING THE BEG "CH 2" AS THE FINAL DC IN THE ROUND: If there is a "ch 2" at the beg of a round, it will stand in as the last dc in the round. This avoids having a noticeable seam. If the repeat ends on a dc at the end of the round, don't make that last dc because the "ch 2" is there and will look like a dc when you join to the top of it. If the repeat ends with 2 dc worked in one stitch, make the first dc in the same stitch as the "ch 2." This will look almost exactly the same as working 2 dc in one stitch.

JOINING IN THE "TOP" OF THE CH 2: If there is any confusion on where to join at the end of each round, use the following method: Complete the first ch 2 of the round, then add a stitch marker around the loop that is on the hook. At the end of the round, this is the stitch that will be used for joining.

BABY WINTER FROST CHUNKY BEANIE

Use #5 chunky yarn and 7 mm hook, or match gauge checkpoint after Rnd 4.

RND 1: Magic Ring, ch 2 (counts as dc), 11 dc in ring, join with sl st in top of ch 2. (12)

OR ch 2, work 12 dc in 2nd ch from hook, join with sl st in first dc. (12)

RND 2: ch 2 (counts as dc), *fpdc around ea of next 2 dc, dc in top of same post just used*, repeat between *...* to end of rnd, last fpdc will be around ch 2 from prev rnd, beg ch 2 counts as last dc, join with sl st in top of ch 2. (18)

RND 3: ch 2 (counts as dc), *fpdc around next 2 fpdc, fpdc around next dc, dc in top of same post just used*, repeat between *...* to end of rnd, last fpdc will be around ch 2 from prev rnd, beg ch 2 counts as last dc, join with sl st in top of ch 2. (24)

NOTE: *From this point on, the first fpdc of EVERY round is worked as follows: fpsc around post of first fpdc from prev rnd, ch 2. The "fpsc + ch 2" creates a stitch that looks like a fpdc. Crochet the fpsc tightly around the post so it doesn't bulge at the base of the ch 2. It is correct if it looks very similar to a fpdc. Starting the round in this fashion (instead of a standard ch 2) will result in a seam that is almost completely invisible. This fpsc + ch 2 combo counts as the first fpdc of every round from this point. All hdc in "3rd loop" are worked in the back 3rd loop (see Special Stitches Definitions, page 187).*

RND 4: *fpdc around ea of next 3 fpdc, fpdc around next dc, hdc in top of same post just used*, repeat between *...* to end of rnd, join with sl st in top of ch 2. (30)

GAUGE CHECKPOINT: *Diameter of the circle should measure approximately 4" (10 cm) here. (Different brands of chunky yarn can vary considerably. Adjust hook size if needed.)*

RND 5: *fpdc around ea of next 4 fpdc, 2 hdc in 3rd loop of next hdc*, repeat between *...* to end of rnd, join with sl st in top of ch 2. (36)

RND 6: *fpdc around ea of next 4 fpdc, hdc in 3rd loop of next hdc, 2 hdc in 3rd loop of next hdc*, repeat between *...* to end of rnd, join with sl st in top of ch 2. (42)

RND 7: *fpdc around ea of next 4 fpdc, hdc in 3rd loop of ea of next 2 hdc, 2 hdc in 3rd loop of next hdc*, repeat between *...* to end of rnd, join with sl st in top of ch 2. (48)

RND 8: *fpdc around ea of next 2 fpdc, hdc in top of same post just used, fpdc around ea of next 2 fpdc, hdc in 3rd loop of ea of next 2 hdc, hdc2tog in 3rd loops of next 2 hdc*, repeat between *...* to end of rnd, join with sl st in top of ch 2. (48)

RND 9: *fpdc around ea of next 2 fpdc, 2 hdc in 3rd loop of next hdc, fpdc around ea of next 2 fpdc, hdc in 3rd loop of next hdc, hdc2tog in 3rd loops of next 2 hdc*, repeat between *... *to end of rnd, join with sl st in top of ch 2. (48)

RND 10: *fpdc around ea of next 2 fpdc, hdc in 3rd loop of next hdc, 2 hdc in 3rd loop of next hdc, fpdc around ea of next 2 fpdc, hdc2tog in 3rd loops of next 2 hdc*, repeat between *...* to end of rnd, join with sl st in top of ch 2. (48)

RND 11: fpdc around **2nd** fpdc of prev rnd, *hdc in 3rd loop of ea of next 2 hdc, 2 hdc in 3rd loop of next hdc, fpdc around next fpdc, sk next fpdc and next hdc, fptr around next fpdc, working **over** first one made, fptr around skipped fpdc**, fpdc around next fpdc*, repeat between *...* to end of rnd, end last repeat at **, join with sl st in top of ch 2. (48)

RND 12: starting with the last fptr of the prev rnd, *fpdc around ea of next 2 sts, hdc in 3rd loop of ea of next 2 hdc, hdc2tog in 3rd loops of next 2 hdc, fpdc around ea of next 2 sts (use fptr on bottom), hdc in top of same post just used*, repeat between *...* to end of rnd, join with sl st in top of ch 2. (48)

RND 13: *fpdc around ea of next 2 fpdc, hdc in 3rd loop of next hdc, hdc2tog in 3rd loops of next 2 hdc, fpdc around ea of next 2 fpdc, 2 hdc in 3rd loop of next hdc*, repeat between *...* to end of rnd, join with sl st in top of ch 2. (48)

RND 14: *fpdc around ea of next 2 fpdc, hdc2tog in 3rd loops of next 2 hdc, fpdc around ea of next 2 fpdc, hdc in 3rd loop of next hdc, 2 hdc in 3rd loop of next hdc*, repeat between *...* to end of rnd, join with sl st in top of ch 2. (48)

RND 15: *fpdc around next fpdc, sk next fpdc and next hdc, fptr around next fpdc, working **over** one just made, fptr around skipped fpdc, fpdc around next fpdc, hdc in 3rd loop of ea of next 2 hdc, 2 hdc in 3rd loop of next hdc*, repeat between *...* to end of rnd, join with sl st in top of ch 2. (48)

RND 16: *fpdc around ea of next 2 sts (use fptr on bottom), hdc in top of same post just used, fpdc around ea of next 2 sts, hdc in 3rd loop of each of next 2 hdc, hdc2tog in 3rd loops of next 2 hdc*, repeat between *...* to end of rnd, join with sl st in top of ch 2. (48)

REPEAT RNDS 9–16 until the hat measures approximately 6.5 to 7" (17 to 18 cm) from top to bottom.

> **NOTE:** *Measure the circumference before completing the edging round. If it's not within the size range listed on page 185, adjust the hook size as necessary.*

EDGING: ch 1, sc in same st as ch 1 and ea st to end of rnd, fasten off with invisible join (or sl st) in first sc. Weave in ends. (48)

OPTIONAL: Add a pom-pom to the top of the hat.

TODDLER AND CHILD WINTER FROST CHUNKY BEANIE

Use #5 chunky yarn and 6.5 mm hook, or match gauge checkpoint after Rnd 4.

RND 1: Magic Ring, ch 2 (counts as dc), 13 dc in ring, join with sl st in top of ch 2. (14)

OR ch 2, work 14 dc in 2nd ch from hook, join with sl st in first dc. (14)

RND 2: ch 2 (counts as dc), *fpdc around ea of next 2 dc, dc in top of same post just used*, repeat between *...* to end of rnd, last fpdc will be around ch 2 from prev rnd, beg ch 2 counts as last dc, join with sl st in top of ch 2. (21)

RND 3: ch 2 (counts as dc), *fpdc around next 2 fpdc, fpdc around next dc, dc in top of same post just used*, repeat between *...* to end of rnd, last fpdc will be around ch 2 from prev rnd, beg ch 2 counts as last dc, join with sl st in top of ch 2. (28)

> **NOTE:** *From this point on, the first fpdc of EVERY round is worked as follows: fpsc around post of first fpdc from prev rnd, ch 2. The "fpsc + ch 2" creates a stitch that looks like a fpdc. Crochet the fpsc tightly around the post so it doesn't bulge at the base of the ch 2. It is correct if it looks very similar to a fpdc. Starting the round in this fashion (instead of a standard ch 2) will result in a seam that is almost completely invisible. This fpsc + ch 2 combo counts as the first fpdc of every round from this point. All hdc in "3rd loop" are worked in the back 3rd loop (see Special Stitches Definitions page 187).*

RND 4: *fpdc around ea of next 3 fpdc, fpdc around next dc, hdc in top of same post just used*, repeat between *...* to end of rnd, join with sl st in top of ch 2. (35)

> **GAUGE CHECKPOINT:** *Diameter of the circle should measure approximately 4.25 to 4.5" (about 11 cm) here. (Different brands of chunky yarn can vary considerably. Adjust hook size if needed.)*

RND 5: *fpdc around ea of next 4 fpdc, 2 hdc in 3rd loop of next hdc*, repeat between *...* to end of rnd, join with sl st in top of ch 2. (42)

RND 6: *fpdc around ea of next 4 fpdc, hdc in 3rd loop of next hdc, 2 hdc in 3rd loop of next hdc*, repeat between *...* to end of rnd, join with sl st in top of ch 2. (49)

RND 7: *fpdc around ea of next 4 fpdc, hdc in 3rd loop of ea of next 2 hdc, 2 hdc in 3rd loop of next hdc*, repeat between *...* to end of rnd, join with sl st in top of ch 2. (56)

RND 8: *fpdc around ea of next 2 fpdc, hdc in top of same post just used, fpdc around ea of next 2 fpdc, hdc in 3rd loop of ea of next 2 hdc, hdc2tog in 3rd loops of next 2 hdc*, repeat between *...* to end of rnd, join with sl st in top of ch 2. (56)

RND 9: *fpdc around ea of next 2 fpdc, 2 hdc in 3rd loop of next hdc, fpdc around ea of next 2 fpdc, hdc in 3rd loop of next hdc, hdc2tog in 3rd loops of next 2 hdc*, repeat between *... * to end of rnd, join with sl st in top of ch 2. (56)

RND 10: *fpdc around ea of next 2 fpdc, hdc in 3rd loop of next hdc, 2 hdc in 3rd loop of next hdc, fpdc around ea of next 2 fpdc, hdc2tog in 3rd loops of next 2 hdc*, repeat between *...* to end of rnd, join with sl st in top of ch 2. (56)

RND 11: fpdc around **2nd** fpdc of prev rnd, *hdc in 3rd loop of ea of next 2 hdc, 2 hdc in 3rd loop of next hdc, fpdc around next fpdc, sk next fpdc and next hdc, fptr around next fpdc, working **over** first one made, fptr around skipped fpdc**, fpdc around next fpdc*, repeat between *...* to end of rnd, end last repeat at **, join with sl st in top of ch 2. (56)

RND 12: starting with the last **fptr** of the prev rnd, *fpdc around ea of next 2 sts, hdc in 3rd loop of ea of next 2 hdc, hdc2tog in 3rd loops of next 2 hdc, fpdc around ea of next 2 sts (use fptr on bottom), hdc in top of same post just used*, repeat between *...* to end of rnd, join with sl st in top of ch 2. (56)

RND 13: *fpdc around ea of next 2 fpdc, hdc in 3rd loop of next hdc, hdc2tog in 3rd loops of next 2 hdc, fpdc around ea of next 2 fpdc, 2 hdc in 3rd loop of next hdc*, repeat between *...* to end of rnd, join with sl st in top of ch 2. (56)

RND 14: *fpdc around ea of next 2 fpdc, hdc2tog in 3rd loops of next 2 hdc, fpdc around ea of next 2 fpdc, hdc in 3rd loop of next hdc, 2 hdc in 3rd loop of next hdc*, repeat between *...* t to end of rnd, join with sl st in top of ch 2. (56)

RND 15: *fpdc around next fpdc, sk next fpdc and next hdc, fptr around next fpdc, working **over** one just made, fptr around skipped fpdc, fpdc around next fpdc, hdc in 3rd loop of ea of next 2 hdc, 2 hdc in 3rd loop of next hdc*, repeat between *...* to end of rnd, join with sl st in top of ch 2. (56)

RND 16: *fpdc around ea of next 2 sts (use fptr on bottom), hdc in top of same post just used, fpdc around ea of next 2 sts, hdc in 3rd loop of ea of next 2 hdc, hdc2tog in 3rd loops of next 2 hdc*, repeat between *...* to end of rnd, join with sl st in top of ch 2. (56)

REPEAT RNDS 9–16 until the hat reaches the following measurement:

TODDLER	Approximately 7–7.5″ (18–19 cm) from top to bottom
CHILD	Approximately 7.5–8″ (19–20 cm) from top to bottom

NOTE: *Measure the circumference before completing the edging round. If it's not within the size range listed on page 185, adjust the hook size as necessary.*

EDGING: ch 1, sc in same st as ch 1 and ea st to end of rnd, fasten off with invisible join (or sl st) in first sc. Weave in ends. (56)

OPTIONAL: Add a pom-pom to the top of the hat.

TEEN/ADULT AND LARGE ADULT WINTER FROST CHUNKY BEANIE

Use #5 chunky yarn and "K" (6.5 mm) hook, or match gauge checkpoint after Rnd 4.

RND 1: Magic ring, ch 2 (counts as dc), 7 dc in ring, join with sl st in top of ch 2. (8)

OR, ch 2, work 8 dc in 2nd ch from hook, join with sl st in first dc. (8)

RND 2: ch 2 (counts as dc), *fpdc around next dc, dc in top of same post just used*, repeat between *...* to end of rnd, last fpdc will be around ch 2 from prev rnd, beg ch 2 counts as last dc, join with sl st in top of ch 2. (16)

RND 3: ch 2 (counts as dc), *fpdc around next fpdc, fpdc around next dc, dc in top of same post just used*, repeat between *...* to end of rnd, last fpdc will be around ch 2 from prev rnd, beg ch 2 counts as last dc, join with sl st in top of ch 2. (24)

RND 4: ch 2 (counts as dc), *fpdc around next 2 fpdc, fpdc around next dc, dc in top of same post just used*, repeat between *...* to end of rnd, last fpdc will be around ch 2 from prev rnd, beg ch 2 counts as last dc, join with sl st in top of ch 2. (32)

> **GAUGE CHECKPOINT:** *Diameter of the circle should measure approximately 4" (10 cm) here. (Different brands of chunky yarn can vary considerably. Adjust hook size if needed.)*

> **NOTE:** *From this point on, the first fpdc of EVERY round is worked as follows: fpsc around post of first fpdc from prev rnd, ch 2. The "fpsc + ch 2" creates a stitch that looks like a fpdc. Crochet the fpsc tightly around the post so it doesn't bulge at the base of the ch 2. It is correct if it looks very similar to a fpdc. Starting the round in this fashion (instead of a standard ch 2) will result in a seam that is almost completely invisible. This fpsc + ch 2 combo counts as the first fpdc of every round from this point. All hdc in "3rd loop" are worked in the back 3rd loop (see Special Stitches Definitions, page 187).*

RND 5: *fpdc around ea of next 3 fpdc, fpdc around next dc, hdc in top of same post just used*, repeat between *...* to end of rnd, join with sl st in top of ch 2. (40)

RND 6: *fpdc around ea of next 4 fpdc, 2 hdc in 3rd loop of next hdc*, repeat between *...* to end of rnd, join with sl st in top of ch 2. (48)

RND 7: *fpdc around ea of next 4 fpdc, hdc in 3rd loop of next hdc, 2 hdc in 3rd loop of next hdc*, repeat between *...* to end of rnd, join with sl st in top of ch 2. (56)

RND 8: *fpdc around ea of next 4 fpdc, hdc in 3rd loop of ea of next 2 hdc, 2 hdc in 3rd loop of next hdc*, repeat between *...* to end of rnd, join with sl st in top of ch 2. (64)

RND 9: *fpdc around ea of next 2 fpdc, hdc in top of same post just used, fpdc around ea of next 2 fpdc, hdc in 3rd loop of ea of next 2 hdc, hdc2tog in 3rd loops of next 2 hdc*, repeat between *...* to end of rnd, join with sl st in top of ch 2. (64)

RND 10: *fpdc around ea of next 2 fpdc, 2 hdc in 3rd loop of next hdc, fpdc around ea of next 2 fpdc, hdc in 3rd loop of next hdc, hdc2tog in 3rd loops of next 2 hdc*, repeat between *...* to end of rnd, join with sl st in top of ch 2. (64)

RND 11: *fpdc around ea of next 2 fpdc, hdc in 3rd loop of next hdc, 2 hdc in 3rd loop of next hdc, fpdc around ea of next 2 fpdc, hdc2tog in 3rd loops of next 2 hdc*, repeat between *...* to end of rnd, join with sl st in top of ch 2. (64)

RND 12: fpdc around **2nd** fpdc of prev rnd, *hdc in 3rd loop of ea of next 2 hdc, 2 hdc in 3rd loop of next hdc, fpdc around next fpdc, sk next fpdc and next hdc, fptr around next fpdc, working **over** first one made, fptr around skipped fpdc**, fpdc around next fpdc*, repeat between *...* to end of rnd, end last repeat at **, join with sl st in top of ch 2. (64)

RND 13: starting with the last fptr of the prev rnd, *fpdc around ea of next 2 sts, hdc in 3rd loop of ea of next 2 hdc, hdc2tog in 3rd loops of next 2 hdc, fpdc around ea of next 2 sts (use fptr on bottom), hdc in top of same post just used*, repeat between *...* to end of rnd, join with sl st in top of ch 2. (64)

RND 14: *fpdc around ea of next 2 fpdc, hdc in 3rd loop of next hdc, hdc2tog in 3rd loops of next 2 hdc, fpdc around ea of next 2 fpdc, 2 hdc in 3rd loop of next hdc*, repeat between *...* to end of rnd, join with sl st in top of ch 2. (64)

RND 15: *fpdc around ea of next 2 fpdc, hdc2tog in 3rd loops of next 2 hdc, fpdc around ea of next 2 fpdc, hdc in 3rd loop of next hdc, 2 hdc in 3rd loop of next hdc*, repeat between *...* to end of rnd, join with sl st in top of ch 2. (64)

RND 16: *fpdc around next fpdc, sk next fpdc and next hdc, fptr around next fpdc, working **over** one just made, fptr around skipped fpdc, fpdc around next fpdc, hdc in 3rd loop of ea of next 2 hdc, 2 hdc in 3rd loop of next hdc*, repeat between *...* to end of rnd, join with sl st in top of ch 2. (64)

RND 17: *fpdc around ea of next 2 sts (use fptr on bottom), hdc in top of same post just used, fpdc around ea of next 2 sts, hdc in 3rd loop of ea of next 2 hdc, hdc2tog in 3rd loops of next 2 hdc*, repeat between *...* to end of rnd, join with sl st in top of ch 2. (64)

REPEAT RNDS 10–17 until the hat reaches the following measurement:

| TEEN/ADULT | Approximately 8–8.5″ (20–22 cm) from top to bottom |
| LARGE ADULT | Approximately 8.5–9″ (22–23 cm) from top to bottom |

> **NOTE:** *Measure the circumference before completing the edging round. If not within the size range listed on page 185, adjust the hook size as necessary.*

EDGING: ch 1, sc in same st as ch 1 and ea st to end of rnd, fasten off with invisible join (or sl st) in first sc. Weave in ends. (64)

OPTIONAL: Add a pom-pom to the top of the hat.

WINTER FROST CHUNKY COWL

This cowl is the perfect accessory for the Winter Frost Chunky Beanie (page 185). It can be made in any size from toddler to adult, and it is sure to keep you warm!

SKILL LEVEL: ⬤▮☐ **INTERMEDIATE**

MATERIALS

TOOLS	Measuring tape, yarn needle
YARN	20 oz (566 g) or less of #5 chunky weight yarn
GAUGE	Gauge is not critical. Keep tension loose. Use hook size that allows tension to remain loose.
HOOK SIZE	"M/N" (9 mm) or "P" (10 mm) hook (Different brands may vary. Match mm size, not letter)

SIZE CHART

Suggested lengths; can be customized for any size. For younger children, these sizes will work best: 24" (61 cm) (looped once) or 48" (122 cm) (looped twice), or for a very snug fit (looped twice), try the 36" (91 cm) length for toddlers.

24" (61 CM) LENGTH	Nice short length for a quick, close-fitting cowl, looped once around the neck.
36" (91 CM) LENGTH	Works well for wearing looped once around the neck, but hangs lower.
48" (122 CM) LENGTH	With a thinner width, this works great for either looping twice, or looped once, hanging low.
60" (152 CM) LENGTH	Great standard length to loop twice around the neck, any width.

ABBREVIATIONS USED

ST(S)	stitch(es)
CH	chain stitch
SC	single crochet
HDC	half double crochet
DC	double crochet
FDC	Foundationless Double Crochet
FPSC	front post single crochet
FPDC	front post double crochet
FPTR	front post treble crochet
HDC2TOG	half double crochet 2 stitches together
SL ST	slip stitch
RND(S)	round(s)
SK	skip
SP	space
EA	each
BEG	beginning
PREV	previous
YO	Yarn Over

SPECIAL STITCHES DEFINITIONS

FRONT POST SINGLE CROCHET (FPSC): Insert hook from the front side of the work (right to left) under the post of the indicated stitch, YO and pull up a loop, YO and draw through 2 loops.

FRONT POST DOUBLE CROCHET (FPDC): Working from the front side of the work, YO and insert the hook from right to left under the post of the double crochet indicated from the previous round, YO and pull up a loop, [YO and draw through 2 loops] twice.

FRONT POST TREBLE CROCHET (FPTR): YO hook twice, insert hook from right to left under the post of the stitch indicated, YO and pull up loop, [YO and draw through 2 loops] 3 times.

HALF DOUBLE CROCHET IN 3RD LOOP: There are 2 main loops in a stitch—the "V" on the top—referred to as the front and back loop. With a hdc, the YO (before the hook is inserted into the next stitch) creates a 3rd loop on the back side of the stitch. In this pattern, all hdc in the 3rd loop will be worked in the BACK 3rd loop. The only difference is where the stitch is placed, not how it is worked. (See hdc2tog definition.)

HALF DOUBLE CROCHET 2 STITCHES TOGETHER (HDC2TOG): [YO, insert hook in next stitch, YO and pull up a loop] twice, YO and draw through all 5 loops on hook.

SPECIAL TECHNIQUES

JOINING IN THE "TOP" OF THE CH 2: If there is any confusion on where to join at the end of each round, use the following method: Complete the first ch 2 of the round, then add a stitch marker around the loop that is on the hook. At the end of the round, this is the stitch that will be used for joining.

WINTER FROST CHUNKY COWL

NOTE: *To adjust the Foundation Round for other sizes/gauges, work any multiple of 8 (the beginning ch 3 counts as the first stitch). Using the suggested number of stitches below, the finished cowl should approximately match the circumference listed and can be made to any height (12" [30 cm] is suggested). This cowl is worked in rounds with an invisible seam. Measure after completing 2 or 3 rounds to make sure gauge is correct.*

SUGGESTED SIZES

24" (61 CM) CIRCUMFERENCE	56 stitches
36" (91 CM) CIRCUMFERENCE	88 stitches
48" (122 CM) CIRCUMFERENCE	112 stitches
60" (152 CM) CIRCUMFERENCE	136 stitches

FOUNDATION RND: (Leave a tail end of 6–8" [15–20 cm]vto close up the join) ch 3 (counts as dc), work (55, 87, 111, 135) FDC, join in top of ch 3 to form a circle. (56, 88, 112, 136)

NOTE: *From this point on, the first fpdc of EVERY round is worked as follows: fpsc around post of first fpdc from prev rnd, ch 2. The "fpsc + ch 2" creates a stitch that looks like a fpdc. Crochet the fpsc tightly around the post so it doesn't bulge at the base of the ch 2. It is correct if it looks very similar to a fpdc. Starting the round in this fashion (instead of a standard ch 2) will result in a seam that is almost completely invisible. This fpsc + ch 2 combo counts as the first fpdc of every round from this point. All hdc in "3rd loop" are worked in the back 3rd loop (see Special Stitches Definitions at left).*

RND 1: *fpdc around ea of next 2 dc, 2 hdc in next dc, fpdc around ea of next 2 dc, hdc in next dc, hdc2tog over next 2 dc*, repeat between *...* to end of rnd, join with sl st in top of ch 2. (56, 88, 112, 136)

RND 2: *fpdc around ea of next 2 fpdc, hdc in 3rd loop of next hdc, 2 hdc in 3rd loop of next hdc, fpdc around ea of next 2 fpdc, hdc2tog in 3rd loops of next 2 hdc*, repeat between *...* to end of rnd, join with sl st in top of ch 2. (56, 88, 112, 136)

RND 3: fpdc around **2nd** fpdc of prev rnd, *hdc in 3rd loop of ea of next 2 hdc, 2 hdc in 3rd loop of next hdc, fpdc around next fpdc, sk next fpdc and next hdc, fptr around next fpdc, working **over** first one made, fptr around skipped fpdc**, fpdc around next fpdc*, repeat between *...* to end of rnd, end last repeat at **, join with sl st in top of ch 2. (56, 88, 112, 136)

RND 4: starting with the last fptr of the prev rnd, *fpdc around ea of next 2 sts, hdc in 3rd loop of ea of next 2 hdc, hdc2tog in 3rd loops of next 2 hdc, fpdc around ea of next 2 sts (use fptr on bottom), hdc in top of same post just used*, repeat between *...* to end of rnd, join with sl st in top of ch 2. (56, 88, 112, 136)

RND 5: *fpdc around ea of next 2 fpdc, hdc in 3rd loop of next hdc, hdc2tog in 3rd loops of next 2 hdc, fpdc around ea of next 2 fpdc, 2 hdc in 3rd loop of next hdc*, repeat between *...* to end of rnd, join with sl st in top of ch 2. (56, 88, 112, 136)

RND 6: *fpdc around ea of next 2 fpdc, hdc2tog in 3rd loops of next 2 hdc, fpdc around ea of next 2 fpdc, hdc in 3rd loop of next hdc, 2 hdc in 3rd loop of next hdc*, repeat between *...* to end of rnd, join with sl st in top of ch 2. (56, 88, 112, 136)

RND 7: *fpdc around next fpdc, sk next fpdc and next hdc, fptr around next fpdc, working **over** one just made, fptr around skipped fpdc, fpdc around next fpdc, hdc in 3rd loop of ea of next 2 hdc, 2 hdc in 3rd loop of next hdc*, repeat between *...* to end of rnd, join with sl st in top of ch 2. (56, 88, 112, 136)

RND 8: *fpdc around ea of next 2 sts (use fptr on bottom), hdc in top of same post just used, fpdc around ea of next 2 sts, hdc in 3rd loop of ea of next 2 hdc, hdc2tog in 3rd loops of next 2 hdc*, repeat between *...* to end of rnd, join with sl st in top of ch 2. (56, 88, 112, 136)

RND 9: *fpdc around ea of next 2 fpdc, 2 hdc in 3rd loop of next hdc, fpdc around ea of next 2 fpdc, hdc in 3rd loop of next hdc, hdc2tog in 3rd loops of next 2 hdc*, repeat between *...* to end of rnd, join with sl st in top of ch 2. (56, 88, 112, 136)

REPEAT RNDS 2-9 until the cowl reaches 6-12″ (15-30 cm) (or desired height).

EDGING

Ch 1, sc in same st as ch 1 and ea st to end of rnd, fasten off with invisible join (or sl st) in first sc. (56, 88, 112, 136) Weave in ends.

SNOW BUNNY HAT

Made with a unique "loopy" stitch, this hat is a fun addition to any little girl's wardrobe. Pair it with the matching Snow Bunny Boot Cuffs (page 201) for an adorable set for toddlers through adults, or match it with the Snow Bunny Baby Booties (page 51) for the little ones.

SKILL LEVEL: 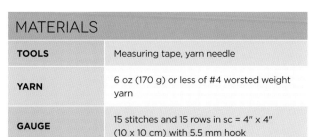 **EASY**

MATERIALS

TOOLS	Measuring tape, yarn needle
YARN	6 oz (170 g) or less of #4 worsted weight yarn
GAUGE	15 stitches and 15 rows in sc = 4" x 4" (10 x 10 cm) with 5.5 mm hook
HOOK SIZE	"I" (5.5 mm) crochet hook

HAT SIZE CHART

0-3 MONTHS	12-14" (30-36 cm) circumference, approximately 5.5" (14 cm) from crown to brim
3-6 MONTHS	14-16" (36-41 cm) circumference, approximately 5.5-6" (14-15 cm) from crown to brim
6-12 MONTHS	16-18" (41-46 cm) circumference, approximately 6.5-7" (17-18 cm) from crown to brim
TODDLER/CHILD	18-20" (46-51 cm) circumference, approximately 7.5-8" (19-20 cm) from crown to brim
TEEN/ADULT	20-22" (51-56 cm) circumference, approximately 8-8.5" (20-22 cm) from crown to brim
LARGE ADULT	22-24" (56-61 cm) circumference, approximately 8.5-9" (22-23 cm) from crown to brim

ABBREVIATIONS USED

ST(S)	stitch(es)
CH	chain stitch
DC	double crochet
DC2TOG	double crochet 2 stitches together
SL ST	slip stitch
RND(S)	round(s)
SK	skip
SP	space
EA	each
BLO	Back Loop Only
FLO	Front Loop Only
YO	Yarn Over

SPECIAL STITCHES DEFINITIONS

DOUBLE CROCHET 2 STITCHES TOGETHER (DC2TOG):
YO and insert hook in stitch indicated, YO and draw up a loop, YO and draw through 2 loops, YO and insert hook in next st, YO and draw up another loop, YO and draw through 2 loops, YO again and draw through all 3 loops on hook.

SNOW BUNNY HAT (ALL SIZES)

Use #4 worsted weight yarn and an "I" (5.5 mm) hook.

BOTTOM RIBBING

> **NOTE:** *This hat is worked from the bottom up. The beg chain determines the "height" of the bottom ribbing and can be adjusted to any size desired. The number of times Row 2 is repeated determines the circumference of the hat.*

ROW 1: ch (7, 8, 9, 10, 11, 12, 13), sl st in 2nd ch from hook (use back loops of ch) and ea ch to end of row. (6, 7, 8, 9, 10, 11, 12)

ROW 2: ch 1, turn, sl st in BLO of ea st to end of row. (6, 7, 8, 9, 10, 11, 12)

REPEAT ROW 2 until the following measurement is reached (measure lightly stretched):

(The sl st ribbing is very stretchy. If you are not sure on size, go smaller.)

0-3 MONTHS	10-11" (25-28 cm)
3-6 MONTHS	12-13" (30-33 cm)
6-12 MONTHS	14-15" (36-38 cm)
TODDLER	15-16" (38-41 cm)
CHILD	16-17" (41-43 cm)
TEEN/ADULT	18-19" (46-48 cm)
LARGE ADULT	19-20" (48-51 cm)

SEAM: ch 1 and sl st the short ends of the ribbing together (using 1 loop from each end). Turn right side out. Pattern is now worked in rounds instead of rows.

FOUNDATION RND: ch 2 (counts as dc), work (44, 48, 52, 60, 64, 68, 72) dc evenly around ribbing, join with sl st in first dc.

> **NOTE:** *Each round is actually made up of two rounds and will be worked in two parts by first using the FLO for the "loops" (Rnd 1), then going around again and using the unused back loop (Rnd 2) for the dc stitches that provide the height of the hat.*

RND 1: ch 6, sl st in FLO of same st as ch 6, *ch 6, sl st in FLO of next st*, repeat between *...* to end of rnd, join with sl st in back loop of first st. (43, 47, 51, 59, 63, 67, 71 loops)

RND 2: ch 2 (counts as a dc), dc in BLO in same st as ch 2 and ea st from Rnd 1, join with sl st in top of ch 2. (44, 48, 52, 60, 64, 68, 72)

REPEAT RNDS 1–2 until the hat reaches the following measurement (end with Rnd 1):

0–3 MONTHS	3–3.5″ (8–9 cm)
3–6 MONTHS	3.5–4″ (9–10 cm)
6–12 MONTHS	4–4.5″ (10–11 cm)
TODDLER	4.5–5″ (11–13 cm)
CHILD	5–5.5″ (13–14 cm)
TEEN/ADULT	5.5–6″ (14–15 cm)
LARGE ADULT	6–6.5″ (15–17 cm)

(DECREASING) RND 3: ch 2 (counts as dc), dc in same st as ch 2, dc2tog, *dc in ea of next 2 sts, dc2tog*, repeat between *...* to end of rnd, join with sl st in top of ch 2.

RND 4: ch 6, sl st in FLO of same st as ch 6, *ch 6, sl st in FLO of next st*, repeat between *...* to end of rnd, join with sl st in back loop of first st.

(DECREASING) RND 5: ch 2 (counts as dc), dc2tog, *dc in next st, dc2tog*, repeat between *...* to end of rnd, join with sl st in top of ch 2.

RND 6: Repeat Rnd 4.

(DECREASING) RND 7: pull up a longer loop to work first stitch, *dc2tog*, repeat between *...* to end of rnd, join with sl st in top of first st.

RND 8: Repeat Rnd 4.

REPEAT RND 7 AND RND 4 until there are only approximately 6 stitches left, turn inside out and close up remaining sts using BLO and yarn needle. Fasten off. Weave in ends.

SNOW BUNNY BOOT CUFFS

A perfect complement to the Snow Bunny Hat (page 197), these "loopy" stitch boot cuffs are easy to customize for any size.

SKILL LEVEL: **EASY**

MATERIALS

TOOLS	Measuring tape, yarn needle
YARN	4 oz (113 g) or less of #4 worsted weight yarn
GAUGE	17 stitches and 18 rows in sc = 4" x 4" (10 x 10 cm) with 5 mm hook
HOOK SIZE	"H" (5 mm) for ribbing, "I" (5.5 mm) for texture section of cuff

SIZE CHART

Please note that sizes are approximate. Measure when possible for best fit! For the correct fit, measure around leg at the same height as the top of the boots. Make ribbing of boot cuff 1–2" (3–5 cm) smaller than leg measurement to allow for stretching.

TODDLER	7–8" (18–20 cm) leg circumference
CHILD	9–11" (23–28 cm) leg circumference
SMALL ADULT	11–12" (28–30 cm) leg circumference
MEDIUM ADULT	13–14" (33–36 cm) leg circumference
LARGE ADULT	15–16" (38–41 cm) leg circumference

ABBREVIATIONS USED

ST(S)	stitch(es)
CH	chain stitch
SC	single crochet
SL ST	slip stitch
RND(S)	round(s)
SK	skip
SP	space
EA	each
BEG	beginning
PREV	previous
BLO	Back Loop Only
FLO	Front Loop Only
YO	Yarn Over

SNOW BUNNY BOOT CUFFS (ALL SIZES)

Use "H" (5 mm) hook, or to match gauge.

RIBBING SECTION (BOTTOM OF BOOT CUFF)

> **NOTE:** *This section of the boot cuff can be easily adjusted for any height by changing the beginning ch number.*

TODDLER SIZES	ch 9
CHILD SIZES	ch 11
ADULT SIZES	ch 15

ROW 1: (See numbers above for beg ch), sl st in 2nd ch from hook (use back loops of ch) and ea ch to end of row. (Stitch count will be 1 number less than beg ch number.)

ROW 2: ch 1, turn, sl st in BLO of ea st to end of row.

REPEAT ROW 2 until the following measurement is reached (measure lightly stretched):

(The sl st ribbing is very stretchy. If you are not sure about size, go smaller.)

TODDLER	7–8" (18–20 cm), or 1–2" (3–5 cm) smaller than actual leg circumference
CHILD	9–11" (23–28 cm), or 1–2" (3–5 cm) smaller than actual leg circumference
SMALL ADULT	11–12" (28–30 cm), or 1–2" (3–5 cm) smaller than actual leg circumference
MEDIUM ADULT	13–14" (33–36 cm), or 1–2" (3–5 cm) smaller than actual leg circumference
LARGE ADULT	15–16" (38–41 cm), or 1–2" (3–5 cm) smaller than actual leg circumference

NOTE: *Record how many rows were made so the second cuff will match.*

SEAM: ch 1 and sl st the short ends of the ribbing together (using 1 loop from each end). Turn right side out. The pattern is now worked in rounds instead of rows.

NOTE: *To adjust the stitch count for ANY size or gauge, end with an even number (counting the dc) in the Foundation Rnd. Because the gauge and different brands of yarn can vary so much, specific stitch counts are not provided. I work my*

dc in between the "ridges" that are created by the slip stitch ribbing, and I space approximately 3 dc in the spaces between 2 sets of ridges. For example, "work 2 dc in between first 2 ridges, work 1 dc in between next 2 ridges," repeat to end of rnd. When ribbing is slightly stretched out, the top should not "flare."

FOUNDATION RND: ch 2 (counts as a dc), dc evenly around ribbing (see Note above), join with sl st in first dc.

NOTE: *Record how many stitches were used for the Foundation Rnd so the second boot cuff will match.*

CONTINUE with the Loopy Section.

LOOPY SECTION

Switch to "I" (5.5 mm) hook, or one hook size larger than gauge.

NOTE: *Each of the following rounds is actually made up of two parts and will be worked in two rounds by first using the FLO for the "loops" (Rnd 1), then going around again and using the unused back loop (Rnd 2) for the dc stitches that provide the height of the boot cuff.*

RND 1: ch 6, sl st in FLO of same st as ch 6, *ch 6, sl st in FLO of next st*, repeat between *...* to end of rnd, join with sl st in BLO of first st.

RND 2: ch 2 (does not count as a st), dc in BLO of same st as ch 2 and BLO of ea st to end of rnd, join with sl st in top of ch 2.

REPEAT RNDS 1 and 2 until the top of the boot cuff is the same height or slightly taller than the ribbing. Fasten off with an invisible join in top of ch 2.

WEAVE in ends. Repeat instructions for second boot cuff.

MINI HARLEQUIN POM-POM EARFLAP HAT

Incorporating a uniquely twisted texture, the Mini Harlequin Pom-Pom Earflap Hat comes in an array of sizes for the entire family! Customize your hat with options such as braids or ties with yarn or faux fur pom-poms attached to the end. Add a huge pom-pom on top to finish the look!

SKILL LEVEL: INTERMEDIATE

MATERIALS

TOOLS	Measuring tape, yarn needle, pom-pom(s) or pom-pom maker (optional)
YARN	7 oz (198 g) or less of #4 worsted weight yarn
GAUGE	See gauge checkpoint in pattern after Rnd 4 or 5 for each size
HOOK SIZE	"J" (6 mm) hook, smaller hook may be needed for edging

HAT SIZE CHART

0-3 MONTHS	12-14" (30-36 cm) circumference, approximately 5.5" (14 cm) from crown to brim.
3-6 MONTHS	14-16" (36-41 cm) circumference, approximately 5.5-6" (14-15 cm) from crown to brim.
6-12 MONTHS	16-18" (41-46 cm) circumference, approximately 6.5-7" (17-18 cm) from crown to brim.
TODDLER/CHILD	18-20" (46-51 cm) circumference, approximately 7.5-8" (19-20 cm) from crown to brim.
TEEN/ADULT	20-22" (51-56 cm) circumference, approximately 8-8.5" (20-22 cm) from crown to brim.
LARGE ADULT	22-24" (56-61 cm) circumference, approximately 8.5-9" (22-23 cm) from crown to brim.

ABBREVIATIONS USED

ST(S)	stitch(es)
CH	chain stitch
SC	single crochet
DC	double crochet
FPSC	front post single crochet
FPDC	front post double crochet
BPDC	back post double crochet
FPTR	front post treble crochet
SL ST	slip stitch
RND(S)	round(s)
SK	skip
SP	space
EA	each
BEG	beginning
PREV	previous
YO	Yarn Over

SPECIAL STITCHES DEFINITIONS

FRONT POST SINGLE CROCHET (FPSC): Insert hook from the front side of the work (right to left) under the post of the indicated stitch, YO and pull up a loop, YO and draw through 2 loops.

FRONT POST DOUBLE CROCHET (FPDC): Working from the front side of the work, YO and insert the hook from right to left under the post of the double crochet indicated from the previous round, YO and pull up a loop, [YO and draw through 2 loops] twice.

BACK POST DOUBLE CROCHET (BPDC): Working from the back side of the work, YO and insert the hook from right to left over the post of the double crochet indicated from the previous round, YO and pull up a loop, [YO and draw through 2 loops] twice.

FRONT POST TREBLE CROCHET (FPTR): YO hook twice, insert hook from right to left under the post of the stitch indicated, YO and pull up loop, [YO and draw through 2 loops] 3 times.

SPECIAL TECHNIQUES

USING THE BEG "CH 2" AS THE FINAL DC IN THE ROUND: If there is a "ch 2" at the beg of a round, it will stand in as the last dc in the round. This avoids having a noticeable seam. If the repeat ends on a dc at the end of the round, don't make that last dc because the "ch 2" is there and will look like a dc when you join to the top of it. If the repeat ends with 2 dc worked in one stitch, make the first dc in the same stitch as the "ch 2." This will look almost exactly the same as working 2 dc in one stitch.

0-3 MONTHS MINI HARLEQUIN POM-POM EARFLAP HAT

Use a "J" (6 mm) hook, or match gauge checkpoint after Rnd 4.

NOTE: *The beginning ch 2 counts as the final dc in each round and is included in the stitch count for this section. See note on page 207.*

RND 1: Magic ring, ch 2, work 9 dc in ring, join with sl st in top of ch 2. (10)

OR ch 2, 10 dc in 2nd ch from hook, join with sl st in first dc. (10)

RND 2: ch 2, *fpdc around next dc, dc in top of same post that was just used*, repeat between *...* to end of rnd, last fpdc will be around ch 2 from prev rnd, beg ch 2 counts as last dc, join with sl st in top of ch 2. (20)

RND 3: ch 2, *fpdc around next fpdc, fpdc around next dc, dc in top of same post just used*, repeat between *...* to end of rnd, last fpdc will be around ch 2 from prev rnd, beg ch 2 counts as last dc, join with sl st in top of ch 2. (30)

RND 4: ch 2, *fpdc around ea of next 2 fpdc, 2 dc in next dc*, repeat between *...* to end of rnd, beg ch 2 counts as last dc, join with sl st in top of ch 2. (40)

GAUGE CHECKPOINT: *Diameter of the circle should measure approximately 4" (10 cm) here.*

RND 5: fpsc around post of first fpdc from prev rnd, ch 2 (serves as first fpdc), dc in sp between first 2 fpdc from prev rnd, fpdc around next fpdc, dc in sp between next 2 dc, *fpdc around next fpdc, dc in sp between 2 fpdc from prev rnd, fpdc around next fpdc, dc in sp between next 2 dc*, repeat between *...* to end of rnd, join with sl st in top of ch 2. (40)

RND 6: fpsc around post of first fpdc from prev rnd, ch 3 (serves as first fptr), now working **over** fptr, go back 2 sts into prev rnd just completed (skip dc) and work a fptr around last fpdc ("x" completed), now moving forward again (past "x" just created), work 2 dc in next dc, *sk next fpdc and next dc, fptr around next fpdc, now working **over** fptr just made, work fptr around skipped fpdc, now moving forward again (past "x" just created), work 2 dc in next dc*, repeat between *...* to end of rnd, join with sl st in top of ch 3. (40)

RND 7: fpsc around post of first fptr from prev rnd (bottom of twist), ch 2 (serves as first fpdc), dc in sp between first 2 fptr from prev rnd, fpdc around next fptr, dc in sp between next 2 dc, *fpdc around next fptr (the post on the bottom), dc in sp between the 2 fptr, fpdc around next fptr, dc in sp between next 2 dc*, repeat between *...* to end of rnd, join with sl st in top of ch 2. (40)

RND 8: fpsc around post of first fpdc from prev rnd, ch 3 (serves as first fptr), now working **under** fptr, go back 2 sts into prev rnd just completed (skip dc) and work a fptr around last fpdc ("x" completed), now moving forward again (past "x" just created), work 2 dc in next dc, *sk next fpdc and next dc, fptr around next fpdc, now working **under** fptr just made, work fptr around skipped fpdc, now moving forward again (past "x" just created) work 2 dc in next dc*, repeat between *...* to end of rnd, join with sl st in top of ch 3. (40)

RND 9: fpsc around post of first fptr from prev rnd (top of twist), ch 2 (serves as first fpdc), dc in sp between first 2 fptr from prev rnd, fpdc around next fptr, dc in sp between next 2 dc, *fpdc around next fptr (the post on top), dc in sp between the 2 fptr, fpdc around next fptr, dc in sp between next 2 dc*, repeat between *...* to end of rnd, join with sl st in top of ch 2. (40)

REPEAT RNDS 6-9 until the hat measures approximately 4.5" (11 cm) from crown to brim.

CONTINUE with the Brim on page 215.

3-6 MONTHS MINI HARLEQUIN POM-POM EARFLAP HAT

Use a "J" (6 mm) hook, or match gauge checkpoint after Rnd 4.

RND 1: Magic ring, ch 2, work 11 dc in ring, join with sl st in top of ch 2. (12)

OR ch 2, 12 dc in 2nd ch from hook, join with sl st in first dc. (12)

RND 2: ch 2, *fpdc around next dc, dc in top of same post that was just used*, repeat between *...* to end of rnd, last fpdc will be around ch 2 from prev rnd, beg ch 2 counts as last dc, join with sl st in top of ch 2. (24)

RND 3: ch 2, *fpdc around ea of next 4 sts, dc in top of same post just used*, repeat between *...* to end of rnd, last fpdc will be around ch 2 from prev rnd, beg ch 2 counts as last dc, join with sl st in top of ch 2. (30)

RND 4: ch 2, *fpdc around ea of next 2 fpdc, dc in top of same post just used, fpdc around ea of next 2 fpdc, dc in next dc*, repeat between *...* to end of rnd, beg ch 2 counts as last dc, join with sl st in top of ch 2. (36)

> **GAUGE CHECKPOINT:** *Diameter of the circle should measure approximately 4" (10 cm) here.*

RND 5: ch 2, *fpdc around ea of next 2 fpdc, 2 dc in next dc*, repeat between *...* to end of rnd, beg ch 2 counts as last dc, join with sl st in top of ch 2. (48)

> **NOTE:** *The "fpsc + ch 2" (or "fpsc + ch 3") combo at the beginning of the following rounds creates a stitch that looks like a fpdc/fptr (and it also counts as the first fpdc/fptr). Be sure to crochet the fpsc tightly around the post so it doesn't bulge at the base of the ch 2. It is correct if it looks very similar to a fpdc/fptr. Starting the round in this fashion (instead of a standard ch 2) will result in a seam that is almost completely invisible.*

RND 6: fpsc around post of first fpdc from prev rnd, ch 2 (serves as first fpdc), dc in sp between first 2 fpdc from prev rnd, fpdc around next fpdc, dc in sp between next 2 dc, *fpdc around next fpdc, dc in sp between 2 fpdc from prev rnd, fpdc around next fpdc, dc in sp between next 2 dc*, repeat between *...* to end of rnd, join with sl st in top of ch 2. (48)

> **NOTE:** *The (fpsc + ch 2) or (fpsc + ch 3) combo at the beginning of each round counts as the **first** fpdc/fptr for the **next** round.*

RND 7: fpsc around post of first fpdc from prev rnd, ch 3 (serves as first fptr), now working **over** fptr, go back 2 sts into prev rnd just completed (skip dc) and work a fptr around last fpdc ("x" completed), now moving forward again (past "x" just created), work 2 dc in next dc, *sk next fpdc and next dc, fptr around next fpdc, now working **over** fptr just made, work fptr around skipped fpdc, now moving forward again (past "x" just created), work 2 dc in next dc*, repeat between *...* to end of rnd, join with sl st in top of ch 3. (48)

RND 8: fpsc around post of first fptr from prev rnd (bottom of twist), ch 2 (serves as first fpdc), dc in sp between first 2 fptr from prev rnd, fpdc around next fptr, dc in sp between next 2 dc, *fpdc around next fptr (the post on the bottom), dc in sp between the 2 fptr, fpdc around next fptr, dc in sp between next 2 dc*, repeat between *...* to end of rnd, join with sl st in top of ch 2. (48)

RND 9: fpsc around post of first fpdc from prev rnd, ch 3 (serves as first fptr), now working **under** fptr, go back 2 sts into prev rnd just completed (skip dc) and work a fptr around last fpdc ("x" completed), now moving forward again (past "x" just created), work 2 dc in next dc, *sk next fpdc and next dc, fptr around next fpdc, now working **under** fptr just made, work fptr around skipped fpdc, now moving forward again (past "x" just created) work 2 dc in next dc*, repeat between *...* to end of rnd, join with sl st in top of ch 3. (48)

RND 10: fpsc around post of first fptr from prev rnd (top of twist), ch 2 (serves as first fpdc), dc in sp between first 2 fptr from prev rnd, fpdc around next fptr, dc in sp between next 2 dc, *fpdc around next fptr (the post on top), dc in sp between the 2 fptr, fpdc around next fptr, dc in sp between next 2 dc*, repeat between *...* to end of rnd, join with sl st in top of ch 2. (48)

REPEAT RNDS 7–10 until the hat measures approximately 5" (13 cm) from crown to brim.

CONTINUE with the Brim on page 215.

6-12 MONTHS MINI HARLEQUIN POM-POM EARFLAP HAT

Use a "J" (6 mm) hook, or match gauge checkpoint after Rnd 5.

NOTE: *The beginning ch 2 counts as the final dc in each round and is included in the stitch count for this section. See Note on page 210.*

RND 1: Magic ring, ch 2, work 13 dc in ring, join with sl st in top of ch 2. (14)

OR ch 2, 14 dc in 2nd ch from hook, join with sl st in first dc. (14)

RND 2: ch 2, *fpdc around ea of next 2 dc, dc in top of same post that was just used*, repeat between *...* to end of rnd, last fpdc will be around ch 2 from prev rnd, beg ch 2 counts as last dc, join with sl st in top of ch 2. (21)

RND 3: ch 2, *fpdc around ea of next 3 sts, dc in top of same post just used, repeat between *...* to end of rnd, last fpdc will be around ch 2 from prev rnd, beg ch 2 counts as last dc, join with sl st in top of ch 2. (28)

RND 4: ch 2, *fpdc around ea of next 4 sts, dc in top of same post just used, repeat between *...* to end of rnd, last fpdc will be around ch 2 from prev rnd, beg ch 2 counts as last dc, join with sl st in top of ch 2. (35)

RND 5: ch 2, *fpdc around ea of next 2 fpdc, dc in top of same post just used, fpdc around ea of next 2 fpdc, dc in next dc*, repeat between *...* to end of rnd, last fpdc will be around ch 2 from prev rnd, beg ch 2 counts as last dc, join with sl st in top of ch 2. (42)

GAUGE CHECKPOINT: *Diameter of the circle should measure approximately 4.5" (11 cm) here.*

NOTE: *The next round increases by more than the usual number of stitches.*

RND 6: ch 2, *fpdc around ea of next 2 fpdc, 2 dc in next dc*, repeat between *...* to end of rnd, beg 'ch 2' counts as last dc, join with sl st in top of ch 2. (56)

NOTE: *The "fpsc + ch 2" (or "fpsc + ch 3") combo at the beginning of the following rounds creates a stitch that looks like a fpdc/fptr (and it also counts as the first fpdc/fptr). Be sure to crochet the fpsc tightly around the post so it doesn't bulge at the base of the ch 2. It is correct if it looks very similar to a fpdc/fptr. Starting the round in this fashion (instead of a standard ch 2) will result in a seam that is almost completely invisible.*

RND 7: fpsc around post of first fpdc from prev rnd, ch 2 (serves as first fpdc), dc in sp between first 2 fpdc from prev rnd, fpdc around next fpdc, dc in sp between next 2 dc, *fpdc around next fpdc, dc in sp between 2 fpdc from prev rnd, fpdc around next fpdc, dc in sp between next 2 dc*, repeat between *...* to end of rnd, join with sl st in top of ch 2. (56)

> **NOTE:** The (fpsc + ch 2) or (fpsc + ch 3) combo at the beginning of each round counts as the **first** fpdc/fptr for the **next** round.

RND 8: fpsc around post of first fpdc from prev rnd, ch 3 (serves as first fptr), now working **over** fptr, go back 2 sts into prev rnd just completed (skip dc) and work a fptr around last fpdc ("x" completed), now moving forward again (past "x" just created), work 2 dc in next dc, *sk next fpdc and next dc, fptr around next fpdc, now working **over** fptr just made, work fptr around skipped fpdc, now moving forward again (past "x" just created), work 2 dc in next dc*, repeat between *...* to end of rnd, join with sl st in top of ch 3. (56)

RND 9: fpsc around post of first fptr from prev rnd (bottom of twist), ch 2 (serves as first fpdc), dc in sp between first 2 fptr from prev rnd, fpdc around next fptr, dc in sp between next 2 dc, *fpdc around next fptr (the post on the bottom), dc in sp between the 2 fptr, fpdc around next fptr, dc in sp between next 2 dc*, repeat between *...* to end of rnd, join with sl st in top of ch 2. (56)

RND 10: fpsc around post of first fpdc from prev rnd, ch 3 (serves as first fptr), now working **under** fptr, go back 2 sts into prev rnd just completed (skip dc) and work a fptr around last fpdc ("x" completed), now moving forward again (past "x" just created), work 2 dc in next dc, *sk next fpdc and next dc, fptr around next fpdc, now working **under** fptr just made, work fptr around skipped fpdc, now moving forward again (past "x" just created) work 2 dc in next dc*, repeat between *...* to end of rnd, join with sl st in top of ch 3. (56)

RND 11: fpsc around post of first fptr from prev rnd (top of twist), ch 2 (serves as first fpdc), dc in sp between first 2 fptr from prev rnd, fpdc around next fptr, dc in sp between next 2 dc, *fpdc around next fptr (the post on top), dc in sp between the 2 fptr, fpdc around next fptr, dc in sp between next 2 dc*, repeat between *...* to end of rnd, join with sl st in top of ch 2. (56)

REPEAT RNDS 8–11 until the hat measures approximately 5.5" (14 cm) from crown to brim, end with either Rnd 9 or 11.

CONTINUE with the Brim on page 215.

TODDLER/CHILD MINI HARLEQUIN POM-POM EARFLAP HAT

Use a "J" (6 mm) hook, or match gauge checkpoint after Rnd 5.

> **NOTE:** The beginning ch 2 counts as the final dc in each round and is included in the stitch count for this section. See Note on page 211.

RND 1: Magic ring, ch 2, work 7 dc in ring, join with sl st in top of ch 2. (8)

OR ch 2, 8 dc in 2nd ch from hook, join with sl st in first dc. (8)

RND 2: ch 2, *fpdc around next dc, dc in top of same post that was just used*, repeat between *...* to end of rnd, last fpdc will be around ch 2 from prev rnd, beg ch 2 counts as last dc, join with sl st in top of ch 2. (16)

RND 3: ch 2, *fpdc around ea of next 2 sts, dc in top of same post just used, repeat between *...* to end of rnd, last fpdc will be around ch 2 from prev rnd, beg ch 2 counts as last dc, join with sl st in top of ch 2. (24)

RND 4: ch 2, *fpdc around ea of next 3 sts, dc in top of same post just used for last fpdc*, repeat between *...* to end of rnd, last fpdc will be around ch 2 from prev rnd, beg ch 2 counts as last dc, join with sl st in top of ch 2. (32)

NOTE: *The next two rounds increase by more than the usual number of stitches.*

RND 5: ch 2, *fpdc around ea of next 2 fpdc, dc in top of same post just used, fpdc around next fpdc, fpdc around next dc, dc in top of same dc just used*, repeat between *...* to end of rnd, last fpdc will be around ch 2 from prev rnd, beg ch 2 counts as last dc, join with sl st in top of ch 2. (48)

GAUGE CHECKPOINT: *Diameter of the circle should measure approximately 4 to 4.5" (10 to 11 cm) here.*

RND 6: ch 2, *fpdc around ea of next 2 fpdc, 2 dc in next dc*, repeat between *...* to end of rnd, beg ch 2 counts as last dc, join with sl st in top of ch 2. (64)

NOTE: *The "fpsc + ch 2" (or "fpsc + ch 3") combo at the beginning of the following rounds creates a stitch that looks like a fpdc/fptr (and it also counts as the first fpdc/fptr). Be sure to crochet the fpsc tightly around the post so it doesn't bulge at the base of the ch 2. It is correct if it looks very similar to a fpdc/fptr. Starting the round in this fashion (instead of a standard ch 2) will result in a seam that is almost completely invisible.*

RND 7: fpsc around post of first fpdc from prev rnd, ch 2 (serves as first fpdc), dc in sp between first 2 fpdc from prev rnd, fpdc around next fpdc, dc in sp between next 2 dc, *fpdc around next fpdc, dc in sp between 2 fpdc from prev rnd, fpdc around next fpdc, dc in sp between next 2 dc*, repeat between *...* to end of rnd, join with sl st in top of ch 2. (64)

NOTE: *The (fpsc + ch 2) or (fpsc + ch 3) combo at the beginning of each round counts as the **first** fpdc/fptr for the **next** round.*

RND 8: fpsc around post of first fpdc from prev rnd, ch 3 (serves as first fptr), now working **over** fptr, go back 2 sts into prev rnd just completed (skip dc) and work a fptr around last fpdc ("x" completed), now moving forward again (past "x" just created), work 2 dc in next dc, *sk next fpdc and next dc, fptr around next fpdc, now working **over** fptr just made, work fptr around skipped fpdc, now moving forward again (past "x" just created), work 2 dc in next dc*, repeat between *...* to end of rnd, join with sl st in top of ch 3. (64)

RND 9: fpsc around post of first fptr from prev rnd (bottom of twist), ch 2 (serves as first fpdc), dc in sp between first 2 fptr from prev rnd, fpdc around next fptr, dc in sp between next 2 dc, *fpdc around next fptr (the post on the bottom), dc in sp between the 2 fptr, fpdc around next fptr, dc in sp between next 2 dc*, repeat between *...* to end of rnd, join with sl st in top of ch 2. (64)

RND 10: fpsc around post of first fpdc from prev rnd, ch 3 (serves as first fptr), now working **under** fptr, go back 2 sts into prev rnd just completed (skip dc) and work a fptr around last fpdc ("x" completed), now moving forward again (past "x" just created), work 2 dc in next dc, *sk next fpdc and next dc, fptr around next fpdc, now working **under** fptr just made, work fptr around skipped fpdc, now moving forward again (past "x" just created) work 2 dc in next dc*, repeat between *...* to end of rnd, join with sl st in top of ch 3. (64)

RND 11: fpsc around post of first fptr from prev rnd (top of twist), ch 2 (serves as first fpdc), dc in sp between first 2 fptr from prev rnd, fpdc around next fptr, dc in sp between next 2 dc, *fpdc around next fptr (the post on top), dc in sp between the 2 fptr, fpdc around next fptr, dc in sp between next 2 dc*, repeat between *...* to end of rnd, join with sl st in top of ch 2. (64)

REPEAT RNDS 8-11 until the hat measures approximately 6 to 6.5" (15 to 17 cm) from crown to brim.

CONTINUE with the Brim on page 215.

TEEN/ADULT MINI HARLEQUIN POM–POM EARFLAP HAT

Use a "J" (6 mm) hook, or match gauge checkpoint after Rnd 5.

> **NOTE:** *The beginning ch 2 counts as the final dc in each round and is included in the stitch count for this section. See Note on page 213.*

RND 1: Magic ring, ch 2, work 8 dc in ring, join with sl st in top of ch 2. (9)

OR ch 2, 9 dc in 2nd ch from hook, join with sl st in first dc. (9)

RND 2: ch 2, *fpdc around next dc, dc in top of same post that was just used*, repeat between *...* to end of rnd, last fpdc will be around ch 2 from prev rnd, beg ch 2 counts as last dc, join with sl st in top of ch 2. (18)

RND 3: ch 2, *fpdc around ea of next 2 sts, dc in top of same post just used, repeat between *...* to end of rnd, last fpdc will be around ch 2 from prev rnd, beg ch 2 counts as last dc, join with sl st in top of ch 2. (27)

RND 4: ch 2, *fpdc around ea of next 3 sts, dc in top of same post just used, repeat between *...* to end of rnd, last fpdc will be around ch 2 from prev rnd, beg ch 2 counts as last dc, join with sl st in top of ch 2. (36)

> **NOTE:** *The next two rounds increase by more than the usual number of stitches.*

RND 5: ch 2, *fpdc around ea of next 2 fpdc, dc in top of same post just used, fpdc around next fpdc, fpdc around next dc, dc in top of same dc just used*, repeat between *...* to end of rnd, last fpdc will be around ch 2 from prev rnd, beg ch 2 counts as last dc, join with sl st in top of ch 2. (54)

> **GAUGE CHECKPOINT:** *Diameter of the circle should measure approximately 4 to 4.5" (10 to 11 cm) here.*

RND 6: ch 2, *fpdc around ea of next 2 fpdc, 2 dc in next dc*, repeat between *...* to end of rnd, beg ch 2 counts as last dc, join with sl st in top of ch 2. (72)

> **NOTE:** *The "fpsc + ch 2" (or "fpsc + ch 3") combo at the beginning of the following rounds creates a stitch that looks like a fpdc/fptr (and it also counts as the first fpdc/fptr). Be sure to crochet the fpsc tightly around the post so it doesn't bulge at the base of the ch 2. It is correct if it looks very similar to a fpdc/fptr. Starting the round in this fashion (instead of a standard ch 2) will result in a seam that is almost completely invisible.*

RND 7: fpsc around post of first fpdc from prev rnd, ch 2 (serves as first fpdc), dc in sp between first 2 fpdc from prev rnd, fpdc around next fpdc, dc in sp between next 2 dc, *fpdc around next fpdc, dc in sp between 2 fpdc from prev rnd, fpdc around next fpdc, dc in sp between next 2 dc*, repeat between *...* to end of rnd, join with sl st in top of ch 2. (72)

> **NOTE:** *The (fpsc + ch 2) or (fpsc + ch 3) combo at the beginning of each round counts as the* **first** *fpdc/fptr for the* **next** *round.*

RND 8: fpsc around post of first fpdc from prev rnd, ch 3 (serves as first fptr), now working **over** fptr, go back 2 sts into prev rnd just completed (skip dc) and work a fptr around last fpdc ("x" completed), now moving forward again (past "x" just created), work 2 dc in next dc, *sk next fpdc and next dc, fptr around next fpdc, now working **over** fptr just made, work fptr around skipped fpdc, now moving forward again (past "x" just created), work 2 dc in next dc*, repeat between *...* to end of rnd, join with sl st in top of ch 3. (72)

RND 9: fpsc around post of first fptr from prev rnd (bottom of twist), ch 2 (serves as first fpdc), dc in sp between first 2 fptr from prev rnd, fpdc around next fptr, dc in sp between next 2 dc, *fpdc around next fptr (the post on the bottom), dc in sp between the 2 fptr, fpdc around next fptr, dc in sp between next 2 dc*, repeat between *...* to end of rnd, join with sl st in top of ch 2. (72)

RND 10: fpsc around post of first fpdc from prev rnd, ch 3 (serves as first fptr), now working **under** fptr, go back 2 sts into prev rnd just completed (skip dc) and work a fptr around last fpdc ("x" completed), now moving forward again (past "x" just created), work 2 dc in next dc, *sk next fpdc and next dc, fptr around next fpdc, now working **under** fptr just made, work fptr around skipped fpdc, now moving forward again (past "x" just created) work 2 dc in next dc*, repeat between *...* to end of rnd, join with sl st in top of ch 3. (72)

RND 11: fpsc around post of first fptr from prev rnd (top of twist), ch 2 (serves as first fpdc), dc in sp between first 2 fptr from prev rnd, fpdc around next fptr, dc in sp between next 2 dc, *fpdc around next fptr (the post on top), dc in sp between the 2 fptr, fpdc around next fptr, dc in sp between next 2 dc*, repeat between *...* to end of rnd, join with sl st in top of ch 2. (72)

REPEAT RNDS 8–11 until the hat measures approximately 7" (18 cm) from crown to brim.

CONTINUE with the Brim on page 215.

LARGE ADULT MINI HARLEQUIN POM-POM EARFLAP HAT

Use a "J" (6 mm) hook, or match gauge checkpoint after Rnd 5.

> **NOTE:** *The beginning ch 2 counts as the final dc in each round and is included in the stitch count for this section. See Note on page 214.*

RND 1: Magic ring, ch 2, work 9 dc in ring, join with sl st in top of ch 2. (10)

OR ch 2, 10 dc in 2nd ch from hook, join with sl st in first dc. (10)

RND 2: ch 2, *fpdc around next dc, dc in top of same post that was just used*, repeat between *...* to end of rnd, last fpdc will be around ch 2 from prev rnd, beg ch 2 counts as last dc, join with sl st in top of ch 2. (20)

RND 3: ch 2, *fpdc around ea of next 2 sts, dc in top of same post just used, repeat between *...* to end of rnd, last fpdc will be around ch 2 from prev rnd, beg ch 2 counts as last dc, join with sl st in top of ch 2. (30)

RND 4: ch 2, *fpdc around ea of next 3 sts, dc in top of same post just used, repeat between *...* to end of rnd, last fpdc will be around ch 2 from prev rnd, beg ch 2 counts as last dc, join with sl st in top of ch 2. (40)

NOTE: *The next two rounds increase by more than the usual number of stitches.*

RND 5: ch 2, *fpdc around ea of next 2 fpdc, dc in top of same post just used, fpdc around next fpdc, fpdc around next dc, dc in top of same dc just used*, repeat between *...* to end of rnd, last fpdc will be around ch 2 from prev rnd, beg ch 2 counts as last dc, join with sl st in top of ch 2. (60)

GAUGE CHECKPOINT: *Diameter of the circle should measure approximately 4.5 to 5" (11 to 13 cm) here.*

RND 6: ch 2, *fpdc around ea of next 2 fpdc, 2 dc in next dc*, repeat between *...* to end of rnd, beg ch 2 counts as last dc, join with sl st in top of ch 2. (80)

NOTE: *The "fpsc + ch 2" (or "fpsc + ch 3") combo at the beginning of the following rounds creates a stitch that looks like a fpdc/fptr (and it also counts as the first fpdc/fptr). Be sure to crochet the fpsc tightly around the post so it doesn't bulge at the base of the ch 2. It is correct if it looks very similar to a fpdc/fptr. Starting the round in this fashion (instead of a standard ch 2) will result in a seam that is almost completely invisible.*

RND 7: fpsc around post of first fpdc from prev rnd, ch 2 (serves as first fpdc), dc in sp between first 2 fpdc from prev rnd, fpdc around next fpdc, dc in sp between next 2 dc, *fpdc around next fpdc, dc in sp between 2 fpdc from prev rnd, fpdc around next fpdc, dc in sp between next 2 dc*, repeat between *...* to end of rnd, join with sl st in top of ch 2. (80)

NOTE: *The (fpsc + ch 2) or (fpsc + ch 3) combo at the beginning of each round counts as the **first** fpdc/fptr for the **next** round.*

RND 8: fpsc around post of first fpdc from prev rnd, ch 3 (serves as first fptr), now working **over** fptr, go back 2 sts into prev rnd just completed (skip dc) and work a fptr around last fpdc ("x" completed), now moving forward again (past "x" just created), work 2 dc in next dc, *sk next fpdc and next dc, fptr around next fpdc, now working **over** fptr just made, work fptr around skipped fpdc, now moving forward again (past "x" just created), work 2 dc in next dc*, repeat between *...* to end of rnd, join with sl st in top of ch 3. (80)

RND 9: fpsc around post of first fptr from prev rnd (bottom of twist), ch 2 (serves as first fpdc), dc in sp between first 2 fptr from prev rnd, fpdc around next fptr, dc in sp between next 2 dc, *fpdc around next fptr (the post on the bottom), dc in sp between the 2 fptr, fpdc around next fptr, dc in sp between next 2 dc*, repeat between *...* to end of rnd, join with sl st in top of ch 2. (80)

RND 10: fpsc around post of first fpdc from prev rnd, ch 3 (serves as first fptr), now working **under** fptr, go back 2 sts into prev rnd just completed (skip dc) and work a fptr around last fpdc ("x" completed), now moving forward again (past "x" just created), work 2 dc in next dc, *sk next fpdc and next dc, fptr around next fpdc, now working **under** fptr just made, work fptr around skipped fpdc, now moving forward again (past "x" just created) work 2 dc in next dc*, repeat between *...* to end of rnd, join with sl st in top of ch 3. (80)

RND 11: fpsc around post of first fptr from prev rnd (top of twist), ch 2 (serves as first fpdc), dc in sp between first 2 fptr from prev rnd, fpdc around next fptr, dc in sp between next 2 dc, *fpdc around next fptr (the post on top), dc in sp between the 2 fptr, fpdc around next fptr, dc in sp between next 2 dc*, repeat between *...* to end of rnd, join with sl st in top of ch 2. (80)

REPEAT RNDS 8–11 until the hat measures approximately 7.5" (19 cm) from crown to brim.

CONTINUE with the Brim below.

BRIM (ALL SIZES)

Switch to "I" (5.5 mm) hook (or one hook size smaller than gauge).

> **NOTE:** *The pattern is now worked back and forth in rows instead of rounds.*

ROW 1: ch 2 (counts as first dc), dc in next (27, 33, 41, 45, 51, 57) sts, leave remaining sts unworked. (28, 34, 42, 46, 52, 58)

ROW 2: ch 2, turn, *bpdc around next st, fpdc around next st*, repeat between *...* to end of row, dc in top of turning ch. (28, 34, 42, 46, 50, 56)

0–3 MONTHS/3–6 MONTHS/6–12 MONTHS	Repeat Row 2 one more time.
TODDLER/CHILD/TEEN/ ADULT AND LARGE ADULT	Repeat Row 2 three more times.

CONTINUE with the Edging Options.

EDGING OPTIONS

Select one of the following two Edging Options to finish off the hat.

EDGING WITHOUT CROCHETED TIES

ch 1, with right side facing, sc around entire edge of hat (2 sc in corners), fasten off with invisible join in first sc. Add braids (see right) if desired.

EDGING WITH CROCHETED TIES

ch 1, with right side facing, sc around entire edge of hat (2 sc in corners), at each corner of brim, use multiple strands of yarn to desired thickness (for ties only), ch desired length for tie, sl st in 2nd ch from hook and ea ch back up to hat, fasten off with invisible join in first sc. Can attach pom-poms on ends of ties or leave as is.

BRAIDS

(Follow steps for Edging without Crocheted Ties first.)

Cut twenty-four 24 to 30" (61 to 76 cm) strands. Divide the strands into two groups, one for each braid. Take 12 strands and pull through bottom corner of the brim. Pull the strands so they are even on each side. Divide so there are three groups of four strands, one from each side of the hat. Braid tightly; secure with an overhand knot. Repeat for the second braid. Trim the ends so they are even. (I make my braids about 6 to 12" [15 to 30 cm] long, depending on the size of the hat, and not counting the fringe at the end.)

OPTIONAL POM-POM

Attach a pom-pom on top of the hat and/or to ends of the crocheted ties. Pom-poms can be purchased, made by hand using materials you have at home, or made with a purchased pom-pom maker such as Clover brand pom-pom maker.

RESOURCES

SYMBOLS

[ ] Work instructions within brackets as many times as directed.

( ) Work instructions within parentheses as many times as directed.

... Repeat the instructions between asterisks as many times as directed, or repeat from a given set of instructions.

** Located within a set of single asterisks, the double asterisks are used when the last repeat of the sequence ends early. For example: *sk next 3 ch, work fan in next ch, sk next 3 ch, sc in next ch**, ch 1, sk next ch, sc in next ch*, repeat between *...* to end of row, end last repeat at **.

" Measurement of inches

SKILL LEVELS

EASY: ⬤▬▬ Easy projects using basic stitches, repetitive stitch patterns, simple color changes and simple shaping and finishing.

INTERMEDIATE: ⬤⬤▬ Intermediate projects with a variety of stitches, midlevel shaping and finishing.

CROCHET TERMINOLOGY

All patterns in this book are written with U.S. Terminology.

UNITED STATES VS. INTERNATIONAL	
SL ST (slip stitch)	**SC** (single crochet)
SC (single crochet)	**DC** (double crochet)
DC (double crochet)	**TR** (treble crochet)
HDC (half double crochet)	**HTR** (half treble crochet)
TR (treble crochet)	**DTR** (double treble crochet)
DTR (double treble crochet)	**TTR** (triple treble crochet)
SKIP	**MISS**

YARN

Can't find a yarn listed in a pattern? Search on yarnsub.com to easily find a substitute.

STITCH DEFINITIONS

BACK POST DOUBLE CROCHET (BPDC): Working from the back side of the work, YO and insert the hook from right to left over the post of the double crochet indicated from the previous round, YO and pull up a loop, [YO and draw through 2 loops] twice.

BACK TWIST: Fptr around each of next 2 stitches, skip next 2 stitches, fptr around each of next 2 stitches, working under (behind) first 2 stitches just made, fptr around first skipped stitch, fptr around second skipped stitch.

CLUSTER: 3 fpdc worked around a sc. (This term is used for stitch count purposes only in the Windchill Hooded Button-Up Baby Cocoon Pattern [page 39].)

CROSS STITCH (CROSS-ST): Skip next ch-2 space, dc in next ch-2 space, working behind first dc, dc in skipped ch-2 space.

DOUBLE CROCHET (DC): YO, insert hook in st, YO, pull up a loop, [YO, draw through 2 loops] twice.

DOUBLE CROCHET 2 STITCHES TOGETHER (DC2TOG): YO and insert hook in stitch indicated, YO and draw up a loop, YO and draw through 2 loops, YO and insert hook in next st, YO and draw up another loop, YO and draw through 2 loops. YO again and draw through all 3 loops on hook.

DOUBLE CROCHET 3 STITCHES TOGETHER (DC3TOG): YO and insert hook in stitch indicated, YO and draw up a loop, YO and draw through 2 loops, *YO and insert hook in next st, YO and draw up another loop, YO and draw through 2 loops*, repeat between *...* in next st, YO and draw through all 4 loops on hook.

FOUNDATIONLESS DOUBLE CROCHET: ch 3, *YO, insert hook into first ch made (3rd ch from hook, use back loop of ch), YO and pull up a loop (3 loops on hook), YO and pull through 1 loop (this creates the base ch upon which to build the next stitch and is used in the repeat), now finish as a normal double crochet stitch: [YO, draw through 2 loops] twice*. Repeat steps between *...*, using the base ch. If unfamiliar with this method, you may want to mark the base ch (or hold it with your thumb) until you are used to finding that stitch for the next double crochet.

FRONT POST DOUBLE CROCHET (FPDC): Working from the front side of the work, YO and insert the hook from right to left under the post of the double crochet indicated from the previous round, YO and pull up a loop, [YO and draw through 2 loops] twice.

FRONT POST DOUBLE CROCHET DECREASE (FPDC DECREASE): Work 1 fpdc around both posts of indicated stitches from previous round at the same time. (This is used in place of a standard fpdc2tog, and it is only used in the Making Waves Beanie and Making Waves Baby Cocoon [page 165] or Swaddle Sack [page 39] patterns.)

FRONT POST SINGLE CROCHET (FPSC): Insert hook from the front side of the work (right to left) under the post of the indicated stitch, YO and pull up a loop, YO and draw through 2 loops.

FRONT POST TREBLE CROCHET (FPTR): YO hook twice, insert hook from right to left under the post of the stitch indicated, YO and pull up loop, [YO and draw through 2 loops] 3 times.

FRONT TWIST: Skip next 2 stitches, fptr around each of next 2 stitches, working over (in front of) first 2 stitches, fptr around first skipped stitch, fptr around second skipped stitch, fptr around each of next 2 stitches.

HALF DOUBLE CROCHET (HDC): YO, insert hook in st, YO, pull up a loop, YO, draw through all 3 loops on hook.

HALF DOUBLE CROCHET IN 3RD LOOP: There are 2 main loops in a stitch—the "V" on the top—referred to as the front and back loops. With a hdc, the YO (before the hook is inserted into the next stitch) creates a 3rd loop on the back side of the stitch. In this book, all hdc in the 3rd loop will be worked in the BACK 3rd loop. The only difference is where the stitch is placed, not how it is worked. (See hdc and hdc2tog definitions.)

HALF DOUBLE CROCHET 2 STITCHES TOGETHER (HDC2TOG): [YO, insert hook in next stitch, YO and pull up a loop] twice, YO and draw through all 5 loops on hook.

INVISIBLE JOIN: Cut yarn (leave a tail end of about 6–8″ [15–20 cm]), thread yarn through yarn needle. Locate first stitch in rnd, insert needle under both top loops of this stitch (from front to back), now insert needle into the top of the last stitch made (straight down into the eye formed by both loops), be sure to insert through the horizontal loop behind the stitch as well. Pull yarn through just tightly enough that the false stitch formed looks the same as every other stitch. Weave in end.

JOINING WITH SC: Begin with a slipknot on hook, insert hook in stitch indicated, YO and pull up a loop, YO and draw through both loops.

MAGIC RING: Making a large loop with the yarn, cross the end of the yarn over the working strand. Holding the loop with your fingers, insert hook into the loop and pull the working strand through, ch 2 (for dc), continue to work the indicated number of stitches into the loop. Pull on the strand's end to close the loop.

MINI BEAN STITCH (MB ST): Insert hook in next st, YO, draw up a loop (2 loops on hook), YO, insert hook in same st, YO, draw up a loop (4 loops on hook), YO, pull through all 4 loops on hook, ch 1 (counts as "top" of the mini bean stitch).

PUFF STITCH (PUFF ST): [YO, insert hook in indicated stitch, YO, draw up loop] 3 times in same stitch, YO, draw through all 7 loops on hook.

PUFF STITCH SHELL (PUFF ST SHELL): [(puff st, ch 3) twice, puff st] in indicated stitch or space.

SINGLE CROCHET (SC): Insert hook in st, YO, pull through st, YO, draw through both loops on hook.

SINGLE CROCHET 2 STITCHES TOGETHER (SC2TOG): Insert hook in stitch indicated, YO and draw up a loop, insert hook in next st, YO and draw up another loop, YO again and draw through all 3 loops on hook.

SINGLE CROCHET 3 STITCHES TOGETHER (SC3TOG): Pull up a loop in each of next 3 stitches, YO and draw through all 4 loops on hook.

SLIP STITCH (SL ST): Insert hook in stitch or space indicated, YO and draw through stitch **and** through loop on hook.

TREBLE CROCHET (TR): YO hook twice, insert hook in indicated st and pull up a loop (4 loops on hook), YO and draw through 2 loops (3 loops on hook), YO hook and draw through 2 loops (2 loops on hook), YO hook and draw through last 2 loops.

V-STITCH (V-ST): (dc, ch 1, dc) in indicated stitch or space.

ACKNOWLEDGMENTS

Thank you to Sarah, Will and the rest of the hardworking team at Page Street Publishing for another wonderful opportunity to write a book about what I love to do—create crochet patterns! I am extremely grateful for your continued support and guidance through this amazing adventure.

Thank you to my family for being patient through the process of writing this second book. I love all of you!

Thank you also to every one of my family and friends who modeled in this book: Jon Dougherty, Taryn Dougherty, Katrina Sertich, David Sertich, Tyler Sertich, Ryan Sertich, April Patterson, Elleanore Patterson, Vikki Pavlovich, Mike Pavlovich, Ashlyn Pavlovich, Levi Pavlovich, Hannah Wright, JJ Wright and Harlee Wright. I would also like to thank the many wonderful clients of AppleTree Photography who graciously allowed their beautiful children to be in this book.

Thank you to April Patterson of AppleTree Photography for her incredible skill and vision and for always being willing to work with me on the final look of the photography. April always makes all of my patterns look amazing!

I would like to thank all of these wonderful women who tested these patterns for accuracy:

- Jenny Doke of Twin Stitches

- Debbie Constable of Waddlesworth's Knit & Crochet Shop

- Kyla Grexton of Keep Me in Stitchez

- Lois Everett of ForEverett Crocheting

- Nakesha Haschke of Bean Sprout Boutique

- Beth Masog of Heavenly Handmade Crochet by Beth

- Kaycee Sterling of Lovable Lids

- Chelsea Relander of OKAMommy

- Francie Christensen of The Mad Capper

- Becky Williamson of Twittle Monkeys

- Sheena Crothers of Meadowlark & Co.

- Jessica Bicknese of That's Sew Crochet

- Kayla Hemingway of Hooks & Twists

- Krissy Shively of Little Bear, Little Bug

- Liane Claassen of LCCrochet

- Lacey Berres of Mama Bear Designs

- Jamie Olson of Northern Lights Crochet

- Jennifer Neerhof of Willow Works

- Patcharee Clinch of Mai's Stitches

And last but not least, a huge thank you to Kate Wagstaff for her continual support and friendship. I'm blessed to call such a talented designer my treasured friend and confidante.

ABOUT THE AUTHOR

Jennifer Dougherty has been a lifelong crocheter, but she didn't find her true calling as a pattern designer until her mid-thirties. Within a few short years, she built up a thriving online business. She published her first book, *Crochet Style*, in November 2016.

Jennifer has several pattern stores online, including Etsy, Ravelry, Craftsy and Loveknitting. She has an active Facebook page for Crochet by Jennifer and also manages several crochet groups online. Jennifer's patterns have been specially featured by Etsy and have also appeared in crochet magazines and blogs worldwide. She has won several pattern competitions in *Happily Hooked Magazine* and has been featured by The Crochet Cafe. More information can be found on Jennifer's website: www.crochetbyjennifer.com.

When not crocheting, Jennifer enjoys reading and spending time with her family—a husband, two daughters, a son-in-law and two adorable grandsons.

INDEX